SEASCAPES: SHAPED BY THE SEA

In memory of Russell Brown (1937–2011),
who fostered and supported
a love of the sea

Seascapes: Shaped by the Sea

Embodied Narratives and Fluid Geographies

Edited by

MIKE BROWN
University of Waikato, New Zealand

and

BARBARA HUMBERSTONE
Buckinghamshire New University, UK

Routledge
Taylor & Francis Group

LONDON AND NEW YORK

First published 2015 by Ashgate Publishing

Published 2016 by Routledge
2 Park Square, Milton Park, Abingdon, Oxon OX14 4RN
711 Third Avenue, New York, NY 10017, USA

First issued in paperback 2018

Routledge is an imprint of the Taylor & Francis Group, an informa business

British Library Cataloguing in Publication Data
A catalogue record for this book is available from the British Library

The Library of Congress has cataloged the printed edition as follows:
Brown, Mike.
  Seascapes: shaped by the sea / by Mike Brown and Barbara Humberstone.
    pages cm
  Includes bibliographical references and index.
  ISBN 978-1-4724-2433-4 (hardback: alk. paper)
1. Ocean – Social aspects. 2. Ocean and civilization. I. Humberstone, Barbara.
II. Title.

  GC11.2.B78 2015
  551.46--dc23

                                                                    2014023413

ISBN 13: 978-1-138-54666-0 (pbk)
ISBN 13: 978-1-4724-2433-4 (hbk)

Contents

Notes on Contributors

Jon Anderson is a senior lecturer in Human Geography at Cardiff University. His research interests focus on the relations between culture, place and identity, particularly the geographies, politics and practices that emerge from these. His key publications include: *Understanding Cultural Geography: Places and Traces* (2010), *Water Worlds: Human Geographies of the Ocean* (with K. Peters, 2014), and *Page and Place: Ongoing Compositions of Plot* (2015).

Karen Barbour is a senior lecturer in Dance in the Faculty of Education, The University of Waikato. Her research focuses on embodied ways of knowing in dance and explorations of cultural identity through autoethnographic writing and performance. She is the editor of *Dance Research Aotearoa* (http://www.dra.ac.nz), author of *Dancing across the Page: Narrative and Embodied Ways of Knowing* (Intellect Books, 2011) and co-editor of *Ethnographic Worldviews: Social Justice and Transformation* (Springer, 2014).

Mike Brown, PhD, is a senior lecturer in the Faculty of Education, The University of Waikato, New Zealand. He is co-author of *A Pedagogy of Place: Outdoor Education for a Changing World* (2011) and editor of the *NZ Journal of Outdoor Education*. Introduced to boating at a young age, he has been involved in sail training in the UK and cruised the SW Pacific by sailboat. He is an occasional sea kayaker, diver and open water swimmer. He currently enjoys sailboat cruising in the Hauraki Gulf, Auckland.

elke emerald is a senior lecturer at Griffith University, Australia. She teaches research methods in the Faculty of Education. elke's research has interrogated the construction of categories in social life and the real lived impact on individuals of society's insistence on maintaining limited and limiting ways of being. Her book *Stories from the Margins* (2009) examines the experiences of mothers of children with disability. elke's co-authored book, *Participatory Activist Research*, was released in 2013 (Springer). Her current research uses narrative, ethnographic and autoethnographic methods to investigate the resilience of researchers in the academy.

Fiona Ewing has a Bachelor of Science in Biological Oceanography and postgraduate qualifications in Fisheries Science. She has extensive 'at sea' experience in a number of fisheries. She has worked onboard both foreign and domestic fishing boats, providing compliance data to fisheries management agencies, technical support to fisheries research and leading research sampling programmes. Fiona presently works in environmentally sustainable fish farming. As Tasmania's 'State Rural Woman of the Year', she researched projects to revive remote communities through sustainable fish farming enterprises.

Barbara Humberstone, PhD, is a professor of Sociology of Sport and Outdoor Education at Buckinghamshire New University, UK. Her research interests include: embodiment and nature-based sport, and well-being and outdoor pedagogies. She co-edited *Whose Journeys? The Outdoors and Adventure as Social and Culture Phenomena* (2003) and has published papers in a variety of journals. She is the managing editor of *Journal of Adventure Education and Outdoor Learning* and was Chair of the European Institute for Outdoor Adventure Education and Experiential Learning. She is a keen windsurfer and walker.

The Pacific Ocean has played a large part in **lisahunter**'s life. 'E* currently researches and lectures in Aotearoa New Zealand in the fields of education, health, sport and leisure. Time spent with the sea has regrettably diminished due to increasingly long work hours, which is a downside of neo-liberal agendas in tertiary education. As such, this chapter was written as a freelance academic outside 'normal' work time due to increasing work demands.

Over the past decade **Mihi Nemani** has been passionately involved in the sport of bodyboarding at national and international levels, through competing and assisting in the running of competitions. While training for competitions, she has had many experiences that have influenced her life and made her reflect on her identity in and out of the surf. Her research interests involve investigating the roles ethnicity and gender play when participating in lifestyle sports such as bodyboarding. In her role as principal lecturer in the School of Sport at Manukau Institute of Technology she is able to draw on her experiences and research to help her students understand the importance of their own identities in relation to sport.

Robbie Nicol is a senior lecturer in Outdoor and Environmental Education and Head of Institute for Education, Teaching and Leadership at Moray House School of Education, the University of Edinburgh. His life motivation comes from the realisation that human activities are fundamentally altering the planet's ability to sustain us in the long term. As an educator, he believes that the outdoors provides places where people can rediscover their direct dependence on the planet through embodied experiences. His teaching and research interests are directed towards the theoretical development and practical implementation of environmental education, sustainability education and epistemological diversity particularly in the outdoors.

---

*   lisahunter has chosen to use gender non-specific language: ''E' rather than 'she'.

Peter Reason is Emeritus Professor at the University of Bath. During his academic career he made significant contributions to the development of participative approaches to action research in the human sciences and in management, approaches variously referred to as 'co-operative inquiry', 'participatory action research' and 'action science' or 'action inquiry'. Since retiring Peter has focused less on action research and more on 'nature writing for an ecology in crisis'. He blogs regularly at onthewesternedge.wordpress.com and has just published *Spindrift: A Wilderness Pilgrimage at Sea* (Vala Publishing Cooperative), the story of a sailing voyage and an investigation of our human place in the ecology of the planet.

Karen Throsby is a lecturer in the School of Sociology and Social Policy at the University of Leeds. Her research is broadly in the areas of gender, technology and the body, and she is the author of *When IVF Fails: Feminism, Infertility and the Negotiation of Normality* (Palgrave, 2004) and co-editor (with Flora Alexander) of *Gender and Interpersonal Violence: Language, Action and Representation* (Palgrave, 2008). She has written extensively on the new reproductive technologies and on the surgical management of obesity. Her most recent research is on the embodied experiences of long-distance open water swimmers.

Brian Wattchow is a senior lecturer in the Faculty of Education, Monash University. His research focus for the last decade has been about land, identity and place-responsive education. The major publication that arose from this research has been a co-authored book, *A Pedagogy of Place: Outdoor Education for a Changing World*. He has also researched how human experiences of place are represented through image and text, and how this process is pivotal in outdoor and experiential education. In 2010 he published *The Song of the Wounded River*, a narrative and poetic representation of a 2,500 km canoe journey along the Murray River. His most recent book, *The Socio-Ecological Educator*, involved collaboration with colleagues across the physical, health, environmental and outdoor education disciplines. In a recent shift, he has returned his attention to the sea and the coast, and is currently writing a book about a series of journeys on the south coast of Australia, which attempts to chart the personal, familial, cultural and ecological dimensions of sea-places.

Robyn Zink has spent the last 20 years working with groups in the outdoors, researching and writing about outdoor education. She is currently spending time playing in the outdoors.

Foreword

On a cold rainy night on a Liverpool quayside
In the years before the great war
The world was in shock at the loss of Titanic,
So proud had they been days before;
Relatives gathered for news of the loved ones,
To read through the list of the dead,
When into the throng came a sad eyed old polar bear:
And to the clerk at the counter he said:

Have you got any news of the iceberg?
My family were on it you see:
Have you got any news of the iceberg?
They mean the whole world to me.

My wife and my children were coming from Greenland,
To be by my side at the zoo:
Belinda's my wife, and the eldest's called Bernard:
And Billy, well, he's only two.
I know on the ship there were hundreds of people,
And I know that the iceberg's not yours:
The polar bear's eyes held the start of his teardrops:
He covered his face with his paws.

Have you got any news of the iceberg?
My family were on it you see:
Have you got any news of the iceberg?
They mean the whole world to me.
  —Les Barker, *Have you got any news of the iceberg?*[1]

In *Have you got any news of the iceberg?* Les Barker fuses the familiar with the unbelievable. On the one hand, the poem naturalises and reaffirms basic structures of human empathy and familial ties. Indeed, it extends these characteristics to the non-human world. Listening to the polar bear's story, we can relate to his anxious plea for news, even bad news, amidst the dread of uncertainty. But we also cannot help but acknowledge the unbelievability of a talking, family-loving, grief-laden polar bear. By fusing these elements in the package of an absurdist

---

1   Reproduced with the permission of the author, Les Barker.

narrative, Barker enables the reader to see things from a different perspective. The poem upends our understandings by pointing out that for a polar bear an iceberg is a site of refuge, and a ship brings danger. And as a result we not only have an enhanced understanding of polar bear livelihoods; we also receive a new impetus for questioning our common sense assumptions about the ways in which we encounter and know a fundamental space of human experience: the sea.

By throwing our perceptual framework into disarray Barker's poem leads us to reconsider the sea as something much more complex than its usual depiction as the surface upon which elements including icebergs and ships float, occasionally meeting up with each other to disastrous effect. In *Have you got any news of the iceberg?* the sea is a space of both sanctuary and danger. It is an alien environment but also a habitat. It is a surface for crossings but also a site of distinct points (some of which are hazards, or refuges, or both). Those points themselves are mobile, which, in turn, challenges their ontological status as 'places' in the ordinary, static sense. Furthermore, we learn from Barker's story that the sea is not simply liquid water. It is also ice. And although Barker does not develop this point, it is also air, including the mist that complicated initial sightings of the iceberg by the Titanic and later sightings of the Titanic by rescue ships. And it is seabed, where the remains now lie.

Additionally, although the ocean in *Have you got any news of the iceberg?* is beyond land, it exists in constant interaction with land. In part, these connections with land are cultural, as in the voyages of cruise ships like the Titanic where land-based social rituals are transplanted to water. But they are also geophysical: the iceberg that sunk the Titanic consisted of glacial ice that almost certainly had calved off the coast of Greenland. In Barker's story we learn that the sea is forever (it is a timeless grave), but we also learn that it is a space of fleeting encounters and geophysical recompositions. Indeed, today, 100 years after sinking the Titanic, the iceberg that is the subject of Barker's poem in all probability no longer exists.

Perhaps most significantly, however, we learn from Barker's poem that the sea is a space of multiple, and at times contradictory, *experiences*. Whether experienced tactilely (e.g. by polar bears), visually (e.g. by cruise ship passengers), or virtually (e.g. by readers of the poem), the sea is a space where singular stories are told about a multiplicitous environment.

Barker's poem thus provides a fitting entry point for this book about the various ways in which we experience the sea and make sense of those maritime encounters. To be certain, not all of the themes suggested by Barker receive equal coverage in *Seascapes*. When the editors, Mike Brown and Barbara Humberstone, state in their opening chapter that they intend to focus on how 'experiences [of the ocean] might inform collective interpretations and how collective representations influence their lived experiences', they appear to be restricting their focus to *human* experiences. There are no polar bears in this book, and if they were to appear they almost certainly would not be talking. But even the human experience, especially at sea, has a more-than-human element to it. Consider one of the quotations from Bernard Moitessier that appears in Brown and Humberstone's introductory chapter: 'I watch this fantastic sea, breathe in its spray, and feel blossoming here in the wind and space something that needs the immensity of the universe to come to fruition.' Moitessier's experience may be specifically human, but it is an experience of something that both *exceeds* and *becomes* himself.

In other words, even when experienced virtually, the ocean is encountered as a profoundly *real* space, a characteristic that is sometimes lost in nineteenth-century romantic accounts of the ocean sublime. The authors in this book not only think *with* the sea, they think *in* the sea, and, because the sea is immersive, it is, as Brown and Humberstone stress, also transformative of who we are and how we think. When we sense the awesome power of an undertow or a crashing wave or a glistening horizon, we are changed and our understanding of the world is changed, whether or not we get wet.

Indeed, distance can sometimes enhance the encounter by providing a critical perspective. I became aware of this around 1999 when I was living in Florida and became friends with a somewhat bored computer network administrator who was seeking certification to fly recreational single-engine aircraft. I joined him in the cockpit on a few training runs and, probably in violation of Federal Aviation Administration rules, occasionally took over the controls. As we flew over the barrier islands of North Florida's Gulf Coast and I mischievously dipped the wings, I observed a diminishing series of sand bars in the water, parallel to land, each less distinct (and deeper) than the previous, trailing away from the coast. I had read previously about dunes migrating toward land, progressively forming new generations of barrier islands, cyclically disrupting and reproducing the coastal geomorphology as wave action pushes sediment ever coastward. I understood the process intellectually. But from the air I could actually *see* the temporality of the sea, not just in the circulations of waves and tides (which I had previously experienced on the ground) but in the long-term movements of sand. These movements, I realised, were a part of the sea, just as much as the shorter-term movements of water expressed through waves and tides. I understood, as never before, how the ocean is dynamic with sediment as well as water.

It was also at this moment that I truly understood that although the barrier island functionally appears to be *of the land* (one can walk on a barrier island, build a home there, and, perhaps most importantly, register that home with a civic authority as 'property'), ecologically it is *of the sea*. Prior to that day, I had spent many hours standing on barrier islands pondering the sea's awesome, transformative force and attempting to connect with it in successive expressions of an overreaching romanticism. But only now, by experiencing the sea from a new, distanced perspective, could I take this to the next step. Only now was I able to comprehend the limits of a perspective wherein one fragment of space is designated 'sea', another fragment is designated 'land', and wherein one is defined as a creature who thinks that one of these two categories of space is his natural habitat and that the other is inherently alien.

Was my aerial encounter with the ocean truly an *experience*? I acknowledge that it was distanced. Furthermore, it was limited to only one sense (the visual) and at no point during the flight did I have a phenomenological experience of being 'one with the water' (which is probably a good thing!). But who truly has an authentic sea experience? The SCUBA diver looking through a face mask? The ship passenger gazing out from a deck? The surfer who for but a fleeting moment exists at the intersection of its various components – the making and breaking of waves, the movement of molecules, the joy of uplift? The swimmer who is counting breaths? Even for Les Barker's polar bear the immersive experience of the ocean is mediated by a cognitive focus on distinct objects: the iceberg, the family members, the memories of home.

Of course, we can never truly know the thoughts of a polar bear, the elusive cyborg of this foreword. But we can think *through* the polar bear, just as we can think *through* the ocean, using these alternative (but nonetheless real) assemblages of space, time, and matter to upend our assumptions and change ourselves. The chapters of this book provide a key starting point for this project. Ultimately they are not so much chapters about the sea or even about our experiences of the sea as they are chapters about humans who are thinking, reactive creatures who navigate their place in the world as they navigate the oceans. No compass can guide this journey. Indeed, the journey never resolves itself in a 'place': the sea's dynamism confounds our everyday understandings of a point as something to which we can return. If you define the ocean as your home, then, like Les Barker's polar bear, you can recall it only in its dissipation and in its ultimate disappearance. But if one doesn't have a destination, one can never be truly lost. Rather, the ocean is a journey of experiences filled with partial knowledges. And that is where this book begins.

Professor Philip Steinberg,
Durham University

Acknowledgements

Our sincere thanks are extended to the contributors who willingly embraced the ideas that we are trying to achieve through this project. That this idea was worthy of effort was readily evidenced by the enthusiasm displayed by all the contributors. We thank you for your openness, willingness to convey your thoughts and experiences, and hitherto personal aspects of your lives, with a wider audience.

Our thanks to Valerie Rose at Ashgate Publishing for supporting our initial proposal, which did not sit easily within disciplinary boundaries. Thank you for seeing the possibilities of how our approach could enrich understandings of human–sea relationships.

Our thanks to the University of Waikato, Faculty of Education Research and Leave Committee for funding to assist in preparing the manuscript for submission.

To Jane Burnett, thank you for your patience with the proofreading and formatting. You lifted a considerable weight from our shoulders.

Mike would like to thank Barbara for her support and for broadening his understanding of the power of embodied narratives. Once again, thanks to Paula for bringing another project to a successful conclusion and for indulging me with my sailing addiction.

Barbara would like to thank Mike for his enthusiasm, drive and considerable knowledge of seafaring.

Introduction

Mike Brown and Barbara Humberstone

In the same year that humans stood on the moon for the first time, an intrepid group of sailors were attempting to complete the first non-stop solo sailing circumnavigation. On the home straight, seven months after departing England, the potential race winner Bernard Moitessier withdrew from the event. At the time of his withdrawal he had already crossed his outward path. After abandoning the race, Moitessier continued sailing for another three months, finally arriving in Tahiti in June 1969. In his communication to the race officials Moitessier simply stated, 'I am continuing non-stop to the Pacific Islands because I am happy at sea, and perhaps also to save my soul' (1974, p. 169).

Moitessier's *The Long Way* is a classic account of an individual's desire to escape what he saw as the corrupting influences of modernity and find peace at sea. It sits within a long tradition of sea narratives that are heavily influenced by the Romantic movement, which saw the sea as one of the last great wildernesses. Jessica Watson's (2010) *True Spirit: The Aussie Girl Who Took on the World* is a more recent manifestation of the continued appeal of this genre. Stories of adventure, self-discovery, of daring rescues and exotic destinations, continue to resonate with readers and audiences in Western societies (for example, the movies *All is Lost, Captain Phillips, Life of Pi*). As Phelan has noted, the 'received metaphors and literary allusions' (2007, p. 8) contained within literature of the sea, coupled with our direct experiences, have become an integral component of how we perceive the sea.

Accounts of people's encounters with the sea, as narratives of discovery, escape from humdrum existence or competitive endeavours are plentiful, as are scientific, historical and archaeological accounts of seafarers and maritime technologies. These diverse approaches to writing *about* or *of* the sea shape the way we engage with the sea and the nature of our relationship with it. Different genres of writing and disciplinary traditions present the sea in very different ways. For example, Moitessier's evocative 'I watch this fantastic sea, breathe in its spray, and feel blossoming here in the wind and space something that needs the immensity of the universe to come to fruition' (1974, p. 138) provides a very different account or perspective from that of the United States Geological Survey, which reports that the volume of the world's seas is 1,338,000 km^3 or 0.12 per cent of the planet's volume (see Steinberg, 2014).

In the chapters that follow, we have drawn together a range of different perspectives of being *with* the sea. The central theme running through the book is the way that lived experiences with the sea shape who we are. Rather than writing about the 'idea of the sea' (Mack, 2011, p. 25) through the use of metaphors, the authors have conveyed their experiences of the sea as a lived reality. They have been required to grapple with the challenges presented by sea writing, or thassalography (Steinberg, 2014), in representing embodied personal experiences within a broader social framework.

The authors have linked their personal experiences of the sea with a variety of theoretical perspectives to reflect on how our relationship with the sea shapes our understanding of both the human and non-human world. As editors, our brief to contributors was simple: write about your experiences of the sea and how they have contributed to your way of being in the world and how this might connect to broader issues in society. The authors seek to understand how personal experiences might inform collective interpretations and how collective representations influence their lived experiences. Strang highlights the reciprocity between the individual and collective thus:

> Although located in the individual, sensory experience incorporates the learned perspectives and interpretations that are the product of collective social and environmental interaction. Thus the meanings engendered by experience are simultaneously part of the cultural landscape that every person enters and exits over an individual lifetime. As many ethnographies have shown, shared meanings are upheld – and continually developed – through a range of cultural forms, including myth, art, ritual and everyday practice. (Strang, 2004, p. 67)

The felt and lived experiences of being *with* the sea act as the grounding for what has been written. This collection of ethnographically inspired narratives provides an approach focus, which complements existing works that represent the human–sea relationship.

A Collaborative Endeavour

Mike's Starting Point

My path and Barbara's have crossed at various conferences, in airport lounges and via emails, as editors and reviewers for journals over the past decade. As individuals with long-standing involvement with the sea, we inevitably found points of common interest relating to being *on* or *in* the water. In 2012 I had the opportunity to take study leave. I spent some time in Edinburgh and wrote a chapter in *Outdoor Adventure and Social Theory* (Pike and Beames, 2013). Whilst struggling to think about how I might connect Durkheim – the social theorist I was asked to write about – to adventure, I went for a run and found myself drawn to the docks. I came across the 60-foot yacht of the Scottish entrant in the 2012 Vendee Global Ocean race. Designed for single-handed racing, these are highly specialised ocean-racing machines. I memorised the internet address on the side of the boat and, after visiting the website, I found a solution to my writing block. The material presented provided avenues to explore how social cohesion might be achieved through appeals to national identity. Ideals of being a true Scot or being of Scots descent were used to encourage support for the Scottish entrant (see Brown, 2013). It was shortly thereafter that I met up with Barbara again at a conference at the University of Edinburgh. With my current writing project still on the go, coupled with my earlier work on place, belonging and identity (Wattchow and Brown, 2011), ideas that I had been mulling over for some time started to coalesce. Fuelled by my interest in the ideological messages contained on the Team Vendee Scotland website, my academic background, coupled with my own lived experiences of the sea, I was increasingly interested in exploring how people experienced the sea and how it shaped their sense of self. The Scottish Vendee Globe public relations person portrayed the sea, and one's relationship with it, in a way that differed greatly from Moitessier's sea. Was 'the sea' that I experienced mine alone or was there commonality with others? How had it shaped me? Why, in a new city, did I seek out the docks, marinas and maritime museums (from Halifax, Nova Scotia to Freemantle, Australia)? How did other people experience the sea and what did it mean for them? Knowing of Barbara's windsurfing experiences and research interests, I broached the subject of editing a book with her. Her enthusiastic response, based on my initial rough outline, has helped bring this edited collection to fruition.

Barbara's Commentary

Mike approached me at the conference to co-edit a book exploring the sea through narrative. Surprised and intrigued, having had no idea of Mike's seafaring background, I considered the invitation with great interest. I had met with Mike intermittently on a number of occasions, and a former PhD student of mine had appreciated time spent with him. As time went on and we became occupied further with the project, it became clear that, although our various experiences of the sea are different, there is much in common, particularly in relation to the importance of the sea to our consciousness. My particular current research interest in the sea is to do with bodily kinetic engagement with the sea when windsurfing and the possibilities and potentialities of 'kinetic empathy' (Thrift, 2008). This specific interest emerged from my academic curiosity in embodiment, movement in nature and the senses, which had been stimulated through themes proposed for a European Institute 'Youth for Europe' conference in Germany, the focus of which was 'experiencing water'. Thus my lifelong engagement with the sea initially came together as an academic piece, which attempted to evoke the experience of windsurfing through the narrative form. Mike had identified the possibility of combining our academic commitments, and our collaboration uncovered our lifelong shared connections with the sea. Thus our common and diverse interests in the sea underpin the production of this edited collection.

The Sea is Integral to our Everyday Lives

Peters argues that in contemporary society the sea continues to be 'a vital space and one that is integral to the workings of the world as we currently know it' (2010, p. 1260). This book's focus is on how the sea, as an embodied cultural and material 'vital space', is experienced in the lives of a number of individuals. By reflecting on personal experiences, situated within broader discourses, the contributors explicate the 'dynamic and recursive relationship' (Strang, 2008, p. 52) with the sea that shapes us as human beings, both individually and collectively.

Whilst conducting research for this book it became evident that there has been an increase in scholarly attention on the human–sea relationship (for example, Anderson and Peters, 2014; Ford and Brown, 2006; Mack, 2011). As Anderson and Peters have stated recently, 'Our world is a water world. The oceans and seas are entwined, often invisibly but nonetheless importantly, with our everyday lives' (2014, p. 3). Their opening chapter entitled 'A Perfect and Absolute Blank: Human Geographies of Water Worlds' details human geography's turn to the sea as a topic worthy of study. Critiques of the terrestrial bias in human geography are comprehensively discussed elsewhere (see Anderson, 2012; Lambert, Martins and Ogborn, 2006; Peters, 2010) and we see little purpose in reiterating critiques, while an explication of the possibilities of understanding the human–sea relationship from ethnographic perspectives offers an avenue for thinking about what is, or what can be, rather than what was. A number of writers have provided eloquent and persuasive arguments to validate the importance of the human–sea relationship in contemporary life (see Anderson and Peters, 2014; Cooney, 2003; Ford and Brown, 2006; Mack, 2011; Peters, 2010; Steinberg, 1999, 2001, 2013). The focus of this book is to further Lambert et al.'s quest for greater consideration to be given to 'the imaginative, aesthetic and sensuous geographies of the sea', thereby opening up 'new experiential dimensions and new forms of representation' (2006, p. 479). In doing so we seek to

> demonstrate the ways in which the sea is not a material or metaphorical void, but alive with embodied human experiences, more-than-human agencies and as well as being a space in and of itself that has material character, shape and form. (Anderson and Peters, 2014, p. 4)

Ethnography and Embodiment

Through the use of autoethnography, the contributors reflect on how the sea has shaped their sense of who they are and their relationship to the human and non-human world. The significance of autoethnographic approaches in understanding human beings' engagement with the sea has considerable potential to enhance 'empathetic forms of understanding' (Sparkes, 1999, p. 19), which can add to the existing literature on the sea from the natural and social sciences. The contributors' narratives of embodied experiences with the sea enable an enriched understanding of what it is to 'be' engaged with the sea. For as Anderson and Peters note, both individuals and cultures 'understand and experience the sea as a "place" with character, agency and personality' (2014, p. 9). These narratives have the 'potential to challenge disembodied ways of knowing' that can take us 'into the intimate, embodied world of the other in a way that stimulates us to reflect upon our own lives in relation to theirs' (Sparkes, 1999, p. 25). Autoethnography enables each narrator to (re)present their lived, sentient, corporeal experiences through the ways in which they describe their sensual and emotional relations with the sea. This approach to locating ourselves, through representations of lived experiences that portray our relationship with the sea, provides one version of a 'different kind of "map"' that Steinberg (2014, p. xv) calls for as we attempt to write of the sea as a non-objectified arena.

The focus on embodiment is important, for as Shields has noted, 'There is tremendous complicity between the body and the environment and the two interpenetrate each other' (1991, p. 14). The use of embodied accounts as a way of conveying lived experiences, and the integration of relevant theoretical frames for understanding the broader cultural implications, provide new opportunities to understand the sea. Sparkes and Smith have recently stated that, 'The development of a more sensory research agenda along with sensual scholarship invites new forms of knowing and routes into the experiences of others and ourselves' (2012, p. 186). In *The Sea: A Cultural History*, John Mack argued that

> if we are to take seriously the observation that the understanding of the sea is predicated on an understanding of the people who inhabit the sea, accounts of mariners must clearly play a large part in what follows here … It [ethnography] has rarely reported on the experience of being on the seas; instead, to the extent that reference is made to the sea at all, it has almost always focused on the implications of being close to the sea, of having a relationship to it, not actually of being *on* it. (Mack, 2011, p. 23)

We concur with Mack that autoethnographic research has until recently rarely been adopted in understanding people's experiences of *being with* the sea. *Seascapes: Shaped by the Sea* makes a significant contribution to enriching our understanding of the sea through multiple voices and perspectives of engaging with the sea, and to the emergent field constituting 'mobile methodologies' (Finch, McGuinness and Murray, 2010) by drawing on the embodied lived experiences of the authors that Mack recognised as being so important. The approach adopted by many of the contributors provides not only for a focus on the 'inner realm of individuals but on narratives as a *vehicle* through which our world, lives and selves are articulated, and the ways in which such narratives function within *social relationships*' (Sparkes and Smith, 2008, p. 298). Thus these autoethnographic accounts provide a way to understand how aspects of 'understanding, knowing and knowledge'

(Pink, 2009, p. 8) of the sea shape both individual and collective identities. Our understandings of the sea and our relationships with it are vitally important as these have an impact on how we utilise and allocate resources, regulate its management, determine territorial authority, and work to preserve or deplete non-human life (Steinberg, 2013).

Chapter Outlines

This book features contributions from scholars who are actively engaged with sea. Each author has been approached because of a combination of scholarly expertise and lived experiences with the sea. Thus each author was required to directly engage with the sea's 'fluid mobility and its tactile materiality' (Steinberg, 2013, p. 157). Written by scholars from a variety of fields (for example, geography, sociology, education) and theoretical backgrounds, drawing on a wide range of theorists (for example, Bourdieu, Delueze, Thrift), these chapters offer new insights and approaches to thinking about the ways in which we might understand our relationship with the sea.

In the opening chapter Mike Brown provides an overview of the various ways that the sea has been represented in Western societies. He integrates personal experiences – as a way of reflecting on some of the key representations – with the growing body of research that has called for a re-examination of the human–sea relationship. The concept of *seascapes* as a way of moving beyond the visual to incorporate embodied, lived experiences is elaborated. He argues that seascapes are not 'outside' us but rather 'they are part of us as we are part of them' (p. 24). In building a case for the sea as a scape, he sets the scene for the reader to consider how seascapes have influenced the lives and thinking of the contributors whose voices come through strongly in the following chapters.

In Chapter 2, Barbara Humberstone expands on the importance of embodied narratives, the senses and subjectivities. She details how autoethnographic accounts can give rise to a greater appreciation of sensuous and embodied knowledge. Through recounting her own sensuous encounters with the sea, she shares with us the way in which the sea can be viewed as the 'seat of the senses' (p. 30). Barbara details how scholars from a variety of disciplinary areas (for example, cultural geography, sport and physical culture, tourism studies) have both recognised and engaged with embodied narratives to elucidate the entwinement between the senses, the body and social thought. This chapter lays the foundations on which the autoethnographic narratives in the succeeding chapters build.

In the following chapter, lisahunter takes us above, on, in and under the water as she shares with us her experiences as a board rider, lifesaver and helicopter rescue swimmer. Her accounts of explorations to understand 'who am I?' and how the sea has shaped this learning are captivating. Drawing on a range of theories, lisahunter offers us a 'glimpse into the life of a spatio-sensorial embodied mind' (p. 41). As lisahunter illustrates, the sea and activities associated with it (for example, rescue work) provide opportunities to reflect on important sociological issues, such as, agency and oppression, life and death, embodiment and abstraction. 'E's chapter encourages us to consider the role of the sea in our lives as we attempt to understand the often competing, contradictory and discontinuous discourses that permeate us across our lives.

In Chapter 4, Jon Anderson uses his experiences of sea swell (surf) to consider the way in which surfing technologies mediate the way in which we experience the sea. Through recounting his own experiences, Jon describes different ways of 'dwelling-in-motion' (p. 58) that is the essence of embodied practices of surfing. His accounts of different ways of engaging with surf illustrate the way that technologies mediate one's relationship with the dynamic fluid wave. Jon's chapter contains multiple links to video clips that allow the reader to move beyond the written word and gain a greater appreciation of the complexities and intricacies involved in different modalities of surfing. As a 'water person', Jon invites us to think anew about the human–sea (surf) relationship that is a place where he belongs.

In Chapter 5, Robyn Zink explores what makes sailing 'feel right'. Her reflections of sailing across Cook Strait (between the North and South Islands in New Zealand) provide a focal point for considering explanations of why she returns to the sea. Her explorations move beyond simplistic accounts of being 'free at sea' or Romantic notions of the sea as a wilderness where one might find one's true self. Robyn's voyage takes us through phenomenology into the work of Foucault, and she finds resonance in the writings of Deleuze and Guattari. Drawing on the notion of assemblage and affect, she considers how these elucidate her lived experiences of being on watch on her night passage. Robyn's insightful examination of what 'feels right' draws on her embodied *being* in an assemblage of relationships that are not divisible into individual elements. For Robyn, it is the sea that affords opportunities to be in relationships that call her back time and time again.

Mihi Nemani's opening narrative in Chapter 6 draws us into a world in which the hierarchies of surfing subculture, gender and race are confronted and challenged through skilful performance. Mihi's account of marginalisation, as a brown female bodyboarder, is thoughtfully analysed through the lens provided by Pierre Bourdieu. Her chapter highlights how one might, through necessity or choice, conform to or subvert existing expectations across a range of contexts. Mihi's chapter highlights how prejudice and bias do not necessarily disappear at the water's edge. As is conveyed through her account, the freedom to be oneself must be fought for at sea, as in other spheres, through displays of competence and mastery. Mihi's journey provides us with an insight into the power of sociological theory in making sense of one's lived experiences, and it potentially challenges us, as readers, to think reflexively about how we position and 'other' those who do not fit within our frames of reference.

Sailing provides Peter Reason with the opportunity to reflect on Bateson's ideas concerning the errors of Western epistemology in Chapter 7. Peter draws our attention to issues of ecological sustainability, and his passages aboard *Coral* provide him with ample opportunity to think about his, and humanity's, relationship with the sea. In the voyage that he shares with us, he relates Bateson's ideas to his own experiences of being with the sea and his preference to work with the elements (tides and wind) rather than pushing against or through them. It is when one has experienced the difference between working with the tide, rather than against it, that the sense of working in harmony or rhythm becomes clear. Peter's reflections on what progress might actually mean and our choices about how we use technology (for example, a diesel engine) provide readers with an example of the tensions that we all face in making decisions that are ecologically sustainable. Drawing on Bateson, Peter's challenge is to consider how we might think in new ways. Sailing may be one way to 'rediscover the experience of grace' (p. 108) of working with sea-world rather than against it.

In Chapter 8, Karen Barbour traces multiple generations of family migrations by sea to Aotearoa, New Zealand. She interweaves personal stories and family recollections to show how personal and cultural identity in an island nation is shaped by the sea and the voyages that sea travel entails. The narrative of her own voyage by yacht to Fiji forms part of a kaleidoscope of experiences that she has inherited and embodied in her own ways of being in relation to the sea. As a woman of the Pacific, Karen's story encapsulates many elements that might resonate with those whose identity is shaped by seas; seas that both connect and separate us from the places of origin of our forebears. As she points out, familial stories, personal sensory experiences and cultural myths serve to shape our subsequent experiences and choices throughout our lives (Barbour, 2011). One is left wondering about how the young boy, at the end of Karen's chapter, will make sense of his heritage as he makes his way in the world that has undeniably been shaped by the sea

In Chapter 9, Brian Wattchow describes the constant draw of the sea, both metaphorically and literally, as he immerses himself in the Southern Ocean. Brian combines poetry, history and the perspective of a naturalist as he interweaves his encounters with the sea with Australian literature and popular culture. His narrative considers the sea in settler Australian consciousness and the way in which it has contributed to particular forms of national identity that is itself under constant revision. Drawing on literature of place, he reflects on local places, on how one might 'know the sea' in particular, and on the importance of indigenous ways of knowing as we look to the future and our changing relationships with the sea.

In Chapter 10, Robbie Nicol considers the mind/world link from the perspective of his sea kayak. Robbie's chapter raises issues relating to anthropomorphism, ecology and sustainability. His work challenges 'those with a love of seascapes to engage in and promote sustainable living' (p. 152). His reflexive and philosophical writing is interspersed with emotive accounts of his encounters with a variety of wildlife (both living and deceased) that powerfully illustrate the connection between autoethnography and broader social issues and forces at play. Robbie articulates how his relationship with the sea calls for him to be in the world and in so doing understand how one might live a meaningful life.

Karen Throsby's chapter (11) opens with the disclosure that she loathes boats. Her recollection of playing in an inflatable dinghy tethered to the shore by a rope to avoid the perils of being swept out to sea does not appear to bode well for an enduring relationship with the sea. Nor does it provide any inkling of the magnitude of her 'deviant behaviour' as a marathon swimmer. Karen's narratives bring to life the trials and tribulations of becoming and then being a marathon swimmer. Drawing on Becker's study of outsiders and deviant behaviour, Karen details the process of becoming a marathon swimmer through her role as an 'aquatic sociologist'. Her powerful first-hand accounts and her observations of her co-deviants' struggles provide an enthralling portrayal of how one becomes socialised into marathon swimming. The process clearly shapes her sense of who she is, but it goes beyond this to literally shaping her body so that it is capable of withstanding the demands of cold temperatures and prolonged repetitive actions. As Karen acknowledges, hers is a particular relationship with the sea based on the idiosyncratic pleasures of long periods of immersion. It is clearly a relationship that has shaped her in ways that extend our understanding of the human–sea relationship.

elke emerald and Fiona Ewing have collaboratively co-constructed Chapter 12 based on Fiona's experiences on board deep-sea fishing vessels and elke's desire to give voice to her friend's experiences in a 'man's world'. The skilful and elegant combination of voices – elke as researcher/writer and Fiona as story-teller/scientist – permits an intriguing entrée into the life of a woman fisheries officer on foreign fishing vessels. This is a chapter that explores stories that we might use to make meaning of our lives, of how one becomes part of the story rather than being the subject of the story, of finding one's place in a community at sea and on land. It is an account of becoming embraced by a community whose unwritten code needs to be lived rather than just understood. Long periods of life at sea have provided Fiona with lived experiences that have seen her embraced as a seafarer and, through elke's crafting of these stories, we gain an insight into how the seascape shapes relationships beyond the confines of a fishing vessel.

In the final chapter, Barbara Humberstone and Mike Brown invite the reader to reflect upon the evocative narratives presented in this volume, taking the notion of seascape 'as a mobile living energy, a phenomenological part of their being and becoming' (p. 188). They call upon readers to engage in research that is corporeal, sentient, more-than-representational, which might 'interrogate[ing] the world for potentials for social and environmental awareness and action' (p. 188).

As the contributors convey, through diverse experiences with the sea and via different theoretical lenses, it is possible to understand the sea as 'an alternative known world' (Raban, 1987, p. 220). This is something that Moitessier knew well when he wrote

> A sailor's geography is not always that of the cartographer, for whom a cape is a cape, with a latitude and longitude. For the sailor, a great cape is both very simple and an extremely complicated whole of rocks, currents, breaking seas

and huge waves, fair winds and gales, joys and fears, fatigue, dreams, painful hands, empty stomachs, wonderful moments, and suffering at times. A great cape, for us, can't be expressed in longitude and latitude alone. A great cape has a soul, with very soft, very violent shadows and colours. A soul as smooth as a child's, as hard as a criminal's. And that is why we go. (Moitessier, 1974, p. 141)

The contributors' sea may not be your sea but we hope that through their narratives you will gain an understanding of the myriad ways that the seascape has the potential to shape all of us, whether we are aware of it or not.

References

Anderson, J., 2012. Relational places: The surfed wave as assemblage and convergence. *Environment and Planning D: Society and Space*, 30, pp. 570–87, doi: 10.1068/d17910.

Anderson, J. and Peters K., 2014. 'A perfect and absolute blank': Human geographies of water worlds. In: J. Anderson and K. Peters, eds, *Water Worlds: Human Geographies of the Ocean*. Farnham, UK and Burlington, VT: Ashgate, pp. 3–19.

Barbour, K. N., 2011. *Dancing Across the Page: Narrative and Embodied Ways of Knowing*. Bristol, UK: Intellect Books.

Brown, M., 2013. Emile Durkheim: Structural functionalism, adventure and the social order. In: E. Pike and S. Beames, eds, *Outdoor Adventure and Social Theory*. London: Routledge, pp. 23–33.

Cooney, G., 2003. Introduction: Seeing land from the sea. *World Archaeology*, 35(3), pp. 323–8, doi: 10.1080/0043824042000185748.

Ford, N. and Brown, D., 2006. *Surfing and Social Theory: Experience, Embodiment and the Narrative of the Dream Glide*. London: Routledge.

Fincham, B., McGuinness, M. and Murray, L., 2010. Introduction. In: B. Fincham, M. McGuinness and L. Murray, eds, *Mobile Methodologies*. Basingstoke, UK: Palgrave Macmillan, pp. 1–10.

Lambert, D., Martins, L. and Ogborn, M., 2006. Currents, visions and voyages: Historical geographies of the sea. *Journal of Historical Geography*, 32, pp. 479–93.

Mack, J., 2011. *The Sea: A Cultural History*. London: Reaktion Books.

Moitessier, B., 1974. *The Long Way*. London: Granada.

Peters, K., 2010. Future promises for contemporary social and cultural geographies of the sea. *Geography Compass*, 4(9), pp. 1260–72.

Phelan, J., 2007. Seascapes: Tides of thought and being in Western perceptions of the sea. *Goldsmiths Anthropology Research Paper*, 14, pp. 1–23.

Pike, E. and Beames, S., eds, 2013. *Outdoor Adventure and Social Theory*. London: Routledge.

Pink, S., 2009. *Doing Sensory Ethnography*. London: Sage.

Raban, J., 1987. *Coasting*. London: Picador.

Shields, R., 1991. *Places on the Margin: Alternative Geographies of Modernity*. London: Routledge.

Sparkes, A., 1999. Exploring body narratives. *Sport, Education and Society*, 4(1), pp. 17–30.

Sparkes, A. and Smith, B., 2008. Narrative constructionist inquiry. In: J. A. Holstein and J. F. Gubrium, eds, *Handbook of Constructionist Research*. London: The Guilford Press, pp. 295–313.

Sparkes, A. and Smith, B., 2012. Embodied research methodologies and seeking the senses in sport and physical culture: A fleshing out of problems and possibilities. *Qualitative Research on Sport and Physical Culture Research in the Sociology of Sport*, 6, pp. 167–90.

Steinberg, P., 1999. Navigating to multiple horizons: Toward a geography of ocean-space. *Professional Geographer*, 51(3), pp. 366–75.

Steinberg, P., 2001. *The Social Construction of the Ocean*. Cambridge: Cambridge University Press.

Steinberg, P., 2013. Of other seas: Metaphors and materialities in maritime regions. *Atlantic Studies*, 10(2), pp. 156–69.

Steinberg, P., 2014. Foreword on Thalassography. In: J. Anderson and K. Peters, eds, *Water Worlds: Human Geographies of the Ocean*. Farnham, UK and Burlington, VT: Ashgate, pp. xiii–vii.

Strang, V., 2004. *The Meaning of Water*. Oxford: Berghahn.

Strang, V., 2008. Uncommon ground: Landscapes as social geography. In: B. David and J. Thomas, eds, *Handbook of Landscape Archaeology*. Walnut Creek, CA: Left Coast Press, pp. 51–9.

Thrift, N., 2008. *Non-Representational Theory: Space, Politics, Affect*. London: Routledge.

Watson, J., 2010. *True Spirit: The Aussie Girl Who Took On the World*. Sydney: Hachette.

Wattchow, B. and Brown, M., 2011. *Pedagogy of Place: Outdoor Education for a Changing World*. Melbourne: Monash University Publishing.

Chapter 1
Seascapes

Mike Brown

I roll over and knock my shoulder on the shelf that runs down the side of my berth. This space is new to me and I haven't yet adjusted to the confines of the quarter berth. Lying on my back I can just see the underside of the deck that can easily be touched with an outstretched arm. Thirty centimetres to my left is the hull and to my right I can see through a porthole into the cockpit. The berth is only just above the waterline. It is the almost constant slopping of small waves under the stern that has woken me. The wind has obviously changed direction and, with the boat secured fore and aft on a pile mooring, waves from a different angle have released a new cacophony of plopping, burping and gurgling under the stern of the boat. I can feel minute movements as the boat gently responds to the wind and waves. I hear the mooring lines stretch to take up tension and then, when the wind eases, they contract back in relief. I'm conscious of these noises – which are both familiar and new. It's 13 years since I sold my last yacht, a steel ocean cruiser, and my new boat is a fibreglass production vessel designed for coastal passages. I know where these sounds originate and I remember the feeling of constant movement afloat – but there is also a strangeness to them. Waves on fibreglass sound different and her movements are not as sedate, but then she is light in comparison to my last boat that I lived on for three years. I turn over. I feel at home in this constantly moving and chattering world. This is a feeling I have missed and longed for. I needed to return to sea. I recall a line from Jonathan Raban's book Passage to Juneau, 'Being afloat gives me, at least, a heightened sense of being alive moment to moment' (1999, p. 90). It is here that I belong.

Introduction

From his vantage point on the deck of an Atlantic liner, Simon Winchester (2010) commented that, 'From here onward the sea yawned open wide and featureless, and soon took on the character that is generally true of all oceans – being unmarked, unclaimed, largely unknowable, and in a very large measure unknown' (p. 8). Winchester's assertion reflects what Mack (2011) has described as the predominant Western characterisation of the sea as 'a quintessential wilderness, a void without community other than that temporarily established on boats crewed by those with the shared experience of being tossed about on its surface, and a space without ruins or other witness to the events which may have taken place on its surface ...' (Mack, 2011, p. 17).

Fleming (1982) suggests that while a mariner might feel at home on a ship, the ocean cannot be home as it engenders feelings of unease.

> It is too deep, too dark below, too boundless. There is nothing limited or cosy or comfortable about it. Awed by its power and immensity we imbue it with magnified human emotions, behaviour, characteristics. Thus it can be sometimes cruel, hungry, mean, callous, sometimes languid, seductive, inscrutable – but never is it ordinary or trivial; never is it truly innocuous. (Fleming, 1982, p. 29)

Conceptualising the sea as featureless, unknowable or a wilderness is a reflection of ideas, imagery and metaphors that have permeated Western consciousness via literature and art. This contrasts with Mack's (2011) account of how Pacific navigators 'feel' their way on Winchester's 'featureless' ocean. As Mack explains, some Pacific navigators appear to give precedence to the feel of the waves over other navigational indicators such as stars. He recounts how a mariner located the vessel's position by feeling the particular 'signature' of waves generated by changes in the swells as they encountered islands far beyond the horizon. Mack details how mariners may also use other sensory organs to navigate and he recounts the story of a blind mariner who was able to identify his location by taste. It appears that different sections or streams of water have different tastes and the blind mariner's heightened sense of taste allowed him to predict landfall at a particular island group the day before arrival. The sea, or perhaps particular places on the sea, may not be as unknowable or unknown as Winchester suggests. The 'featureless' sea or 'void space' reflect particular readings or interpretations of the sea that fail to resonate with me and, I suspect, with many of the people I have associated with over the years.

I grew up surrounded by boats. My father was introduced to the sea and allure of the Hauraki Gulf (Auckland) via his compulsory military training in the New Zealand Navy. As a young man from the southern city of Dunedin he sought job opportunities in Auckland, where he was based during his time in the navy, and he was transferred north in the early 1960s. As a young boy I went sailing in a series of small centreboard dinghies and over about a decade I helped my father build a 12-metre motorboat. New Zealand and American boating magazines were staple reading at home and, for a period of time, Christmas and birthday presents consisted of books on most matters nautical. In the early 1990s I worked in the United Kingdom for a sailing training organisation on 70-foot boats with a crew of up to 18. On my return to New Zealand I purchased an offshore yacht and cruised the south west Pacific. In more recent years I have sailed Outward Bound cutters (open boats designed along the lines of traditional Royal Naval vessels as used by Captain Bligh), racing yachts and now on my own boat. I have also sea kayaked in Scotland, south east Australia and New Zealand. For me, the sea is far from featureless. The Irish Sea is different from the Hauraki Gulf, which is different from the slow rolling mass of Pacific swells. The colour, the temperature, the shape of the waves, the types of boats and the people who inhabit these sea places differ. The professional Scottish fisher, used to toiling in the Atlantic, is a different character from the Tongan fisher who fishes for family and community from an open canoe, who is in turn different from the Moreton Bay (Australia) recreational fisher in a purpose-built day-boat. Each of these illustrative groups enters into a relationship with the sea on which they fish. This relationship is impacted by the economic importance of their task (occupation, source of necessary nutrition, or leisure activity); the nature of the sea on which they perform their tasks (depth of water, level of exposure to wind/ waves, water temperature); the materiality of their environment (access to steel, timber, aluminium or fibreglass) and their cultural history with the sea (economic resource to be exploited/conserved, a sacred 'spiritscape', or a playground). Each of these examples serves to point out the reciprocity between people and the sea that they inhabit; some by choice and others by necessity.

The meanings that are given to the sea have been referred to as timeless, in that we have always tried to make meaning of our relationship, but they are certainly not changeless (Osborn, 1977). Osborn has argued that 'the changing face of the sea symbol illustrates how even the archetype can be transformed by dramatic changes in human circumstance' (p. 347). In the section that follows I provide a brief outline of some of the major representations of the sea that have shaped Western thought.

Representations of the Sea

Steinberg (1999a) points out that, 'Modern-era representations and regulations of ocean spaces are particular to our society and have their origins in underlying social structures and uses of the sea' (p. 408). A number of authors have provided detailed analyses of the changing representations of the sea in Western thought that are worthy of further exploration (see Auden, 1951; Connery, 2006; Ford and Brown, 2006; Lambert, Martins and Ogborn, 2006; Peters, 2010; Phelan, 2007; Raban, 1992; Steinberg, 2001).

The Sea as Dangerous and Chaotic

Auden (1951) outlines how Western societies have been influenced by the Judaeo-Christian narratives of Genesis and Greek cosmologies to construct a view of the seas that has created a powerful metaphor of the sea as dangerous and chaotic. Connery (2006) details Biblical influences on Western understandings of the sea and notes that Revelation (21:1) portrays an apocalyptic vision in which a new earth will be rid of the disorderly sea. In mapping the influence of these early representations Auden (1951) noted that the sea was positioned as a 'barbaric vagueness and disorder out of which civilisation has emerged and into which, unless saved by the efforts of gods and men, it is always liable to relapse' (pp. 18–19). Early representations reinforced conceptions of the sea as a place of fear and repulsion that are still manifest in contemporary discourses (Ford and Brown, 2006). For example, see Brown and Penney's (2014) analysis of public reaction to Jessica Watson's solo sailing circumnavigation.

Ford and Brown (2006) suggest that Renaissance perspectives (for example, exemplified by Shakespeare) provide a 'bridge between the primarily dark and negative classical and medieval attitudes to the sea and the later more positive perspectives' (Ford and Brown, 2006, p. 10). They suggest that Shakespeare's work illustrates a transition from portraying the sea as a site of fear to one where the sea, and a voyage on it, could become a site for cleansing and transformation. This re-shaping of the sea mixed notions of fear and repulsion with the possibility for redemption in and though the sea (Osborn, 1977).

Sea as a Blank Public Space

Ford and Brown (2006) suggest that advances in science and the development of new technologies have reshaped perceptions of the sea. As our understanding of the natural world increased, ancient myths and misconceptions about the sea were supplemented by more reasoned understandings.

> These advances underlay Europe's 'Age of Discovery' as imperial expansion and state rivalries led to voyages to ever-more distant parts of the globe, fuelled by a sense of adventure, enchantment with and attraction to exotic shores in search of profit and glory. (Ford and Brown, 2006, p. 11)

Imperial agendas and capitalism had a profound effect on the production of sea space as a blank public space. Steinberg (1999a) details the rise of the modern sea-space regime based on the legal principle of *imperium* derived from the Roman control of the Mediterranean. 'According to this doctrine, the ocean is immune to incorporation within the territory of any individual state, but, as an essential space of society …' (Steinberg, 1999a, p. 408). This was expressed in Grotius' 1608 influential treatise *Mare Liberum [Freedom of the Seas]* (Steinberg, 2001). This approach was well suited to the mercantile trade; the sea could not be possessed. According to Steinberg (2001), *mare liberum* was central to capitalist constructions of the ocean-space as an empty, non-territorial domain, an 'asocial space between societies' (p. 208). McNiven (2008) has argued that this emptiness is manifest in the 'cartographic tradition of representing sea-space two dimensionally as homogenized blue space and necessitated a new (arbitrary) geo-referencing grid system of latitude and longitude for European ocean navigation' (p. 150).

'*Mare liberum*' is a construct that has served particular economic and political agendas. McNiven (2008), drawing on Nonie Sharp, suggests that the notion of *mare liberum* concealed more complex and localised associations with particular seascapes in small indigenous communities – including those in Scandinavia.

Likewise Steinberg (1999a) has compared the notion of *mare liberum*, as a social construction of the ocean, to a range of other societies. He notes that in some societies in Oceania, for example, the sea is an integral space of society and is governed like the land. Hence Steinberg's (2001) assertion that what we take to 'be' the ocean, and our understandings of it (for example, the extent of the freedom of the sea and what might fall within the realm of territorial jurisdiction), is a social construction.

Sea as Sublime, Wild Nature

European Romanticism, as a reaction against rationalism, materialism, imperial expansionism, industrialisation and environmental despoliation, gave rise to a new way to view the sea as an exemplar of the sublime. It has been argued that romanticism marked a fundamental change in the symbolic meaning ascribed to the sea (Auden, 1951; Osborn, 1977).

Auden (1951) suggests that the Romantic inclination heralded in a new attitude to the sea. However, Osborn (1977) argues that the Romantic conception was a development of ideas that featured in many of the early epic poems. In these epic accounts, the sea dealt harshly with ships that carried 'wicked or morally polluted persons' (Osborn, 1977, p. 349). Auden (1951) suggests that the Romantic movement stressed firstly, that men of sense and honour should desire to leave the land and city; secondly, 'the sea is the real situation and the voyage is the true condition of man'; and thirdly, 'The sea is where decisive events, the moments of eternal choice, of temptation, fall and redemption occur. The shore life is always trivial' (p. 23).

Romanticism drew on the discontent with industrialisation and the notions of the sea as a blank site where one might be free. Through adventure one might escape the banalities of shore-based life and its contaminating influences.

> Men came to find in the ocean a large-scale, concrete projection of what they felt in grander moments to be their own depth, immensity, mystery, and permanence … For such persons, the sea came to represent freedom, an opportunity for the self-realization which had been denied on shore. (Osborn, 1977, p. 357)

Interestingly, Osborn observed that, though the newer poetic metaphors of the sublime gained traction, elements of traditional perspectives of the sea, as immense and dangerous, remained. This was no placid tamed sea. It was a wilderness that stood in contrast to the domesticated and despoiled landscape.

It was a wilderness in which one could venture and create one's own destiny. As Ford and Brown (2006) note, 'The sea, especially in its wild and stormy incarnation, appeared as a recurring symbol of wild nature beyond the stifling control of reason … the creative contribution of the Romantic movement was to propound a coherent discourse of the sea, which enhanced the emotional strategy of enjoying the seashore' (p. 12).

Ford and Brown (2006) argue that the Romantic image of the sea continues to shape contemporary perceptions. I am reminded of the opening chapter in Jonathan Raban's (1987) *Coasting*, in which he describes the preparations for his sailing trip around the British Isles. Tracing a lineage of coasters who recorded their journeys (McGregor, Middleton and Belloc), Raban describes his search for a suitable boat and the conversations he has with men who share similar dreams. 'What unites us more deeply is a compulsive itch for the escape valve of a wilderness, an open frontier, and that even now Britain does have a last frontier, in the sea' (p. 35).

I wonder if I am 'afflicted' with a dose of romanticism. There is something special and satisfying about rounding a headland and entering the lee of the land, dropping anchor and relaxing after a 'fair old bashing'. Yet I've never thought of the sea as a wilderness – to me wilderness conjures up images of high mountain peaks or dense forests. It involves consciously embarking on an adventure and embracing risks. I've never thought of the sea in this way. At times it fills me with anxiety, and boredom and pleasure. Sometimes when I'm at sea I can think of nothing more pleasant than being in a warm dry café. Sometimes being out here is just shitty, when my stomach has turned itself inside out and I'm cold and tired it's not much fun. I'm not escaping 'civilisation'. I'm not looking to build character or reveal my 'true' nature – being at sea is just what I enjoy – despite the shitty moments. It's not a battle against the elements (I'm far too much of a fair weather sailor to want to conquer anything). The sea is, just as the land is, and the air is. Seasickness quickly dispels the poetic or sublime images of the sea. But I'm also conscious of that which is difficult to articulate, that sense of being that cannot be adequately described in words or rational explanations. To try and progress this chapter I've come to the boat. But I haven't gone anywhere – I'm still gently rocking on the pile moorings. I came here because I knew that the movement, the creaks and groans and the wind in the rigging would help me to think and write.

This brief sketch of key elements in representations of the sea highlights the changing perspectives of the sea, which Ford and Brown suggest act 'as a mirror to humankind and the human condition' (2006, p. 12). Our relationship with the sea reflects the myths, beliefs and knowledge of our times. Through time, our understandings of the sea have changed as a result of social and technological changes in society. However, elements of these conceptions continue to permeate Western attitudes to the sea. For example, Steinberg (1999a) suggests that the seas are still seen 'as an empty void to be annihilated by hypermobile capital' (p. 403). Bespoke sailing events provide amateur adventurers with the opportunity to test themselves against the challenges of the Southern Ocean (for example, www. clipperroundtheworld.com). The sea, as a site of fear and repulsion, continues to feature in movies aimed at the general public (for example, *Deep Blue Sea*, *Adrift* and the various monsters in the *Pirates of the Caribbean* series).

Lambert et al. (2006) remind us that the sea is both a social and material space. Yet Steinberg (2013) issues a caution, conceding that while the sea is a social construction, 'it is not *just* a social construction' (p. 156). He goes on to state that, 'The partial nature of or encounter with the ocean necessarily creates gaps, as the unrepresentable becomes the unacknowledged and the unacknowledged becomes the unthinkable' (p. 157). It is the challenge to represent the under-acknowledged or only partially acknowledged that has provided the catalyst for this book.

Just as the boat bobs on the smallest of waves so to do the sentences and paragraphs on my computer screen. My ideas are in constant flux. Does this sentence/idea belong here or would it be better placed earlier? Is this an essential idea or have I belaboured that point? Like my environment, my thinking is constantly changing. Yet just like my floating office, I too am moored. I am tethered to my cultural assumptions and beliefs. I can move around within certain parameters but what will happen if I let the lines go?

This 'letting go of the lines' is what Steinberg (2014) calls for when he adroitly points out how statistics are used to justify the significance of the oceans as a worthy topic of study. He argues that numbers reduce the ocean to a static and undifferentiated other that can be objectified. Rather than seeing the ocean as 'other' Steinberg (2014) argues that:

> The alternative, if one is to write about the ocean as a non-objectified arena, is to approach it as a space that is not so much *known* as *experienced*; less a space that we live *on* (or, more often, gaze *at*) than we live *in*; less a two-dimensional surface than a four-dimensional sphere; a space that we think *from*. (Anderson, 2012, p. xiv)

It is this notion of experiencing and knowing, in and through direct engagement, that I wish to encapsulate through *Seascapes*.

Seascapes

As indicated above, our views of the sea are fluid rather than fixed and are intertwined with changes in technology and shifts in the composition and nature of society. Raban (1992) notes that the sea 'changes in response to shifts of sensibility as dramatically as it does to the shifts of wind and the phases of the moon' (p. 3).

Connery (1996) has suggested that the liquid or fluid nature of the sea has often been seen as problematic and has led to 'categorical difficulty and ontological uncertainty' (p. 291). Strang (2004) suggests that the 'most constant "quality" of water is that it is not constant' (p. 49). Yet notions of fluidity, movement and change are only problematic if one views stability as the norm by which judgements of worth/value are made.

The post-modern turn (Best and Kellner, 1997; Giddens, 1991), which has disrupted bounded categorisations, established fields of expertise and power/

knowledge relationships, has created space for creatively re-examining existing ontological and epistemological positions in regard to what *is* and, in doing so, has opened up new ways of considering what *might be*. Anderson (2012) argues that changes wrought by globalisation and postmodernity have impacted on conceptualisations of terrestrial place 'not as static or bounded but as mobile and in process' (p. 571), which has had a profound impact on how we think about places. This reconceptualisation has provided an opportunity for greater engagement with the fluidity and dynamism of the sea, which previously set it as distinct from conceptions of (terrestrial) places that were considered stable and defined. The recognition of the fluidity, porosity and mutability of spaces and places opens up room for embracing the sea in ways hitherto on the edges of academic analysis (see Lambert et al., 2006; Peters, 2010). It is the very notion of the fluid, moving and changing nature of the sea that opens up opportunities to consider the sea as a 'scape'; a seascape that shapes us by a myriad of physical and social processes (Steinberg, 1999b).

The Oxford English Dictionary (OED online) defines a seascape as 'a picture of the sea, a sea-piece' and 'a picturesque view or prospect of the sea'. McNiven (2008) suggests that the term seascape is commonly used to refer to visual representations of the sea, the coast or ships. 'Beyond this authoritative and generally accepted view, it is difficult to find more nuanced definitions' (McNiven, 2008, p. 150). Perhaps some of the difficulties that we experience, when trying to develop more nuanced definitions, are rooted in the discourses of the sea to which we are exposed, along with the difficulty in coming to terms with the fluidity and movement that *is* the sea. Consideration of the sea as fluid and 'other' accentuates difference from land-based ways of thinking that have, until recently, been the focus of scholars' attention.

Cooney (2003) suggests that we should consider the sea as a scape that is 'contoured, alive, rich in ecological diversity and in cosmological and religious significance and ambiguity ...' (p. 323). In doing so, he suggests that we can gain a valuable new perspective on how people 'actively create their identities, sense of place and histories' (p. 323). As a scape, the sea 'is a participant in, not a contextual backdrop to, social engagements ... maritime people technologically travel *across* the sea but socially negotiate their way *through* a seascape' (McNiven, 2008, p. 154).

A seascape moves beyond the visual to include the non-human world, embodied lived-experiences, representations of these experiences of being in and on the sea, and the historical and social dimensions that constitute individual and collective consciousness of the sea.

Drawing on Ingold (2000), we can conceive of a seascape not as a representation of something exterior to us but rather as an integral part of who we are. Ingold argues for a rejection of the division between the inner and outdoor worlds of experience and representation, of mind and matter, or meaning and substance.

Cobb and Ransley (2009) re-articulated Ingold's conceptualisation of landscape to highlight the potential of seascapes[1] in shaping our lived experiences.

> The [seascape], I hold, is not a picture in the imagination, surveyed by the mind's eye; nor, however, is it an alien and formless substrate awaiting the imposition of human order ... neither is the [seascape] identical to nature, nor is it on the side of humanity *against* nature. As the familiar domain of our dwelling, it is *with* us, not against us, but it is no less real for that. And through living in it, the [seascape] becomes a part of us, just as we are a part of it. (Ingold, 1993:154; Cobb and Ransley, 2009, p. 3)

As Anderson (2014) highlights, the seascapes we live in 'are dynamic, and form our world views and our lives' (p. 114). Thus seascapes include the materiality of the biophysical world, the cultural lens through which we construct our world view(s) and our lived experiences of being in and on the sea. The sea shapes us and we, in turn, attempt to 'shape it' as we construct various versions of it that reflect our changing relationship with it. Our interaction with the sea is a 'dynamic and recursive relationship' (Strang, 2008, p. 52) that may act as a form of cultural reproduction, but there is also the potential for subversion (see Chapters 3, 6 and 12). Seascapes are integral in the formation of our expressions of personal and cultural identity (Strang, 2008; Tilley, 2006). The social and technological intertwine in our engagement with the sea. Our identities are conditioned by the materiality and cultural logic that constitutes the seascapes we inhabit. Much like the sea, our identities may be 'improvised and changing, rather than fixed and rule-bound, intimately related to experience and context. They are both in the mind and of the world, embodied and objectified through action and material practice' (Tilley, 2006, p. 17). Our relationship with the sea is based on an interactive process where we also conceive of seascapes in culturally specific ways (Lambert et al., 2006; Torrence, 2002). By way of example, Lambert et al. (2006) and Mack (2011) have detailed how Pacific mariners are able to locate their position through feeling differing motions in waves. This is vastly different from sailors who might use electronic signals (for example, Global Positioning System) from satellites to pin-point their position. These ways of determining location indicate 'different relationships between water, land, bodies, knowledge and techniques' (Lambert et al., 2006, p. 487). Thus experiences and knowledge of one's seascape can be markedly different and demonstrate 'different relationships between people, materials and geographies' (Lambert et al., 2006, p. 487). Far from being a 'blank slate' the experiences of seascapes are differentiated by gender, class, race and sexuality (Lambert et al., 2006).

Arguing for the importance of seascapes is not premised on the need to diminish the scholarship connected to the study of landscape(s) nor to establish it 'against' or separate from studies of people's relationship to the land. For, as Anderson and

---

1 They adapted Ingold's original quote, which referred to 'landscape', and replaced it with 'seascape'.

Peters (2014) have recently noted, 'the sea is a space intrinsically connected to and absorbed within a broader network of spaces (earth and air) which are also, likewise porous, open and convergent with each other' (p. 6).

Seascapes as Embodied Experiences

Central to broader a conception of seascapes is the need to take into account embodied ways of knowing and being (see Chapter 2 for an elaboration on narratives, the body and the senses). As Tilley (2006) has noted, identity, memory and meaning 'have their generative source in the lived experience and sensory perception of people as they move in and through the water ...' (p. 21). By thinking of our engagement with the sea as a fluid and moving scape, we have the possibility of considering embodied ways of being and knowing that contribute to who we are or who we might become that are not bound by 'grounded and static categories' (Phelan, 2007, p. 20). By taking into account lived experiences in the seascape, we are able to move beyond the sea as a metaphor and engage in understanding how it 'becomes part of us, just as we become part of it' (Ingold, 2000, p. 191). Steinberg (2013) has expressed concerns that the sea has been

> reduced to a metaphor: a spatial (and thereby seemingly tangible) signifier for a world of shifting, fragmented identities, mobilities, and connections. While metaphors provide powerful tools for thought, spatial metaphors can be pernicious when they detract attention from the actual work of construction ... that transpires to make a space what it is. (p. 158)

The sea is more than a metaphor and Blum (2010) has commented on the danger of writing about the sea in such a way that the actual sea is rendered as immaterial. To counter this, Blum advocates for an approach that is 'attentive to the material conditions and praxis of the maritime world' (p. 670) and which draws on the lives and writings of those for whom the sea is central to their lived experiences. By centring 'the sea as a proprioceptive point of inquiry' (Blum, 2010, p. 671), through a focus of writing *from within* a seascape, we hope to encapsulate the local knowledge(s) and lived experience(s) that 'lie at the heart of the way in which people socialize seascapes' (Cooney, 2003, p. 324). It is our experiences *in* seascapes that constitute our construction of seascapes and our understanding of who we are. For example, the ethnographer Tyrell (2006) describes how the more she went out to sea the more meaningful it became for her and her evolving identity. It is our active involvement in a seascape, as the 'seat of our senses' (Humberstone, 2014, p. 30), that gives depth to the meanings that we might make. Tyrell's study with the Aviarmiut people of Hudson Bay sits alongside the accounts of the authors in this volume, as testimony to how the fluid and dynamic sea can be central to notions of identity and community. Tyrell details how her perspective of the sea changed from being a featureless space, to one that, based on her growing engagement and knowledge, became a seascape 'filled with meaning, connection, emotion and feelings of belonging' (p. 237). Ford and Brown (2006) suggest that, while sensory experiences may be located in the individual, they are constituted by 'the learned perspectives and interpretations that are the product of collective social and environmental interaction. Thus the meanings engendered by experience are simultaneously part of the cultural landscape that every person enters ...' (Ford and Brown, 2006, p. 9).

I look behind me at the wake and as I do so my shoulders twist slightly and I pull on the tiller. The boat alters course slightly and a little zigzag appears in the track we have left on the water. Oops – I push the tiller gently away and we are back on course. It's only a matter of several seconds before the waves and wind have removed all trace of our passing. Unlike walking or mountain biking, there are no visible markers of our movement through this area. There is no footprint or tread pattern as evidence of my presence or passage. I turn back and glance along the side deck. I can see the wind shadow on the water ahead and prepare to easy the mainsheet slightly. I move my foot so that it is resting against the small ridge in the cockpit floor. I know the boat will lean more when the breeze arrives. I'm ready to brace myself and ease the sail should it be necessary. My partner looks at me quizzically as if to say 'what are you doing?' As a sailor I've been here many times before; I can feel minute changes in wind strength, the differences in wave patterns, the 'sweet spot' when the sails are trimmed right and the boat is in 'the groove'. I may not be leaving a visible mark of my passing but being on the sea has imprinted a pattern of knowing, acting and being. The gust hits, the boat leans, the muscles in my leg tense slightly as I maintain my stance. I ease the sail to reduce pressure ... she accelerates slightly and I find myself grinning.

The sea's rapid erasure of signs of human activity[2] should not lead to the assumption that the sea has little or no impact on our understandings of who we are. Barthes's oft-quoted 'Here I am before the sea; it is true that it bears no message' (cited in Connery, 1996, p. 290) has a very hollow ring. Seascapes consist of embodied actions and reciprocal interactions between people and the sea (Cobb and Ransley, 2009, drawing on Ingold, 1993). As Cobb and Ransley (2009) point out, individual biographies, materials and places emerge, are entwined, and enacted by being in seascapes.

Being on/in the sea is to enter into a relationship that requires a response. We have no choice other than to adapt to the movement and rhythms of the sea (Palsson,

---

2 I acknowledge the construction of human artefacts such as the seawalls, sea defences, navigation aids, and more recently wind farms may alter the seascape (and whose presence may outlast an individual's lifespan). However, all such structures require ongoing maintenance to survive in an environment that is largely impervious to their presence. I am also conscious that ocean currents concentrate large quantities of detritus that may become part of the seascape for indefinite periods.

1994). As a familiar domain of our lives, seascapes are with us rather than against us (Ingold, 2000). For the contributors in this collection a seascape is not easily categorised. It is not simply a fearful chaotic place, a blank slate, or sublime nature. Various aspects of these representations may feature, as markers of our cultural heritage, but the accounts that follow attempt to move beyond simplistic descriptions to capture the complexities and nuances of being a person in and of the sea.

Seascapes are not 'outside' us; they are part of us as we are part of them. Like us they are constantly changing and complex. As the authors in the following chapters illustrate, our engagement with seascapes shape who we are.

References

Anderson, J., 2012. Relational places: The surfed wave as assemblage and convergence. *Environment and Planning D: Society and Space*, 30, pp. 570–87, doi: 10.1068/d17910.

———— 2014. What I talk about when I talk about kayaking. In: J. Anderson and K. Peters, eds, *Water Worlds: Human Geographies of the Ocean*. Farnham, UK and Burlington, VT: Ashgate, pp. 103–17.

Anderson, J. and Peters, K., 2014. 'A perfect and absolute blank': Human geographies of water worlds. In: J. Anderson and K. Peters, eds, *Water Worlds: Human Geographies of the Ocean*. Farnham, UK and Burlington, VT: Ashgate, pp. 3–19.

Auden, W., 1951. *The Enchafed Flood, or the Romantic Iconography of the Sea*. London: Faber and Faber.

Best, S. and Kellner, D., 1997. *The Postmodern Turn*. New York: Guilford Press.

Blum, H., 2010. The prospect of oceanic studies. *Proceedings of the Modern Language Association*, 125(3), pp. 670–77, doi: 10.1632/pmla.2010.125.3.670.

Brown, M. and Penney, D., 2014. Solo sailing: An 'ordinary girl', voluntary risk taking and (ir)responsibility. *Sociology of Sport Journal*, 31(3), pp. 267–86.

Cobb, H. and Ransley, J., 2009. Moving beyond the 'scape' to being in the (watery) world, wherever. In: Association of Social Anthrologists Annual Conference, *Anthropological and Archaeological Imaginations: Past, Present and Future*. Bristol, UK, 6–9 April 2009. Available at: http://core.kmi.open. ac.uk/display/23656 [accessed 25 March 2014].

Connery, C., 1996. Oceanic feeling and regional imaginary. In: R. Wilson and W. Dissanayake, eds, *Global/Local: Cultural Production and the Transnational Imaginary*. London: Duke University Press, pp. 284–311.

———— 2006. There was no more sea: The supersession of the ocean from the bible to cyberspace. *Journal of Historical Geography*, 32, pp. 494–511.

Cooney, G., 2003. Introduction: Seeing land from the sea. *World Archaeology*, 35(3), pp. 323–8, doi: 10.1080/0043824042000185748.

Fleming, D., 1982. Seascapes. *Maritime Policy and Management: The Flagship Journal of International Shipping and Port Research*, 9(1), pp. 29–33.

Ford, N. and Brown, D., 2006. *Surfing and Social Theory: Experience, Embodiment and the Narrative of the Dream Glide*. London: Routledge.

Giddens, A., 1991. *Modernity and Self-Identity: Self and Society in the Late Modern Age*. Cambridge: Polity Press.

Ingold, T., 2000. *The Perception of the Environment*. Oxford: Routledge.

Lambert, D., Martins, L. and Ogborn, M., 2006. Currents, visions and voyages: Historical geographies of the sea. *Journal of Historical Geography*, 32, pp. 479–93.

Mack, J., 2011. *The Sea: A Cultural History*. London: Reaktion Books.

McNiven, I., 2008. Sentient sea: Seascapes as spiritscapes. In: B. David and J. Thomas, eds, *Handbook of Landscape Archaeology*. Walnut, CA: Left Coast Press, pp. 149–57.

Osborn, M., 1977. The evolution of the archetypal sea in rhetoric and poetic. *The Quarterly Journal of Speech*, 63(4), pp. 347–63.

OED Online, 2014. *Oxford English Dictionary*. Oxford: Oxford University Press. Available at: http://www.oed.com.ezproxy.waikato.ac.nz/view/Entry/174335? redirectedFrom=seascape [accessed 10 January 2014].

Palsson, G., 1994. Enskilment at sea. *Man*, 29(1), pp. 901–27.

Peters, K., 2010. Future promises for contemporary social and cultural geographies of the sea. *Geography Compass*, 4(9), pp. 1260–72.

Phelan, J., 2007. Seascapes: Tides of thought and being in Western perceptions of the sea. *Goldsmiths Anthropology Research Paper*, 14, pp. 1–23.

Raban, J., 1987. *Coasting*. London: Picador.

——— 1992. Introduction. In: J. Raban, ed., *The Oxford Book of the Sea*. Oxford: Oxford University Press, pp. 1–34.

—— 1999. *Passage to Juneau*. London: Picador.

Steinberg, P., 1999a. The maritime mystique: Sustainable development, capital mobility, and nostalgia in the ocean world. *Environment and Planning D: Society and Space*, 17, pp. 403–26.

——— 1999b. Navigating to multiple horizons: Toward a geography of ocean-space. *Professional Geographer*, 51(3), pp. 366–75.

——— 2001. *The Social Construction of the Ocean*. Cambridge: Cambridge University Press.

——— 2013. Of other seas: Metaphors and materialities in maritime regions. *Atlantic Studies*, 10(2), pp. 156–69.

——— 2014. Foreword on Thalassography. In: J. Anderson and K. Peters, eds, *Water Worlds: Human Geographies of the Ocean*. Farnham, UK and Burlington, VT: Ashgate, pp. xiii–vii.

Strang, V., 2004. *The Meaning of Water*. Oxford: Berg.

——— 2008. Uncommon ground: Landscape as social geography. In: B. David and J. Thomas, eds, *Handbook of Landscape Archaeology*. Walnut Creek, CA: Left Coast Press, pp. 51–9.

Tilley, C., 2006. Introduction: Identity, place, landscape and heritage. *Journal of Material Culture*, 11(1/2), pp. 7–32.

Torrence, R., 2002. Cultural landscapes on Garua Island, Papua New Guinea. *Antiquity*, 76, pp. 766–76.

Tyrell, M., 2006. From placelessness to place: An ethnographer's experience of growing to know places at sea. *Worldviews*, 10(2), pp. 220–38.

Winchester, S., 2010. *Atlantic: A Vast Ocean of a Million Stories*. London: Harper Press.

Chapter 2

Embodied Narratives: Being with the Sea

Barbara Humberstone

Sallyport Lamentation[1]

Sallyport, Oh Sallyport
Oh how we do love thee
From your white walls and rounded stones
Down to the blue-green sea

The 'Bunny Pier' with fishermen
The pier which we jump from
The waves which lash upon the shore
In a place which we call home

What is it about the sea, its shores and its depths, that draws us to it in so many ways? What is it that draws me, body–mind–soul, to the sea and has done so for all my life? In the beginning, it was the smells, the sounds, the lapping of water at my feet and around my body, the ships and boats passing the port entrance, going out to sea or returning back into the harbour.

From a very early age I spent my school holidays on the pebbly beach of, and in the sea at, Sallyport. Mum and I would go down on the bus in the mornings with our towels, sandwiches and a flask of tea, returning home warm, tanned, salt-encrusted and content in the early evening. On high water, we would wade through the sea to get to the small triangle of stones bounded on the other sides by the high Sallyport 'hot' walls. Years later, as Mum cleaned offices at the naval dockyard, I would go on my own or with one or two school friends. We would jump into the sea from the pier, disappearing under the water or swim out from the beach, careful to avoid the pull of the strong currents that ran in and out of the harbour at particular states of tide. Later in the day, my mum would arrive with

---

1   This poem was published in the *Portsmouth Evening News* in the sixties when the author and five of her school friends sent the poem to the paper as we were concerned about the Council pulling down the walls. The piece was entitled 'These six Sallyport girls DO care'. Beneath a photo of us superimposed on Sallyport is the comment, 'Longing for the time when they can swim and sunbathe again at their favourite haunt, Sallyport, are six Portsmouth schoolgirls, who wrote a poem entitled, "Sallyport Lamentation"'.

the sandwiches. Not every mother approved of this 'time-wasting'. When I got to 15, mornings were worked in a local hotel, still going in the afternoons to immerse myself in the cool waters at Sallyport. We would spend the long summer days swimming and diving, lying on the beach, watching the boats go by, at peace with our world. Little did I realise then the significant impact this 'time-wasting' in and by the sea would have on shaping me and my future.

This brief, personal, corporeal, fixed-in-time narrative came to mind as I began to ponder what was needed/might be written for a chapter to introduce the reader to 'Embodied Narratives: Being with the Sea'. Narratives are stories that tell a tale. There are many stories by seafarers telling of their experiences of being on the sea, often solitary journeys taking various routes around the globe. These published works are commonly known as autobiographies. What largely separates these autobiographic narratives from the chapters in this book is that the authors here, amongst other things, draw upon their theoretical knowledge and particular research practices to make connections with broader social, environmental or political concerns that may potentially stimulate critical dialogue and open possibilities. An autobiography is generally made up of reflections of the past, which are drawn together to make an often compelling story. Autoethnography is not only constituted by these past reflections, but also informed by methodological research considerations and socio-cultural theoretical frameworks. Like ethnographies, autoethnographies challenge traditional concepts of what constitutes legitimate knowledge and ways of knowing (Humberstone, 1997). An autoethnography engages in exploring identity politics but additionally it can be concerned with culture, society and/or engagement with landscape (Wylie, 2005). Recently, autoethnography has been the preferred methodology for researching embodiment, 'how the body learns to be in the world' (Humberstone, 2011a, p. 496), and for seeking the senses (Sparkes, 2009).

In this book we explore being with the sea through the embodied narratives of social scholars who are deeply engaged with the sea. Ellis, Adams and Bochner (2010) propose that, 'A researcher uses tenets of autobiography and ethnography to do and write autoethnography. Thus, as a method, autoethnography is both process and product'. The products of authors' engagement in, on or under the sea highlight the considerable diversity of this engagement and the 'multiple layers of consciousness' (Ellis and Bochner, 2000, p. 209) embedded in each of the narratives. Each sea–water narrative is not a 'theory-free' observation but 'socially and historically conditioned' (Sparkes and Smith, 2008, p. 299) and, I would add, spatially habituated.

Often not made explicit in many autoethnographic accounts is how the body is implicated in these narratives. Yet the body being in place, through practice and performance of lived experiences, directs attention to sensuous, embodied knowledge by which the sentient person learns what it means to sense, feel and understand, which for 'sea people' is through our complex relations with sea. Being in or on the sea attends to the whole body, not the (un-)consciousness in isolation but the whole of the corporeal body: mind, senses, their inter-relatedness and particular embodied relationship with the sea. If we challenge traditional Western Cartesian thinking, which has judged consciousness to be ontologically distinct from the outer physical world, as many philosophers have done, we cannot separate embodied activity from our 'intuitiveness' built through our 'lived' sensuous encounters with our material environment; the sea and its permeable edges or liminal spaces.

Amongst many thinkers concerned with non-dualistic thinking has emerged the notion of space or landscape being known through bodily, sensual engagement with the land (Wylie, 2005). For Ingold (2000, p. 207):

> The landscape, in short, is not a totality that you or anyone else can look at, it is rather the world in which we stand in taking up a point of view on our surroundings. And it is within the context of this attentive involvement in the landscape that the human imagination gets to work in fashioning ideas about it.

Likewise, for those of us sea–water people engaged in various diverse practices with the sea, the sea and seascape cannot be divorced from our corporeality and who and what we are. Additionally, we become part of the fluid motion of the sea and are kinaesthetically and emotionally moved by and with it instantaneously and over time, long-term.

The Body, Social Thought and the Senses

The corporeal, material, sentient body is now recognised as of particular significance in many areas of social analysis, and currently is emerging in geographies of the sea (see Merchant, 2011; Anderson, 2012). This bodily turn in the social sciences came about largely with the emergence of critiques of disembodied social theory by a number of social analysts. Whilst Shilling (1993) observed the absence of the material body in sociology, feminist commentaries from writers such as Grosz (1994), Grosz and Probyn (1995), Witz (2000), and Witz and Marshall (2003) have proclaimed that much feminist and social theorising was abstracted, ignoring the 'messy body'. Not only in social theorising of the body but also in empirical research that informs theory, was the material body found to be missing (Wainwright and Turner, 2006). An example of explicit inclusion of the body is found in Sparkes's (1996) 'The Fatal Flaw' narrative account of his former elite athletic body struck by chronic injury. His discursive storytelling challenges what it is to know about the 'sporting' body. We, the readers, come to 'feel' what it is to live this transition from fit athletic body to a body that is no longer 'able' and 'hurts'.

Analysts within the sociology of physical culture and sport (Denison and Markula, 2003; Hargreaves and Vertinsky, 2007; Hockey, 2006; Hockey and Allen-Collinson, 2007; Sparkes, 2000, 2002, 2004, 2010; Woodward, 2009) and tourism studies (Swain, 2004) build on this swell of interest in corporeality and call for an embodied, sentient sociology. In consequence, there is a steady and increasing attention to the senses and body in social research. Sensory features and phenomenological perspectives are explored in a variety of ways in analysis of road and cross-country running (Allen-Collinson, 2011; Allen-Collinson and Hockey, 2011). To enable this, the researchers are deeply engaged in running. This current 'shift towards more sensuous forms of scholarship in sport and physical culture' (Sparkes and Smith, 2012, p. 168) is also evident in explorations of other physical cultures, in dance and forms of martial arts. South American dance, the Tango (Olszewski, 2008) and movement culture, Capoeira (Downey, 2005; 2007) have added to this upsurge. All these autoethnographic narratives are based upon data that are collected by the researcher who has gained, or is gaining, intimate knowledge and experience of kinaesthetic phenomena. Since data concerning feelings generated through the senses when 'doing' are difficult to uncover unless one is deeply engaged in these sentient performances, uncovering the relevant data necessarily requires the researcher to know the kinetic movement along with the social and contextual place in which it is practised. Experiential research through the corporeal, sensing body has brought considerable insights into how the body learns to be in the world, its being and becoming in 'the here and now of bodily existence and presence' (Münch, 1994, p. 151). Thus scholarly sea–water people narrating their embodied tales have much to offer our understanding of human engagement with and 'affordances' by the sea and more.

Ethnography and self-narrative have become the preferred methodologies of the mobile geographies genre which, for the most part, has taken space/place to be land-based (see, for example, Ingold, 2011; Fincham, McGuinness and Murray, 2010). Rarely has the sea been the sensorium, the space for emplaced sensuous embodied scholarship. A recent autoethnography exploring sub-aqua diving has added to a move of scholarship away from a spotlight on land to the sea. Merchant (2011) attends to the senses as beginner divers take to the ocean to develop their practice of sub-aqua exploration in the sea. Water is a constituent of the sensorium that includes the complex relationships through which the body learns kinaesthetically, making sense of this generally 'unfamiliar', fluid environment. 'The sensorium is the sum of a person's perceptions, or "the seat of sensation", of their interpretation of an environment' (Merchant, 2011, p. 57).

'Seat of the Senses' – The Sea

Sparkes (2009), pointing to the particular elevation of sight in Western narrative research, argues for greater attention to be given to other senses such as sound, smell, touch and taste, whilst highlighting the problem of representation of multi-sensory ethnographies. Drawing upon Stoller's evocation of sensuous scholarship, he constructs narratives that evoke the senses, coming some way toward providing a more holistic, less 'dualistic' way of interpreting embodiment. Anthropologist of the senses, Stoller encourages researchers to surrender to their senses, proposing:

> To accept sensuousness is, like the Songhay spirit medium or Sufi Saint, to
> lend one's body to the world and accept its complexities, tastes, structures, and
> smells ... sensuous scholarship is ultimately a mixing of head and heart. It is
> an opening of one's being to the world – a welcoming. (Stoller, 1997, cited in
> Sparkes, 2009, p. 21)

Phenomenologically inspired scholars Hockey and Allen-Collinson (2007) attend
to the five 'dominant' senses – aural, visual, olfactory, haptic and taste – in their
embodied narratives of running selves. Cultural geographer Thrift (2004) observes
that the senses are differently understood in diverse cultures and balance, in
particular, is frequently ignored in Western thought (see also Stoller, 1989):

> So, for example, the interoceptive and proprioceptive sensations get comparatively
> short shrift as formal categories of the senses in Euro-American societies, even
> though their importance can hardly be denied. (Thrift, 2004, p. 602)

These balance senses, for most sea–water people, are significant and allow for
continuous awareness and presence to the minute and subtle shifts of wave,
water, elements, body, board or vessel. Evers's (2004, 2006, 2009) sensuous
autoethnographic accounts of masculine bodies practising surfing (re)present
and capture kinaesthetic experiences, emphasising the constantly changing and
challenging, fluid environment and the ways in which these dynamic seascapes
open up the male sentient body to intuitive movements and affective moments,
where the balance senses are crucial.

> I may have an idea of how a wave could be ridden but the wave, weather and
> bathymetry rarely assemble as expected. This dynamic ecology forces its way into
> my embodied memories, enthusiasms, expectations, gestures and imagination
> by way of sight, taste, smell, touch, hearing and balance. Ecologies never allow
> proprioceptic, kinaesthetic and sensual awareness to settle. This means that
> emergences of masculinity and surfing are full of improvisation, potentials and
> the new, and not just repetition and prediction. (Evers, 2009, p. 898)

Evers's (2004, 2006, 2009) studies more than represent the significance and
complexity of autoethnographic narrative in understanding affective embodiment,
sensuous masculinities and the environmental and the social. Yet, it is not only
male bodies, as much research on surfing tends to suggest, that experience
and sensuously embrace the sea. The women in Spowart, Burrows and Shaw's
(2010) study of mothers who surf, whilst not drawing upon autoethnographic
methodology, provide narratives from the women which tell of their sensual
embodied engagement with the sea. '[For] each of the other women interviewed,
surfing seems to be represented as an embodied identity, something that yields a
visceral pleasure, a jouissance not necessarily dependent on achievement of the
rewards engagement ...' (p. 1193).

Further, Taylor (2007), whose text focuses on spirituality, ecology, the ocean and surfing, cites the perspective of a woman surfer, editor of a women's surf magazine, which points to a more-than-normal sensoria of the kinaesthetic movement. Blending surfing spirituality with an ecofeminist ethos in which it is proposed that women more easily apprehend the spirituality of surfing, Edwards, quoted in Taylor, asserted:

> When I see a female on a wave, I see the connectedness with the wave. Women's emotional energy is about unity. The masculine energy is more independent, more 'me' out front. And that is not true for all men, but sometimes men surf 'on' the wave, whereas women surf 'with' the wave.

Surfing is not about achievement, she continued.

> It is about balance, blend and unity. It is about being a part of, not about dictating or ruling it. The Zen of surfing is about being mindful of the energy you are joining forces with, not conquering it. (Taylor, 2007, p. 937)

As a woman who windsurfs and has done so for some considerable time, I also experience this 'visceral pleasure' and connection with the elemental. Even within the last week of writing this, the perfect conditions occurred in the creek where I sail. North-west wind force 4–5, high water, 5.7-metre sail, I sail back and forth across the short distance at the mouth of the creek from the marshes to the mini-spit where the water is dead flat and a gybe is smooth and flowing, then back across the entrance where small waves can be ridden and manoeuvred upon, absolute bliss despite a knee that is determined to give out.

In the previous year and in less initially inviting conditions, I sailed in the same place but in a south-westerly wind.

> The water edges over my feet and up my legs, a sensation of pulsing around my rubber-encased feet and legs. No one else is around and the wind howls. Stepping right foot, left foot onto the board I take off. The sail fills as I hitch into the harness. Faster and faster outward across the undulating surface, the sail, the board and me balanced in harmony, picking up speed as we begin to skim over the surface, light as a feather blowing in the air. Then, front arm straight, unhook sink down, and we begin to turn away from the wind, body leaning away from the rig as the board and sail turn in an arc away from the wind, back to shore. (Humberstone, 2014, cited in Fox and Humberstone, 2014, p. 8)

Each of these experiences of windsurfing occurred under very different conditions. These self-narratives come someway to expressing the unsettling dynamic and fluidity of elemental forces, yet they also speak to the senses – the balanced harmony of the movement through the water. The interoceptive and proprioceptive sensations become equal and 'visible' partners in the sensoria nexus of being in, on the sea and moving through the sea, windsurfing.

An embodied sea person, being on, by, in or under the sea engages the balance senses with all of other senses in a co-creation of sensuous relations with a mobile sea spaces. Embodiment, as Howes (2005) argues, is an integration of body–mind where the sentient body is situated in time and space constituting interrelationships of body–mind–environment. Developing the notion of fluidity and ethnographies of 'mind–body–environment', Pink (2009), drawing upon phenomenology of perception (Merleau-Ponty, 2002), brings together theories that construct the nexus of senses, embodiment and place. Through her focus on sensuous ethnography and narratives of self, she proposes 'an emplacement ethnography that attends to the question of experience by accounting for the relationships between bodies, minds and materiality and sensoriality of the environment' (Pink, 2009, p. 25). Pink's work largely refers to social and cultural contexts in everyday post-industrial society. Nevertheless, the brief attention paid to embodiment through gardening, provides stimulus for further research that observes complex relationships in embodiment, sensoria and the natural environment.

The turn to seeking the senses amongst sport and physical culture research and cultural-mobile geographers occurred somewhat contemporaneously. The latter much encouraged by Thrift's attempts to move cultural geographical theory beyond the symbolic and representational to more affective and sensuous approaches that recognise the senses and emotions in analysis and discourse. Thrift (2000, p. 216) argued that geographers might 'weave a poetic of the common practices and skills which produce people, selves and worlds' and look 'towards a poetics of encounter' (2008a, p. 148). Unpicking these shifts, there is not only greater emphasis on autoethnographic research and self-narrative but the question of how to (re)present or give expression to these embodied sensuous engagements is also firmly identified. Wylie (2005, p. 237), continues in this vein, with his self-narration of a coastal path walk where he notes 'that forms of narrative – memoir, montage, travelogue, ethnography – are being used both within and beyond academia as creative and critical means of expressing post-humanist philosophies of place'.

The chapters in this book are the authors' narratives of their experiences of being and becoming in their various encounters with the sea. These narratives are 'evocative form(s) of writing that produce(s) highly personalized and revealing texts in which authors tell stories about their own lived experience' (Sparkes, 2002, p. 73). These stories entwining self with the sea are 'more-than-representational' knowledges (Carolan, 2008), bringing to life the ways in which people learn to become in the mobile sensorial seat of the sea.

Back to the Future – Shaped by the Sea

Many years after the 'not particularly good poetry', published in the *Portsmouth Evening News*, my engagement with the sea continues, professionally and emotionally.

Recently, as indicated in the above narratives, I have been exploring embodied engagement with the sea. Further, it could be said that I owe my career in no small way to the 'time-wasting' as a child and adolescent in and by the sea at Sallyport. I pursued a degree at the local polytechnic and first went into school teaching, partly as a way out of limited options of routine factory or shop work, where summers would be spent indoors and not on or near the sea.

Since the early attempt at producing the 'poem' to express our feelings about being by and in the sea, which was stimulated by the local authority's proposal to close off Sallyport, I have been practically engaged with water-based sports. This included teaching dinghy sailing and later windsurfing. I have sailed the English Channel and along the South Coast recreationally and occasionally competitively, as member of a women-only crew in the Three Peaks yacht race. Returning back to a space/time dimension: soon after the *Portsmouth Evening News* 'poem', my access to being on the sea (as opposed to being by and in it), as a girl from a working-class home with few social networks or money, was through the Sea Rangers. This was part of the Girl Guide organisation enabling young women not only to camp away from the city, but also to take responsibility and learn skills associated with maritime activities. I 'learnt how to be in (my) body' through this engagement with the sea. Our group had a whaler (an open rowing boat), which was kept on Whale Island, a tiny island naval base in Portsmouth harbour, at the end of a rather notorious road. On a Sunday afternoon we would cycle over the bridge to the island and row the whaler from the island, some three miles, to a sheltered naval berth near Sallyport. Through this organisation, I learnt to sail, row and kayak. I appreciate now that this provided a significant opportunity for a working-class girl living in a suburb on Portsea Island.

In a real sense the sea surrounded me and I (un-)consciously embodied it. It has always been part of me. By providing a brief narrative of my practical, corporeal experiences and sensations, I hoped through the following narrative to express something of what being on/in the sea was about and how a body – my body – 'learns' to be through practice. But more importantly I wanted to explore the notion of kinetic empathy (Thrift, 2004), through self-narrative around embodiment, and how learning to be in the body in nature might engender environmental awareness and the potential for social/environmental action.

> I am a committed recreational windsurfer. I learnt to windsurf on a board with a removable wooden dagger board and a bamboo boom over 28 years ago. I have also been an ethnographer for most of that time and an ethnographic and, more particularly, an autoethnographic approach to explore embodiment, location and nature seems 'natural'. The main place I windsurf and where I

conduct this research is a relatively safe and very accessible location at the mouth of Southampton water. Here, there is access to the water on three sides of a kilometre-long shingle and earth spit, on which stands a collection of large buildings, which housed sea planes during the 1940s and 1950s and now is a thriving outdoor activities centre. At most states of the tide, except for a few hours around low water, there is a small lagoon (the pond) with usually flat water. The spit looks to the Solent waters and Isle of Wight on one side and a massive chimney and oil refinery on the other. I sail there regularly during the summer months and have spent much time there on and off the water over the last 30 years. For an earlier conference on 'experiencing water' and to evoke a sense of place and the sensuous engagement with nature of windsurfing for me, I wrote my own feelings about windsurfing:

> I feel the water rushing past my feet and legs. The wind in my hair. I sense the wind shifts in strength and direction and move my body in anticipation to the wind and the waves. I feel the power of the wind and the ability of my body to work with the wind and the waves. The delight and sensation when surfing down a small wave with the sail beautifully balanced by the wind. Seeing the sea birds and the fish jump delight further. The smell of salt and mud. The small seal that made its home on the tiny pebble spit.
>
> These are some of the beauties of windsurfing in this liminal space even with a monstrous power station chimney hovering in the distance and the occasional smell of sulphur from the large oil refinery when the wind blows from the north-east. In the summer of 2010, a seal, possibly the original I refer to above, having grown much larger, returned but did not stay. It played around the 'pond' looking for fish whilst we sailed backwards and forwards across the entrance trying to spot the seal in order to both see it and avoid hitting it; a glorious sunny day, the reflected sunshine making the small waves shimmer and dance. (Humberstone, 2011a, pp. 163–4; Humberstone, 2011b, pp. 502–3)

The above brief self-narrative was stimulated by a call for a special issue of *Leisure Studies Journal* that focused on 'leisure and the politics of the environment'. My involvement in teaching and learning in and through the outdoors and, more particularly being a 'water person', generates in me, as perhaps for other sea–water people, a strong feeling for the environment and, through this particular challenge of writing on the politics of the environment, unfolds the 'feelings'/knowledges embedded in Thrift's (2008a) notions of kinetic empathy and politics of hope. That is to say, how we learn to be in our bodies connects us to the wider world and, arguably for us 'sea people', we are subtly connected to and intertwined with the energies of the waves, the sea and the universe. Who we are, and what we become, is bound up within the dynamism of the sea.

Geographies of Subjectivities – Empathy and the Seas

[I]t seems very hard to argue any longer that the geography of subjectivity is rooted in an individual subject, a nation state militantly united in the pursuit of consciousness and marching under the banner of a rationality ... Whether the author is Jacques Derrida or Derek Parfit, pretty well everyone seems to subscribe to the idea that that kind of identity is an invented Western tradition that has had its day. But if that is so, how might we understand where the subject is. That is a much more tricky question. (Thrift, 2008b, p. 84)

Reflecting upon who we (sea–water people) are, on our diverse subjectivities, changing with time, place, choice and chance, leads to considerations of the interconnections between us or the encounters that constitute us, through the rhythmic patternings of embodied practices and movements of the oceans. Thrift, along with philosophers such as Deleuze and Guattari, observes subjectivity as fluid, and ourselves and our bodies not as 'bounded entities' with more or less fixed identities, but as embodied mobile, permeable 'propagating signals': centres of control. Who, what and where we become are constructions not only of social imperatives but also of the places, spaces and durations through which and in which our bodies travel in time.

Shifting patterns of being and becoming as one moves in, on or under the sea provide for and affords us sea–water people with unique situated spaces that are arguably less amenable to control or manipulation by human intervention than most other habituated spaces. Our bodies learn to respond and 'dance' to the sea's movement, learning to be in the body to become part of the sea's mobile energies, learning to become more permeable bodies. My varied encounters with the sea, as first a Portsea islander, later a teacher, then an academic, in different continuous and interrupted durations provide (un)conscious corporeal embodied knowledges, which sustain me and influence who I am and what I became/can become. These emplaced encounters, rehearsed here in my self-narratives of becoming and being, enable subjectivities less bounded by conventional notions and imperatives of what is appropriate and was expected behaviour for me, at one time a working-class young female flourishing through the sea.

Thus the question of subjectivity – 'who I am and who I could become' (Lorraine, 2011, p. x) – is constructed through and within these self-narratives. In some sense, these respond to and give a reading to Thift's (2008b) 'much more tricky question'. For sea–water people, as for me, the 'where' in 'wherewithall' (p. 87) is located in the fluctuating sea.

References

Allen-Collinson, J., 2011. Feminist phenomenology and the woman in the running body. *Sports, Ethics, Philosophy*, 5(3), pp. 297–313.

Allen-Collinson, J. and Hockey, J., 2011. Feeling the way: Notes towards a haptic phenomenology of distance running and scuba diving. *International Review for the Sociology of Sport*, 46, pp. 330–45.

Carolan, M.S., 2008. More-than-representational. Knowledge/s of the countryside: How we think as bodies. *European Society for Rural Sociology*, 48(4), pp. 409–22.

Denison, J. and Markula, P., eds, 2003. *'Moving Writing': Crafting Movement in Sport Research*. New York: Peter Lang.

Downey, G., 2005. *Learning Capoeira: Lessons in Cunning from an Afro-Brazilian Art*. New York: Oxford University Press.

––––––– 2007. Seeing with a 'sideways glance': Visuomotor 'knowing' and the plasticity of perceptions. In: M. Harris, ed, *Ways of Knowing: New Approaches in the Anthropology of Experience and Learning*. Oxford: Berghahn, pp. 202–41.

Ellis, C., Adams, T.E. and Bochner, A.P., 2010. Autoethnography: An Overview. *Forum Qualitative Sozialforschung/Forum: Qualitative Social Research*. Available at: http://www.qualitative-research.net/index.php/fqs/article/view/1589/3095 [accessed 27 June 2013].

Ellis, C. and Bochner, A., 2000. Autoethnography, personal narrative, reflexivity. Researcher as subject. In: N.K. Denzin and Y.S. Lincoln, eds, *Handbook of Qualitative Research*. Thousand Oaks, CA: Sage, pp. 733–68.

Evers, C., 2004. Men who surf. *Cultural Studies Review*, 10(1), pp. 27–41.

––––––– 2006. How to surf (research and methodology). *Journal of Sport and Social Issues*, 30(3), pp. 229–43.

––––––– 2009. The point: Surfing, geography and a sensual life of men and masculinity on the gold coast, Australia. *Social and Cultural Geography*, 10(8), pp. 893–908.

Fincham, B., McGuinness, M. and Murray, L., eds, 2010. Introduction. In: B. Fincham, M. McGuinness and L. Murray, eds, *Mobile Methodologies*. Basingstoke, UK: Palgrave Macmillan, pp. 1–10.

Fox, K.M. and Humberstone, B., 2014. Embodiment, mindfulness and leisure. In: L. Such, ed., *Education, Culture and Justice: Leisure Theory and Insight*. Eastbourne: Leisure Studies Association (LSA) Publication No. 125.

Grosz, E., 1994. *Volatile Bodies: Towards a Corporeal Feminism*. Bloomington: Indiana Press.

Grosz, E. and Probyn, E., eds, 1995. *Sexy Bodies: The Strange Carnalities of Feminism*. London: Routledge.

Hargreaves, J. and Vertinsky, P., 2007. Introduction. In: J. Hargreaves and P. Vertinsky, eds, *Physical Culture, Power, and the Body*. London: Routledge, pp. 1–24.

Hockey, J., 2006. Sensing the run: The senses and distance running. *Senses and Society*, 1(2), pp. 183–202.

Hockey, J. and Allen-Collinson, C., 2007. Grasping the phenomenology of sporting bodies. *International Review for Sociology of Sport*, 42(2), pp. 115–31.

Howes, D., ed., 2005. *Empire of the Senses*. London: Berg.

Humberstone, B., 1997. Challenging dominant ideologies in the research process. In: G. Clarke and B. Humberstone, eds, *Researching Women and Sport.* Macmillan, London, pp. 199–213.

———— 2011a. Engagements with nature: Ageing and windsurfing. In: B. Watson and J. Harpin, eds, *Identities, Cultures and Voices in Leisure and Sport.* Eastbourne: Leisure Studies Association (LSA) Publication No. 116, pp. 159–69.

———— 2011b. Embodiment and social and environmental action in nature-based sport: Spiritual spaces. Special issue – Leisure and the politics of the environment. *Journal of Leisure Studies*, 30(4), pp. 495–512.

Ingold, T., 2000. *The Perception of the Environment: Essays on Livelihood, Dwelling and Skill.* London: Routledge.

———— 2011. *Being Alive.* London: Routledge.

Lorraine, T., 2011. *Deleuze and Guattari's Immanent Ethics: Theory Subjectivity and Duration.* New York: Suny Press.

Merleau-Ponty, M., 2002. *The Phenomenology of Perception.* London: Routledge.

Merchant, S., 2011. The body and the senses: Visual methods, videography and the submarine sensorium. *Body & Society*, 17, pp. 53–72.

Münch, R., 1994. *Sociological Theory: From the 1920s to the 1960s.* Chicago: Nelson Hall.

Olszewskiel, B., 2008. Cuerpo del Baile: The kinetic and social fundaments of Tango. *Body & Society*, 14(2), pp. 63–81.

Pink, S., 2009. *Doing Sensory Ethnography.* London: Sage.

Shilling, C., 1993. *The Body in Social Theory.* London: Sage.

Sparkes, A., 1996. The fatal flaw. *Qualitative Inquiry*, 2(4), pp. 436–94.

———— 2000. Autoethnography and narratives of self: Reflections on criteria in action. *Sociology of Sport Journal*, 17, pp. 21–43.

———— 2002. *Telling Tales in Sport and Physical Activity: A Qualitative Journey.* Leeds: Human Kinetics.

———— 2004. Reflections on an embodied sport and exercise psychology. In: R. Stelter and K. Roessler, eds, *New Approaches to Exercise and Sport Psychology.* Oxford: Meyer & Meyer Sport, pp. 31–54.

———— 2009. Ethnography and the senses: Challenges and possibilities. *Qualitative Research in Sport and Exercise*, 1(1), pp. 21–35.

———— 2010. Performing the ageing body and the importance of place. Some autoethnographic moments. In: B. Humberstone, ed., *'When I am old I will.!' Third Age and Leisure Research: Principles and Practice.* Eastbourne: Leisure Studies Association (LSA) Publication No. 108.

Sparkes, A. and Smith, B., 2008. Narrative constructionist inquiry. In: J.A. Holstein and J.F. Gubrium, eds, *Handbook of Constructionist Research.* London: The Guilford Press, pp. 295–313.

Sparkes, A. and Smith, B., 2012. Embodied research methodologies and seeking the senses in sport and physical culture: A fleshing out of problems and possibilities. *Qualitative Research on Sport and Physical Culture Research in the Sociology of Sport*, 6, pp. 167–90.

Spowarta, L., Burrows, L. and Shaw, S., 2010. 'I just eat, sleep and dream of surfing': When surfing meets motherhood. *Sport in Society*, 13(7), pp. 1186–203.

Stoller, P., 1989. *The Taste of Ethnographic Things*. Philadelphia, PA: University of Pennsylvania Press.

Stoller, P., 1997. *Sensuous Scholarship*. Philadelphia: University of Pennsylvania Press.

Swain, M., 2004. (Dis)embodied experience and power dynamics in tourism research. In: J. Phillimore and L. Goodson, eds, *Qualitative Research in Tourism, Ontology, Epistemologies and Methodologies*. London: Routledge, pp. 102–18.

Taylor, B., 2007. Surfing into spirituality and a new, aquatic nature religion. *Journal of the American Academy of Religion*, 75(4), pp. 923–51.

Thrift, N., 2000. Non-representational theory. In: R.J. Johnston, D. Gregory, G. Pratt and M. Watt, eds, *The Dictionary of Human Geography* (4th ed.). Oxford: Blackwell, pp. 211–19.

———— 2004. Movement-space: The changing domain of thinking resulting from the development of new kinds of spatial awareness. *Economy and Society*, 33(4), pp. 582–604.

———— 2008a. *Non-Representational Theory: Space, Politics, Affect*. London: Routledge.

———— 2008b. I just don't know what got into me: Where is the subject? *Subjectivity*, 22, pp. 82–9.

Wainwright, S.P. and Turner, B.S., 2006. 'Just crumbling to bits'? An exploration of the body, ageing, injury and career in classical ballet dancers. *Sociology*, 40(2), pp. 237–55.

Witz, A., 2000. Whose body matters? Feminist sociology and the corporeal turn in sociology and feminism. *Body & Society*, 6(2), pp. 1–24.

Witz, A. and Marshall, B., 2003. The quality of manhood: Masculinity and embodiment in the sociological tradition. *The Sociological Review*, 51(3), pp. 339–56.

Woodward, K., 2009. *Embodied Sporting Practices, Regulating and Regulatory Bodies*. Basingstoke: Palgrave Macmillan.

Wylie, J., 2005. A single day's walking: Narrating self and landscape on the South West Coast Path. *Transactions of the Institute of British Geographers*, 30, pp. 234–47.

Chapter 3

Seaspaces: Surfing the Sea as Pedagogy of Self

lisahunter

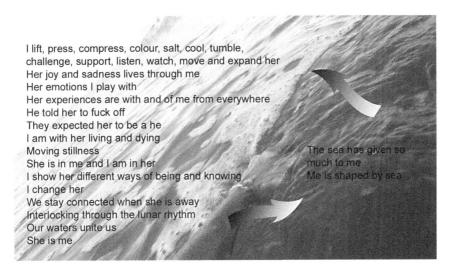

I lift, press, compress, colour, salt, cool, tumble,
challenge, support, listen, watch, move and expand her
Her joy and sadness lives through me
Her emotions I play with
Her experiences are with and of me from everywhere
He told her to fuck off
They expected her to be a he
I am with her living and dying
Moving stillness
She is in me and I am in her
I show her different ways of being and knowing
I change her
We stay connected when she is away
Interlocking through the lunar rhythm
Our waters unite us
She is me

The sea has given so much to me
Me is shaped by sea

Background

The sea has been a medium for learning and knowing 'self': my selves. It is an intersubjective, intersubjecting and intersubjected space that reveals unity and separation. For me, surfing is a metaphor for my interaction with the element of water and specifically the sea, capturing mobility and fluidity as part of my corporeal sensibilities. It is also reflective of this chapter's structure and content. Just as waves in the sea embody time-space, so too do my autoethnographic (Reed-Danahay, 1997; Ellis and Bochner, 2000) experiences explored through two related narratives of my encounters with 'the sea'. Employing habitus (Bourdieu, 1990; Reay, 2004), I offer a glimpse into the life of a spatio-sensorial embodied mind. I use Ellsworth's (2005) notion of 'sensational pedagogies' alongside Mellor and Shilling's 'body pedagogic' (2010) to note encounters that have marked how I have learned who I am in this world. The mobility of these 'spatial stories' (Cresswell and Merriman, 2011, p. 5) is represented as smaller narratives from different perspectives, stitched together as I move through my world in a flight above the sea, standing back with a broader and reflexive view to some of my highly fleshed memory experiences, as an intimate blur. I capture interactions with the sea from helicopter surf rescue (above), to board riding (on), to lifesaving (in), to diving (under), to contemplating or processing death/life (through). These accounts are chosen as being critical in establishing moments of reflexivity for the self, critical in that I was forced to ask questions such as: Who am I? What is 'I'? What is my relationship with the sea? What is my relationship to other people who are different to me, mediated by the sea? These heterogeneous encounters, where 'all of the actors are not human and all of the humans are not "us" however defined' (Haraway, 1992, p. 67), then prompt me to ask more questions of ontological and epistemological nature, and of relation, place and pedagogy.

Surfing indicates a movement with the sea, a partnership that is bigger than the parts. Cresswell and Merriman (2011, p. 5) explain this eloquently saying 'mobile, embodied practices are central to how we experience the world, from practices of writing and sensing, to walking and driving. Our mobilities create spaces and stories – spatial stories'. Through my senses, affects, emotions, my experiences of being, constituted in relation to the sea, I have come to 'know' myself in particular ways. These ways have been mediated socially by other humans who also participate in my seascapes. The sea is mobile and fluid, as the notion of self/selves is, but together something different arises. These assemblages of sea, elements and humanity touch the fields of work, leisure, sport and all aspects of being human.

Seaspace Encounters

The smell of the JetA1 fuel contrasts with the hot salty sea breeze as my colleagues and I don wetsuits and helmets for the afternoon flight. The black tarmac is hot against the soles of my feet as I watch for the pilot's signals and checks during the start-up of the Bell206B helicopter used for surf patrols. This fourth flight for the weekend, each time covering 100 kilometres of pristine subtropical beaches, is one I've done for many years but it is still exciting being lifted into the air and observing the world from 'just above' it. I say just above because we get to fly 'not above 100 (feet)' due to our search and rescue status. On some callouts we climb much higher though as we make our own path between landing site and the next emergency. The anticipation of the usual surf rescue practice at the end of the flight is compensation for the heat I feel as the wetsuit suffocates, the sweat trickling down the back of my neck, exposed arms and legs, gathering in places where the wetsuit creases. The colours of the sea below are patterned by the white breaking waves along the shore, the sandbars paralleling the shore and curving around the river mouths, deepening blues out to sea and clear, faintly green at the shore. I feel the drive of my legs against my surfboard, speeding along the face of the wave as I watch those below do the same.

I sit on the Deep Blue Mirror with only my red log between us, my feet lazily pushing and pulling in opposition against the cool of your water, with my back to the white sandy beach, time standing still in my spiritual space where the past of the last wave ride merges with my still state and this sea. We are water separated only by skin, or are we? I watch the corrugated lines to the horizon, shapes that evoke a rising heartbeat with a sense of excitement as the memory of my last ride of the wave lingers. The new sun for the day arrives as the earth spins towards it. It burns my eyes below the peak of my cap, blinding me so that I have to look away to recover from checking the approaching waves. The big tide triggers me to look for the moon. Opposite, the silhouette of the full moon fades as the other horizon turns away. These rhythms add certainty to this complex world. The gentle westerly offshore breeze teases at the ends of my hair and brushes my wet exposed skin hinting that autumn approaches and it may be time to consider the somewhat warmer garb of the wetsuit as opposed to rashies and boardies. The rise and fall of the swell passing under me, part of the human-board structure, is rhythmical as the ocean breathes in and out and there is no longer a 'me'. Even the trigger of sensing that the next swell line was about to express a face, inviting me to turn to shore, paddle and match the new wave's speed in order to stay with it as we head to shore, brackets space so that the experience is constituted by all captured in the merger, a oneness of time, elements, fibreglass, colour, sound, smell, pressures, flesh, and temperature in the form of a wave ride. But that oneness, the meditative and spiritual spaces are ephemeral as I am quickly reminded of self when there is an interruption, a separation between the wave, the board, the human, me as ... a flick off the wave at the end of the ride, a return to the paddle out position on my belly or knees, an appreciative hoot from one of the two other humans surfing near me, or as a wipe-out ... until a physical equilibrium is found once again in the rhythm of the paddle out and the return to the meditative position where human, board, mirror and world merge, my feet lazily pushing and pulling in opposition against the cool of your water, with my back to the white sandy beach, time standing still in my spiritual space where the past of the last wave ride merges with my still state and this sea. 'What the fuck are you here for?' screeches through my every cell, shattering the spiritual space and calling not only 'me' into being but something more specific. The ongoing rant from the newcomer on his short, white, sharp-nosed board both pointing at me, felt like a missile awaiting launch. 'You fuckin' longboard pieces of shit fuck up everyone's wave and you could kill someone with that. Fuckin' women' he continued, his body seeming to harden, heighten and solidify with tension and aggression. His effect was instant as I shrank, gripped my board tight with my knees and hands as my life shield. I looked about to see if he was annihilating someone else or was he just lining me up as a target?

I can already feel the cooling air I will get as I step out of the chopper onto the skids in a hover above our practice patient, and I anticipate the stimulating cold blast I will get as I jump from the skids of the helicopter into the big ocean 'out the back', rescue tube under my arm. But for now I'm not yet in it. We scan the beaches, shore and water, one of us either side of the craft. The radio bursts forth with announcements from police, ambulance, surf lifesaving, air traffic control and our own base, breaking an otherwise silent space above the blanket of water we call the Coral Sea or Pacific Ocean. Bunches of people congregate around the many flagged lifesaving areas, most are inshore with the occasional swimmer or floater beyond the breaking waves. Another yellow flag indicating caution to the swimmers accompanies the red and yellow lifesaving flag.

I can feel the undertows, the sweeps, the dumping waves and the messiness of the surf that attracts the yellow flag as I've often had to do the 'first swim' of the morning when on beach duty to establish which flag will go up.

I see a group take off together from the shore, jumping onto their racing paddle skis in unison, attacking the water as they pick up speed on what are reportedly the fastest human-powered craft.

I can feel that speed as the sea propels me forward by its resistance against my paddle, an opposition that also propels me through the air as I paddle over an incoming wave, shouting out a hoot of joy, slamming down the other side as it passes under me and I pass over it. It is different to the lift of the wave that catches you on the way back into shore and shoots you forward, paddling only to stay straight or quickly get ahead of a breaking wave before it dumps you on its floor. But today I'm not competing at the Masters competition as my free time to train has declined. Work is getting to be a bigger proportion of my life. It never seems to stop. Without good training time, the challenge of the sea in its tumultuous dance with winds asks too much of me for competition and I prefer to choose the more predictable surf to ride the ski. We climb higher, our pilot noticing the white spurts of water about two kilometres from the shore. The distinctive white spurts alert us to their whereabouts before their black shapes come into view as we move over the top of them. A small pod of three adult whales and two calves slide as black shadows, heading south after the births nearby. We hover at the required 'safe' distance and check that the two motorboats do the same. They seem oblivious to the whales. Such glorious creatures still treated precariously by humanity despite the work of groups like Surfers for Cetaceans.[1] I cop taunts like 'bloody greenie' as I do subscribe to reducing waste and being mindful of our actions with non-humans, constantly negotiating what that means in our land of plenty and relatively pristine environment. The needless slaughter of animals is just one end of a carnivorous and capitalist continuum that we all dance along in some form. I do despair at the tragic human trashing of the seas and the destruction of its inhabitants and I am mindful of the paradox as our Jet fuel fills the air, the thump of our rotors affect the wildlife around us, and my compulsory leather safety boots and oil-based wetsuit contribute to some of that waste and destruction. But I'm in a privileged position to care, a position that requires action not just despair.

From this angle above the sea we see many creatures using the ocean as a travelscape in ways my flesh knows or can imagine. The Sunday afternoon sailing racers tack around the nearby island and back to their river moorings, salt spray crusting on my face; the sharks weaving around the river mouths unbeknown to the kiteboarders, windsurfers, fishing fraternity and occasional swimmers as I have when diving, laughing when I look up at their legs and craft; the manta rays winging their way across the bottom of the sea and settling as huge diamonds on the white sand in the shallows, it looks relaxing; the pods of dolphins surfing the waves in regular spots along the coastline or propelling themselves up into the air in a display I experience as joy and athleticism like when I spring forward body surfing or flick off the back of a wave from my board into the air; the divers below, their white and blue buoy just off the little island, suspended by the mighty ocean as a cinematic experience of colour and movement works across the facemask; the jet skis speeding across the mix of ocean and air, tripping between both in increasingly harder encounters with the ocean as the wind picks up; the fishers bobbing about in their boats, the regular gentle sway hinting at sea sickness that I'm beginning to feel from the hour flight trapped in the hot wetsuit at the end of a busy rescue weekend.

---

1   S4C http://www.s4cglobal.org/.

We quickly drop back to the patrol along the shoreline speeding over the breaking waves just metres below the skids. I feel for the pressure point on my wrist and press my thumb into it to hold off the uncommon yet familiar signs of the beginning of motion sickness. All the while I continue to scan between the sea below and the horizon as our work is not just for the beach zone. Nearing our practice zone at the end of the flight, I radio the lifesaving command centre to notify them of our practice arrangements. We often have pseudo patients planted out beyond the flags and practice a rescue on lifesavers for their own experience and good PR. Lifesaving and all the rescue services are based on goodwill and positive relationships, their success only as good as the professional volunteerism, which is increasingly under pressure with the rise of individualism in these neoliberal times.

Last week the practice was at a club well north of our regular surf patrol area but within our larger rescue area. I did the jump and rescue on a young woman and man, suspended underneath the helicopter by the rescue rope and delivered to the adjoining beach just beyond the lifesavers' flags. They seemed disappointed after we had been settled onto the beach by the chopper. The rescue rope had been released and I had removed their rescue tubes. While I retrieved the rope they chatted to each other, turning to walk with me back to the flagged area saying 'we thought you'd be a man'. I'd heard this before. The expectation of the mythical 'bronzed, buffed, Aussie (male) lifesaver' was still alive, particularly for this more specialised line of rescue service. Our Surf Lifesaving club had a high membership of females and those who did the extensive patrol hours were all shapes, sizes and ages. They were competent but often not competitors so demonstrated their commitment to the club by patrolling and performing other less glamorous tasks. This was in contrast to many competitors who just completed their minimum hours in order to compete. I hear myself explaining that the requirements of helicopter rescue crew were certainly about fitness but more importantly relevant skills, teamwork and problem solving. 'Yes, women are still in the minority in crews but it is more about structural sexism than anything else' was my standard response. I always stopped there though. My comment was often met with a knowing nod, an 'I don't want to know' look, or a blank expression that indicated that conversation was over. People would come from all over to look at the chopper, hear about the high-tech contents and their functions, and ask questions about the sorts of work we do, but very few were interested in discussing sexism. After all, I made it into the crew so I guess anybody could!

Today we had guests as our 'patients' and my next radio communication was with another of our crew on the shore, who was telling our patients to swim out beyond the breaking waves. They are accompanied by the patrol's inflatable rescue boat (IRB) for safety as they enter the increasingly messy water stirred up by the afternoon winds. The increasing safety consciousness gets quite debilitating at times but I know it's our first priority, however liminal or uncertain the lines are between risk and rescue. Something catches my eye out to sea. Two racing skis are stationary several hundred metres from the nearby uninhabited island. I can't put my finger on what is odd but the pilot notes my concern and we bank tightly to the right, the vibration of the blades thudding through my bones and my stomach tumbling as though we were doing a somersault. We circle towards the skis with urgency. One ski is vacant but the second has one man sitting astride it with what seems to be another slumped across the bow. A sense of doom and excitement rushes through me as I prepare to jump. The routine of changing helmets, grabbing the rescue harness, unbelting, opening the door, standing on the skids, closing the door and stepping off the skid once above the patient is done without conscious thought although my focus is very clear. All sense of time changes and I no longer feel the senses I was anticipating earlier with a jump. I do not feel the cool air from the skids, or the cold and wet as I drop into the sea. The upright man yells above the noise and downwash of the helicopter rotors 'he's not breathing', looking to the other he holds awkwardly across the ski but half submerged in the sea. CPR is only a momentary option as the sea envelops the unconscious man's body that flails in the water and rocks across the ski. The land is where we need to be. The sea is heavy as though clawing at the dead weight of my patient and it is difficult to get the harness around him. Choppy waves splash over our heads and into our mouths while I support him away from his companion's ski, a vigorous eggbeater kick finding resistance from the sea. Flashes of other rescues in rougher seas, real and practice, make me grateful for a split second as fear reminds me of the many incidents where the power and unknown of the sea has been life threatening and life taking. I learned that as a kid when a sandbar collapsed beneath me while supporting my little brother, the experience and the thought that we nearly both drowned still palpable today, along with other close calls that always teach me to respect the ocean, its power and its inhabitants. Such a respect seems misplaced by those who rape and pillage the seas yet hold human life to be saved at all costs through rescue services such as our own. The power and magic of the sea has been my motivation to be challenged by it, to learn to read it, and to help others read it before entering or getting out of trouble afterwards. In seconds that felt like minutes after hitting the water, I signal to the pilot with a nod as my bear hug locks the patient into the rescue tube. We are pulled into the air, the pressure of my harness taking over from my freedom in the water. The patient's companion quickly becomes a dot in the vast ocean as we speed towards the shore. Our feet are close to the water and his weight tears at one of my arms to be released from the rescue tube. The sea is our safety and our threat. It may take his body altogether if he slips from me now but it will cushion us if we fall, or if he slips from my hold that locks his arms over the rescue tube. But for safety we never go very high, just enough to avoid being dragged through the top of the swell. For all the wonderful sights we have from the aerial perspective of the chopper, I know how much skill it takes for a pilot to do this while also keeping the chopper from being claimed by the sea. I'm locked in to the rescue rope but only his rescue tube is locked in for expediency of a surf rescue. The tube is not designed for longer lifts such as this but it was a close call between shore distance and urgency, given that he is not breathing. Slipping out is usually not an issue with conscious patients even when they are pretending to be unconscious, but the sea can be hard to hit at any time if contacted at the wrong angle. Injuries from being propelled from an IRB during racing have taught me that.

Close to the shore now our feet are dragging through the water, the resistance turning our bodies of entangled limbs between rescue rope and sea-shackled feet. We are carefully lowered into the shallows, where a gentle wash of the final energy of the wave rocks us forward to the wet sand. The pilot releases the rope then spins to land close by on the beach above the waterline. My colleague alights with defibrillator and oxygen, meeting me as I drag our patient to dry sand. Our CPR relieves him of the sea his flesh has taken in but there is no sign of life as paramedics arrive from our other chopper. I know he will not return but our training is to continue. His form becomes attached to machines, injected with drugs, packaged for flight and I'm momentarily relieved from my duties while the other crew load him into the chopper bound for the hospital. I mechanically recover my rope from nearby lifesavers, rewinding it while washing the sand from it in the sea, ducking below shallow waves, until I can kneel on the ocean's floor and stay below the surface of the water, my tears joining the ocean. Looking up through the sea, watching the breaking wave curl, boil and clear, time stops, then returns to normal. I am the manta ray.

His death that day left traces of sadness in me, not for him but for those who loved him. The sea lays many challenges to my own flesh and to strangers. I knew his body had released 'life', whatever that is, and I felt it. He was a person of the sea though, so I reckoned there would be no better way 'to go' than to have a heart attack while paddling. I feel uncomfortable with such a thought, at the same time comforted that that was the natural order of things with the sea, regardless of human intervention. Unlike those who get into difficulty through a lack of experience or the unpredictability of the seas, and then experience a great struggle through drowning, this had been quick, a heart attack. Despite the sea not being the cause I wondered would the sea still mean the same for his paddling companion and for his friends and family?

I had imagined what it was like to drown after pulling my first body from the sea the day I got my CPR qualification and returned to beach patrol. The nightmares of my little brother's near drowning had returned after that first rescue, fear gripping my chest so that it could not expand. Now, I look through the water up to the sky as it got darker and further away, then a sense of letting go, staring, waiting, and peace. What was I afraid of? The cycle of death? Losing something?

My ontology fell apart when mum died. Her death was not connected with the sea. To aid me in coping with the shock of losing her, coupled with the terrible last few months of her 'life', the sea continued to beckon, support and challenge me. During those months with her, I often found myself drawn to being with the sea in one of my many favoured spots, along the shore, in the water, on my board, to watch the sun rise over it, watch its ebb and flow, its surface glittering in the sunlight, its coolness brushing past my skin, its lapping at the shore washing my feet with grits of sand, its wetness flushing through me with a healing energy, its wildness tumbling me within its waves, its weightlessness dissolving this thing called me, yet me unable to ... breathe? Be? The sea soothed me, my spirit, my flesh, but 'I' felt absent. I felt at once disembodied with the sadness of mum's illness and death but clearly reminded that 'I' was. With no emotion or feeling, after drowning in grief at the hospital by her side and then at home while we waited for family to arrive and dawn to break, I was picked up by my triathlon partner and driven to the competition venue by the sea. The only memory of that day was doing the swim leg in the sea with a technical monotony that took no caution from the waves slapping me in the face, choking on the salty water, crying and screaming below the water, then returning to disbelief that mum was gone. I had to do 'something', not just sit around home, even though my teammates insisted I could skip the race. Doing was being. Swimming, I wanted to let go and become the sea. Drowning seemed a peaceful end to my bursting agony but, despite my paralysed diaphragm, I kept stroking the water.

Fifteen years on and the experience remains in my watery flesh, not just as a cognitive memory, hardly watered down at all despite my many iterations since. It is nearly as clear as it was then, and as I write the trauma returns. The sea kept me, and kept me human.

Death, life, sea and me.

Ongoing Thoughts: Mindful Spatio-Sensational Pedagogics

While I have left out much of the still-felt details of these experiences with the sea, for me their clarity, effect and affect act as a mix of sensational pedagogies (Ellsworth, 2005) and body pedagogics (Mellor and Shilling, 2010); elemental chronospatial assemblages where a self or selves has/have been learned, those that constitute who 'I' might be. At the same time, I suggest that such assemblages raise the question of something that undoes subject positions, where entry into the sublime hints at how our humanness has created blind spots in our perceptions that structure our world. Clearly, I believe the sea has had a significant influence on 'me', on learning my 'self'. This relational interaction of intersubjectivity aids distinction, between an individual 'self' in relation to the sea, between self and other humans, and between humans and my sea-self. But I do not think we ask enough questions about our interaction with the seas, not as something separate to us but as something with us.

There are subject positions made possible by society, and others by my perceptions reclaimed from society or reframed and reconstituted by my practices within it. For example, the many subject positions that have been available to me are nested within social/human categories such as sex (the surfer, the practice rescue) where my practice has illustrated some forms of social agency *and* oppression (female rescue crew). The sea participated in me knowing my 'self' as capable, not female. Those 'others', humans, participated in me knowing my 'self' as female, not capable. Experiences of 'self' are also nested effects of the sensorium and feeling body (haptic, aural, visual, proprioceptive), emotion (fear, joy, peacefulness, doom, spirituality), ways of being that are fragmented yet stitched in this thing called a life (surfing, diving, rescue crewing, lifesaving, competing, relaxing, defending, living, grieving, being lost), and within a liminal cycle or between dimensions of life and death. Reflecting on these recollections, I offer several brief Deleuzian 'lines of flight' (Deleuze and Guattari, 1980 [2004]) for more extensive exploration elsewhere.

Ontologically there is much to consider from studies of practice, focusing on autoethnographic accounts of habitus, one's own dispositions and positionings within the social field. By extending the notion of field to include elements, such as within the sea, as subject not object, calls for greater engagement with the social construction of oceans (see, for example, Steinberg, 2001), with the concept of the personification of the seas (see, for example, ancient and indigenous ontologies of sea spirits, goddesses and gods such as the Inuit Sedna, Māori Tangaroa or Norse AEgir), as a space for 'kinetic empathy' (Thrift, 2008), as a spiritual connection (Humberstone, 2011), or transgressing objectivity to understand the sea as an elemental sensory quality of fluidity. This is related to the sensible physical world that has an inside and outside, but is an abstraction of one of Buddhism's four Great Elements (see Wallace, 2001; Warder, 2000). Such notions also break from dualisms including human–nature, and provide a more complex, unified and relational conception to work within. Drawing on Reay (2004), we could recuperate reflective and creative aspects of practice (Crossley, 2002; Farnell, 2000) and 'inner conversations' (Sayer, 2005) by using habitus as a method of analysis. We can continue to explore our 'being' and our ways of knowing that challenge dominant Western, dualistic humanocentric and ontologically secure notions of self that are more perceptive of, and sensitive to, complex relational understandings. Such ontological shifts are also embedded in some of the current feminist (Whatmore, 2002), nature-based sport (Humberstone, 2011), and place-based (Cresswell and Merriman, 2011; Gruenewald, 2008; McKenzie, 2008) literature.

Engaging with related epistemologies and their knowledges may enhance perceptual and cognitive understandings of the sentient, spatial and elemental relationships that constitute 'I', humanity, society, life and world. Learning to read the world and act upon it, what Bourdieu would refer to as *reflexivity* and Freire as *conscientizacao*, is for the purpose of 'learning to perceive social, political, and economic contradictions, and to take action against the oppressive elements of reality' (Freire, 1972, p. 17). This requires awareness, and perhaps mindfulness, linked to a spiritual ontology, and an ethical commitment to navigate difficult territories shaped by perceptions, the inherited structures Bourdieu situates at once in fields and habitus. What I feel can be further developed is our sensorial capacities alongside perceptual, cognitive and affective awareness. Such learning is embodied and spatial.

Bringing together pedagogics of place (Gruenewald, 2008), sensation (Ellsworth, 2005), and body (Mellor and Shilling, 2010), I consider 'being' to be an assemblage of at least four dimensions of space and time that are manifested in physical, symbolic, discursive and spiritual subject positions. Such positions are embodied in practice, a verb, rather than identities and their categories, nouns. Going beyond conceptualisations of seascapes and places, to (sea)spaces where lived spatialities are social and elemental, their mobility and fluidity can be considered more fully, where 'spaces are not simply contexts, they are actively produced by the act of moving' (Cresswell and Merriman, 2011, p. 7), a consideration directly embodied in the element water. This is an alternative to identities being fixed in individuals and played out in enabling places. Just as DeLyser (2011) shows how embodied flying practices by pioneering women aviators challenged their place, the dominant gendered narratives in their lived spatialities, I too was able to take up subject positions previously unavailable to many females, despite the persistence of patriarchal practices embodied in organisations such as surf rescue and surfing. Like the sea, learning is also a motion towards previously unknown ways of thinking and being in the world, a challenging process that involves letting go of a part of your known self (Ellsworth, 2005). Knowing one's subjective space, as a verb, as possible practices that are mobile, fluid, transitional, emergent, sensorial and pedagogical feels more freeing and reflective of the process of learning, more so than the more fixed notions of place and identity embodied in nouns. Breaking from the tyranny of nouns and focusing on practices makes way for action against oppressive elements of our lived worlds. For me, this was through volunteering for a community good, albeit with ethical dilemmas that required negotiation. It allowed for challenging physical and symbolic violences of the categories and embodying different possibilities for others to witness. And it allowed for me to debate what constitutes life and death, to reveal blind spots that underpin the killings or destruction of other beings, or the actions that facilitate life. But it also allows for the celebration of the spaces of joy, so much of which we have yet to understand as experience.

Conclusion

> As well as habitus coming into view as a mixture of the embodied, the instinctual
> and the unthought, we also glimpse the 'life of the mind', the reflective as well
> as the pre- reflective. (Reay, 2004, p. 441)

Surfing the seaspace is a metaphor for the life of my reflective and pre-reflective
mind. It is a spatio-sensational pedagogy of self; my sensorial, multi-perspective,
intersubjective, lived, embodied experiences assembled in relation to seaspace.
It involves a range of perspectives: above, in, under, through, and with the sea,
shifting as tides and seasons punctuated with recurring practices that mediate
the status quo and change; embedded in the habitus and socio-elemental field
synchronously. Each individual experience is like surfing a different wave from
the same sea of self, a different time-space but nuanced with some of the same
social, physical, and cognitive similarities, with the water taking different shapes
and me interacting from different perspectives dependent upon the assemblage at
that point in time and space. So too is life shaped, made up of many fluid elements
of materiality, symbolism and spirituality including assemblages of time, space,
sex, gender, race and so on. The embodied subjectivities illustrated in the narrative,
the self, learned in relation to and with the sea, prompt me to ask questions of self,
and of physical, social and symbolic space. I look forward to exploring others'
mindful spatio-sensational pedagogics to further my understanding of the sea/
mind, as human, as self, and as not.

Acknowledgements

Thanks to elke emerald for reviewing drafts of this chapter and offering helpful advice. Thanks also to the editors, Mike Brown and Barbara Humberstone, for inviting me to write and then for providing feedback on my draft.

References

Bourdieu, P., 1990. *In Other Words: Essays Towards a Reflexive Sociology.* Stanford, CA: Stanford University Press.

Cresswell, T. and Merriman, P., 2011. Introduction. Geographies of mobilities: Practices, spaces, subjects. In: T. Cresswell and P. Merriman, eds, *Geographies of Mobilities: Practices, Spaces, Subjects.* Farnham, UK and Burlington, VT: Ashgate, pp. 1–15.

Crossley, N., 2002. *Making Sense of Social Movements.* Buckingham: Open University Press.

Deleuze, G. and Guattari, F., 1980 [2004]. *A Thousand Plateaus.* New York: Continuum.

DeLyser, D., 2011. Flying: Feminisms and mobilities – Crusading for aviation in the 1920s. In: T. Cresswell and P. Merriman, eds, *Geographies of Mobilities: Practices, Spaces, Subjects.* Farnham, UK and Burlington, VT: Ashgate, pp. 83–96.

Ellis, C. and Bochner, A., 2000. Autoethnography, personal narrative, reflexivity. In: N. Denzin and Y. Lincoln, eds, *Handbook of Qualitative Research* (2nd ed.). Thousand Oaks, CA: Sage, pp. 733–68.

Ellsworth, E., 2005. *Places of Learning: Media, Architecture, Pedagogy.* New York: RoutledgeFalmer.

Farnell, B., 2000. Getting out of the habitus: An alternative model of dynamically embodied social action. *Journal of the Royal Anthropological Institute,* 6, pp. 397–418.

Freire, P., 1972. *Pedagogy of the Oppressed.* Harmondsworth: Penguin.

Gruenewald, D., 2008. The best of both worlds – a critical pedagogy of place. *Educational Researcher,* 32(4), pp. 3–12.

Haraway, D., 1992. Otherworldly conversations; Terran topics; Local terms. *Science As Culture,* 3(14), pp. 64–98.

Humberstone, B., 2011. Embodiment and social and environmental action in nature-based sport: Spiritual spaces. *Leisure Studies,* 30(4), pp. 495–512.

McKenzie, M., 2008. The places of pedagogy: Or, what we can do with culture through intersubjective experiences. *Environmental Education Research,* 14(3), pp. 361–73.

Mellor, P.A. and Shilling, C., 2010. Body pedagogics and the religious habitus: A new direction for the sociological study of religion. *Religion*, 40, pp. 27–38.

Reay, D., 2004. 'It's all becoming a habitus': Beyond the habitual use of habitus in educational research. *British Journal of Sociology of Education*, 25(4), pp. 431–44.

Reed-Danahay, D. ed., 1997. *Auto/Ethnography: Rewriting the Self and the Social.* Oxford: Berg.

Sayer, A., 2005. *The Moral Significance of Class.* Cambridge: Cambridge University Press.

Steinberg, P., 2001. *The Social Construction of the Ocean.* Cambridge, UK: Cambridge University Press.

Thrift, N., 2008. *Non-Representational Theory: Space, Politics, Affect.* London: Routledge.

Wallace, B.A., 2001. Intersubjectivity in Indo-Tibetan Buddhism. *Journal of Consciousness Studies*, 8(5–7), pp. 1–22.

Warder, A.K., 2000. *Indian Buddhism* (3rd ed.). Delhi: Motilal Banarsidass.

Whatmore, S., 2002. *Hybrid Geographies: Natures, Cultures, Spaces.* London: Sage.

Chapter 4

On Being Shaped by Surfing: Experiencing the World of the Littoral Zone

Jon Anderson

Theirs, briefly, is a perilous excitement
When the current lifts them high
And they stand erect on roofs of water,
Balanced on the summit of a wave.

And there they glide, untouchable,
The moment of flight and their bodies'
Instinctive mastery lasting until
They are somersaulted into the foam
And they creep to shore exhausted,
Barefoot, wincing with the discriminate
Steps of thieves, aware perhaps
Of something they might have won, or stolen
— Minhinnick, 1999, p. 63

Introduction

Although the vast majority of human beings lead land-locked lives (see Anderson, 2012), some people, as Taylor (2005) tells us, always return to the water. For these people the sea is their home, their hope, their past and their future. They are called to it and, as this book suggests, are shaped by it. These people are 'water people' and, as Mattos outlines, these individuals are blessed 'with a total mastery of all oceanic endeavours … [they] can survive entirely on self-harvested ocean bounty, catching [their] food from the very seas [they]'ll surf over when the swell is up' (Mattos, 2004, p. 8).

Speaking personally, I cannot rely on any putative 'mastery of the ocean' to 'self-harvest the ocean bounty'. Fortunately I am not dependent on my water skills to live but simply to make life worth living. As a consequence I am, like other water people, defined by a desire for the 'perilous excitement' derived from surfing the sea 'when the swell is up'. For water people, such direct contact with the sea is vital. Following the poet Walt Whitman (or rather taking him by the hand

and leading him from his *Leaves of Grass* to the sea), water people are drawn to an embodied engagement with 'the original energy' of the ocean, they are 'mad for contact' with this 'nature without check' (Whitman, 1855). For water people, 'there's nothing [like] the tumult of the sea' (Abse, 2009, p. 290). As Booth puts it, water people

> share a collective conscience based on common experiences[:] The 'motion of the waves', 'the instability of the sand beneath their feet' [and] 'the sting of spray in their eyes' ... Indeed, Matt George, a co-star in, and a scriptwriter for, the big-wave surf classic *In God's Hands* (Sony, 1998), believes that 'if you look a real surfer in the eye ... you'll see the tides'. (Booth, 2001, pp. 7–8)

Water people are thus drawn to the motion of the waves, and the vast majority of these waves are accessible at the oceanic margins where the land meets the sea. In this space, surfers are shaped differently to non-water beings. In the words of Kampion (2004), water people feel at home in this 'dynamic give and take of land and sea, swell and tide. The people indigenous to this fluid landscape belong to the global tribe of surfers. They see the ocean differently than inlanders, differently too than the other fringe dwellers who seldom set foot in saltwater' (p. 1).

This chapter investigates how this littoral zone shapes the 'global tribe of surfers'. It will show that this tribe is constituted by an array of different surf riders, including body-, board- and boat-riders, and how the place of the surfed wave is different for each of these surfing neo-tribes (to use Maffesoli's phrase, 1996). Building on related writing (Anderson, 2014a), I will attempt to outline what it is like for these surfers to experience this space and surf its swells. In line with the philosophy of this book, this chapter is therefore positioned from an 'actor-centred perspective' (after Jones, 2009); it attempts to represent the experience gained when one 'engage[s] with the world tactually [and has] a potentially unmediated relationship with it' (Lewis, 2000, p. 59). In short, I seek to give an insight into how individuals, through engaging in the embodied practice of surfing, 'choose to make sense of the world [of the surf zone and how this engagement] constitutes ... [their] reality' (Lewis, 2000, p. 59). In this way, I build on my previous work on the places, cultures and relational senses of surfing (see Anderson, 2012, 2013a, 2014b, forthcoming). The reader is also encouraged to use the Internet links given throughout the text to films that give a visual representation of what it is like to be shaped by the sea through the act of surfing.

Surfing the Edge of Things: Where the Terrestrial and Aquatic Meet

As outlined above, most accessible waves occur in the zone where the land meets the sea, in the 'transitional, highly porous border between the primeval terrestrial and aquatic' (Barilotti, 2002, p. 34).[1] The surf zone is thus a location both between and beyond the land and sea. As such, it can be understood as a liminal space, a space that is not adequately defined simply by the languages and concepts traditionally used to describe the marine or the terrestrial. In this sense, the surf zone can be understood as a new space, one that 'temporarily suspends' the conventional (b)orders of cultural and maritime societies (after Bakhtin, 1984, p. 10). Riding these border or edge zones is crucial to surfers, in both a physical and societal sense. As Booth identifies:

> ... Surfers are edge-riders. We've made a decision ... to live on the fringe of society and not be active citizens and participants in society, unless we want to. The act of going surfing is a very selfish endeavour. It's an experience that has nothing to do with anything except you and the ocean, period (Bill Hamilton, surfboard shaper and legendary rider). (Booth, 2001, p. 84)[2]

To engage on this edge, to live a border life between the land and sea is part of surfing's appeal, especially because it is at this edge that is possible to directly experience the original energy of the ocean. From a hydrological perspective, this edge is a 'littoral' space. McCabe describes littoral spaces as those 'of, relating to, situated, or growing near a shore' (2004, p. 7). From this perspective, the littoral zone is where land, sea and air meet – it is the zone where these physical media interact, clash and combine. What all surfers share is an instinctive magnetism to the energy produced in this littoral space. As Wilson states, surfers are 'shoreaholics' (2008, p. 18); this periphery is their centre, the ephemeral edge is where their action is. In short, they are all 'mad for contact' with the surface crests of this littoral space.

> It will be objected that th[is chapter] deals too much with ... the surface of things ... For my own part I am pleased enough with surfaces – in fact they alone seem to me to be of much importance ... what else is there? What else do we need? (Abbey, 1992, p. xiii)

Surfing is an engagement with the sea that is not premised on accessing depths or traversing huge distances, rather it is the act of riding the surface swell. It is a practice that necessitates the generation and implementation of a high degree of skill to anticipate, be well positioned and successfully ride the waves. This act of wave riding is a thrilling experience and is articulated by surfers with reference to the term 'stoke'. Stoke is described by Duane as 'the light joy of effortless,

---

1   However, it is increasingly possible to go offshore and engage in deep-sea surfing, operationalised through boat charter.

2   This sentiment is echoed in the following short film (Fordham et al., 2013), specifically at 9 minutes, 30 seconds: http://www.guardian.co.uk/travel/video/2013/jun/06/california-road-trip-surfing-culture-video.

combustion-free speed' (1996, p. 11) and by Kampion as 'the real-time neural stimulation and restorative prophylaxis ... resulting in a stunning net profit on time and energy invested' (2004, p. 44). Stoke refers at once to the thrill of personal skill accomplished (that is, of catching and carving a route on a moving mass of water – see Csikszentmihalyi, 1990; and Anderson, 2012), to the relational sensibility of a sublime encounter (see Anderson, 2013a) and a convergent experience (Anderson, 2012) – or as one surfer simply puts it, stoke refers to the 'immense feeling of being carried by the sea' (survey response[3]). Here, however, I would like to emphasise the different means through which surfers surf, and the different technologies that create particular experiences of the surfed wave. Despite Lewis's suggestion (above), surfers' sensuous and tactile experiences of the sea are not wholly *un*mediated, rather they are brokered and influenced by the technologies used by participants to ride the waves. Despite all surfers sharing the call of the surface swell, surfers are not a homogeneous tribe. Surfers can be categorised in terms of those who like to lie to surf (bodysurfers and bodyboarders), those who prefer to sit (surf-skiers, sit-on-top kayakers or surf-kayakers) and those who must stand in order to catch their waves (surfboarders, on either long- or short-boards). Each different technology shapes the experience of the surfed wave. The 'place' of the surfed wave (see Anderson, 2012) for a surf-*kayaker*, for example, is therefore subtly but importantly different from that of the surf*boarder*. Each technology enables a different 'dwelling-in-motion' on the sea (after Sheller and Urry, 2006) and each unique coming together of swell, fetch, geology, wind, surfer and riding-technology 'shapes [their] experience of place, as well as shaping [the] place [of the surfed wave] itself' (after Price, 2013, p. 124). To paraphrase Edensor, the assemblage of the surfing body and riding technology 'weaves a path that is contingent, and accordingly produces contingent notions of place as well as being always partially conditioned by the special and physical characteristics of place' (2010, p. 70). The chapter continues by giving insight into these different experiences of being shaped by the sea through surfing. To do so it draws on my personal experiences and from first-hand accounts articulated by professional surfers and surf-writers.

Being Carried by the Sea: Body(board) Surfing

We had spent the morning sea kayaking from an island in the centre of the Sea of Cortez, Southern California. We had paddled across flat water to a remote bay on

---

3   This survey was undertaken by the author as part of a project funded by the Sports Council for Wales, which investigated participation regimes in surfing in the principality. This research was based on an online questionnaire that was completed by 134 anonymised surfers in Wales as well as interviews with the proprietors of 14 surf schools in Wales, interviews with six surf club secretaries and 20 in-depth interviews with well-travelled, international-standard surfers.

the peninsula of Baja, a few hours south of Loreto. We had covered the distance in three to four hours, racing ahead of the winds, which created a surface chop on the sea. By the time this chop had reached where we were camping that evening, we had set up our tents and the wind's energy had coalesced the sea into a series of waves. This new shore-break was too inviting to ignore. We had no boards with us and the sea kayaks were too long, unwieldy, and packed with provisions to ride such surging swell. I decided to bodysurf the waves.

Perhaps the closest physical encounter one can have with the surfed wave is through the practice of bodysurfing (sometimes known as wave sliding, for examples see Bodysurf, n.d., http://bodysurf.net/). Bodysurfing involves swimming to locate oneself in front of a series of breaking waves and timing your 'swim-in' to catch a wave as it rises behind you. Often undertaken with scuba diving styled fins (although cut short to aid manoeuvrability and give greater propulsion), bodysurfing offers the most unmediated engagement with the surface swell. It is, however, a tricky activity to master.

> The waves were regular but their height and speed made timing my swim-in difficult. I had no fins and so had to kick and paddle like fury in order to generate any sort of speed, especially compared to that produced by the swell. I also had to compete against my lack of natural buoyancy and the absence of a wetsuit, which would trap some air and give me a 'lift'. Nevertheless, with a sandy shore and enough collapsing froth to tamper the energy of the broken waves, the risk of serious impact was low. I was therefore free to clumsily 'porpoise' my way through the waves, being lifted and carried by the crests, my feet rising first, then being shot forward as if down a supercharged children's slide. Although the scale of the waves and their carrying distance were small, being so close to their falloomphing gave a minor charge from what McGinty has called the '24-karat gold monster-cable speaker wire [which has] one end plugged into [the surf] and the other soldered into your adrenal gland'. (Warshaw, 2004, p. xx)

Despite bodysurfing being the least mediated engagement with the surface swell, perhaps the most popular way to be introduced to surfing is through bodyboarding. This form of surfing involves lying prone on a small board, being well-positioned (initially with board and body facing to the shore as a wave approaches) and catching waves as they careen to shore. As with bodysurfing, bodyboarding is commonly undertaken in shallow water and thus frequently constitutes the entry level of surf riding. The bodyboarding encounter is well summed up by the writer Jack London, when reminiscing on his first experience of the sport.

> I shall never forget the first big wave I caught out there in the deep water. I saw it coming, turned my back on it and paddled for dear life. Faster and faster my board went, till it seemed my arms would drop off. What was happening behind me I could not tell. One cannot look behind and paddle the windmill stroke.

I heard the crest of the wave hissing and churning, and then my board was lifted and flung forward. I scarcely knew what happened the first half-minute. Though I kept my eyes open, I could not see anything, for I was buried in the rushing white of the crest. (London, 2004, p. 23)

Due to the proximity of body to sea, a real sense of stoke can be generated through this surfing method, and although bodyboarding is commonly seen as an entry level activity, it is always possible to ride more challenging waves in this fashion (for examples, see ThreeSixty, n.d., http://www.threesixtymag.co.uk/; and Nemani's accounts of bodyboarding in Chapter 6). However, despite this form of engagement with the ocean enabling an embodied and physical encounter of the thrill of stoke, other surfing technologies such as long- or short-boards tend to be employed with greater frequency by the surfing community.

Short- and Long-Boards

It is estimated that there are approximately 23 million surfboarders across the littoral globe (see Surfers Path, 2012, p. 4). This form of engagement with the surface swell has become the mode of practice for the majority of aspiring water people; as Barilotti puts it, 'everyone wants to be a surf[board]er' (2002, p. 89). Surfboards come in a range of sizes with different aims of mobility and speed. Some are long-boards, which are 'ideal for easy wave-catching and smooth-flowing, style-conscious manoeuvres' (Fordham, 2008, p.75); some are 'thrusters' (or short-boards), which enable surfers to 'turn more radically and to take aerial manoeuvres out over the lip of the breaking wave' (Fordham, 2008, p. 154); whilst others are 'guns', which are made for paddling into big waves (see CoastlineTobi, 2013, http://www.youtube.com/watch?v=iC76The-FMU). Although much media focuses on big waves and increasingly exotic or tow-in waves (see dawnrboucher, 2011, http://www.youtube.com/watch?v=EulFrt1rpPA), the vast majority of surfers paddle in to their waves on their long- or short-boards from the local shore break. Surf-writer Drew Kampion introduces us to the experiential world of this tactile, embodied culture. He begins by describing the importance of the ritual of waxing your board (in order to aid friction and grip in the transition to standing), before your entry to the water.

Rub the wax in figure eights onto the deck of the board, stick it in your pocket. Run down the beach, feet sinking an inch or two, the sand moist and grainy and warm where it is wet with the ocean. You come to the rip, wait for a wave to rush up to the crown of the sand, then run with it as it flows back to the sea. Throw the board down, out ahead of you, and slide onto your belly. Paddle as fast as you can till you are outside of the shorebreak, heaving and crashing and splashing out with the rip. A quarter mile in three minutes and you are working your way out of the rip and over into the line-up. Some friends are there, wet already, and they greet you with big smiles. The waves are perfect, one says. Another yawps agreement ... You are flushed with the run and the paddle-out, and exhilarated by the water. (Kampion, 2004, p. 22)[4]

Such stylised accounts may have the effect of convincing the novice – or 'kook' in surfing parlance – that board-riding is easy. As Cornish surfer Fuz Bleakley states 'so many people come to surfing now thinking that they, too, will be deep inside a ... barrel within just a couple of weeks. They've no idea how difficult [board]surfing is, and don't understand the surf media's idealized images don't represent most people's real surfing experience' (Wade, 2007, p. 65). My initial surfboard experience made me realise that the utopia of perfect barrels (see below) and intense stoke were not objectives easily won.

On the back of absurdly cheap flights to the continent we had made a cheeky trip to Biarritz, on the Atlantic coast of France. On the sea front, backed by casinos, wine bars, and expensive restaurants, were the most regular sets of surf I had yet seen. At that point I had no boardriding experience, but my friend had weathered Welsh waters for years and was raring to go. We had the beach to ourselves. We unravelled our wetsuits from our rucksacks and cobbled together the Euros necessary to rent boards from the local surf shop. I'm sure the vendor could read me as a 'kook' simply from how I carried the board from the rack (I had no clue which board which would best suit the conditions, or my lack of skill, so my friend picked me a safe option): on film surfers carry their boards so effortlessly, this monster seemed unwieldy on land, let alone water, and my arms remained too short to carry it with nonchalance, so I bear-hugged it to the sea.

There are no amiable 'good lucks' or last minute advice: my friend is off into the breakers so I have to follow. How hard can it be? There is no rip on this beach, no fluid 'travelator' to take me the easy route beyond the cresting waves; I have to go through them. Or under them! Duck-diving – of course! I can duck under the waves; propel myself down or turn myself over, and let the breaking wave rise without me. I try it, and find capsizing my board whilst clinging to its edges the easiest style to accomplish. Good. The next task is timing: paddle like mad ... gasp a breath ... roll ... withstand the buffet of the breaking wave ... and resurface in clear water to begin again. Phew. Effort and exertion. Rinse and repeat. After time I feel as if I have to be 'out back' by now, but looking around I realise I have hardly made any 'ground' at all. I remain resolutely in the midst of the crests and – what!?! &$%! Despite there being only two of us on the whole beach, my friend zooms across me within inches of my head as he catches his first wave back to shore. Gasping, breathless, exhausted, I realise I am out of my depth in more ways than one.*

---

4   A contemporary example of Kampion's experience is well captured in the following clip: Pollett, N., 2013, http://www.carvemag.com/2013/03/uber-slo-mo-hawaii/#. Ubc7JufFV5Z.

On my first experience of surfing in Biarittz, I had unwittingly committed surfing's cardinal sin. Although I thought my friend had surfed too close to me for the comfort of either of us, it was I who really was in the wrong place. As Steve Bough (former editor of surfing magazine *Wavelength*) states 'surfing's primary rule is that the surfer who is already on the wave has right of way' (Wade, 2007, p. 86). By loitering without intent where the waves were breaking, I had inadvertently 'dropped in' on an incoming surfer's ride, making it impossible for them to continue on their wave unimpeded. On more populated beaches, such indiscretion from kook boardriders results in confrontational incidents (see Montero, 2009, http://www.youtube.com/watch?v=CcyFwnftALQ; and Anderson, 2013a, forthcoming). However, through dedication and perseverance, it is possible to achieve more successful experiences of catching a wave through surf-boarding. As Kampion articulates,

> The guy next to you moves, begins to paddle. You turn and look out to sea. A dark line approaching. A thick, fat hump of water moving soundlessly closer and closer: a bluebird they once called them. You stroke frantically out towards it, praying not to be caught inside ...[5] Outside is another, larger wave. You paddle hard. Fresher than the others, you pull out ahead, and have time to turn while they are still trying to make it over. You stroke towards the shore. You are lifted, lifted. A deep trough sags low before you. The water descends like a wide slide. You feel it catch you, then hurtle you forward with incredible acceleration. You take the drop coming to your feet. You drive down and down, carve around a surfer trying to make it over, but you know he will be caught inside and have to swim because the wave is already coming out over your head. You turn hard at the bottom and draw back tight against the wall of the water and rocket along to your right. You touch a hand to the water surface, and your fingers flap and chatter as if from a speedboat, and when you turn to glance towards the shore, you cannot see it because the wall of water has come out over your head and surrounded you, and there is just a big, fat hole in front of you, and you are going for it and definitely, positively, absolutely nothing else matters. (Kampion, 2004, p. 24)

Kampion describes the space created by this concave, curling wave, which the surfer inhabits and rides. Surfers call this constantly forming and rolling tube of water the 'barrel' or 'green room', the latter named after the chromatography created inside the wave by the sun filtering through the sea-room walls (see GoProCamera, 2010, http://www.youtube.com/watch?v=4T2AG5fIfsc at 60 seconds). This space, although fleeting, seems substantial to the surfer (see Capp, 2004) and the relational affect or sensibility (Anderson, 2009) generated by

---

5   Being caught inside refers to being in front of the wave just after it has broken, leaving you no place to escape to. The experience is well captured in this footage: Howdynews, 2009, http://www.youtube.com/watch?v=nAlAI6UOHoo.

being within it prompts surfers to smile, scream and talk of near religious (see Anderson 2013a; Taylor 2007a, 2007b, 2007c, 2008) and mystical experiences. Shaun Thomson, Surf World Champion in 1977, reflects: 'When you go into a deep barrel you certainly feel as if time's expanded. Life is slowed down. I felt as if I could curve that wall [of water] to my will. I really felt that. It's a magical, magical moment' (quoted in Gosch, 2008).

This feeling of 'mastery' of the sea (as referred to by Minhinnick and Mattos, above) is a component that appears to be more prevalent in surfboarding than other forms of surfing. Standing on the water, walking or dancing on it (as some refer to board-riding, see Winton, 2008, p. 25) often confers a sense of mastery over and conquering of the original energy of the surf zone.[6]

Surf-Kayaking

'Whether 'tis nobler in the mind to stand', is hardly the point. Some of us are kayakers and as such driven by the desire to see what dizzy heights our chosen craft can reach upon the ocean wave. (Mattos, 2004, p. 8)

Despite the potential to 'lord it over all creation' (see London, 2004, p. 13), there is a further alternative to the 'noble' art of surfboarding and that is surf-kayaking. Riding the waves in a kayak or canoe was the original way that humans rode

---

6 Although important, this point should not be overplayed. Some long-boarders, often referred to as soul surfers, would refute any wish to conquer the ocean. However, this component of surfing is clear from the position of the surfer, as well as the shore-side spectator, as perhaps the most famous of Jack London's surf descriptions outlines:

And suddenly, out there where a big smoker lifts skyward, rising like a sea-god from out of the welter of spume and churning white, on the giddy, toppling, overhanging and downfalling, precarious crest appears the dark head of a man. Swiftly he rises through the rushing white. His black shoulders, his chest, his loins, his limbs – all is abruptly projected on one's vision. Where but the moment before was only the wide desolation and invincible roar, is now a man, erect, full-statured, not struggling frantically in that wild movement, not buried and crushed and buffeted by those mighty monsters, but standing above them all, calm and superb, poised on the giddy summit, his feet buried in the churning foam, the salt smoke rising to his knees, and all the rest of him in the free air and flashing sunlight, and he is flying through the air, flying forward, flying fast as the surge on which he stands. He is a Mercury – a brown Mercury. His heels are winged, and in them is the swiftness of the sea ... He has 'bitted the bull-mouthed breaker' and ridden it in, and the pride in the feat shows in the carriage of his magnificent body as he glances for a moment carelessly at you who sit in the shade of the shore ... He is a man, a member of the kingly species that has mastered matter and the brutes and lorded it over creation. (2004, p. 13)

the surface swell, as Mattos states:[7] 'The first people to [surf] were Polynesians in outrigger canoes, a point I'm always happy to make when surfers insist that boardriding is the only original, cool and indeed acceptable way to enjoy waves. Which, unfortunately, happens quite a lot' (Mattos, 2004, p. 13).

Despite being the original means of surfing, surf-kayaking remains a peripheral activity when compared to other forms of surf riding. Along with Mattos, I would describe myself as a primarily a surf-kayaker and I cannot wholly discount that in this peripherality is some of the sport's appeal. Where surfers are on the edge and the alternative to the mainstream, now that 'everybody wants to be surfer' the edge has in some senses *become* the mainstream. Despite this, the kayaker remains on the periphery, practising a marginal sport in a marginal space. And in this marginality, perhaps, lies an important aspect of identity for those who are obstinate about being different, or who are drawn away from the crowds towards some sort of self-reliance (after Emerson, 1994). Despite this marginality, there is something about the sea when experienced in a kayak. Sanford states 'paddlers emphasize their intimacy with the [sea] ... kayakers sit low in the water and are always partially immersed in the water' (2007, p. 882). I feel this intimacy strongly. Through this particular contact with the surface swell, it is possible to feel each rise and fall of the sea through my boat and my body. I am not on the water or under it, but in it, and that few inches of submergence means kayakers cross the boundary between air and depth, and transgress this surface with their bodies. Surfboards do not do this. Surfboards have no depth, no edges or rails (that is, the side sections of the hull of the kayak) and as a consequence surfers experience a *flatter* sense of buoyancy. In short, boarders surf *on* the water, kayakers surf *in* the water.

There are also functional reasons for my preference for engaging with the littoral zone through a kayak, especially in the coastal waters of the North Atlantic. As Finisterre surf products state 'The [surf] lifestyles we continue to see marketed are ones that focus on warm water surf regions. ... Do we really need another board, flip flop, or sunglasses company? There are more cold water surf spots than warm ones and we're surfing them more than ever' (Finisterre, 2012, p. 4).

In a boat, humans become cyborgs. Our human corporeality is physically extended firstly by the boat – through internal padding we sit tight into the kayak hull, with thighs braced and feet wedged against our new exoskeleton;

---

7 Kayaking as the original means through which to engage with surf is confirmed by Captain James Cook (in Warshaw, 2004, p. 4), when he states in his 'Voyage to the Pacific Ocean', that a local 'went out from shore till he was near the place where the swell begins to take its rise; and, watching its first motion very attentively, paddled before it with great quickness, till he found that it overlooked him, and had acquired sufficient force to carry his canoe before it without passing underneath. He then sat motionless, and was carried along at the same swift rate as the wave, till it landed him upon the beach. Then he started out, emptied his canoe, and went in search of another swell. I could not help concluding that this man felt the most supreme pleasure while he was driven on so fast and so smoothly by the sea'.

and secondly by our paddles – adding leverage for our limbs and dexterity to our movements in our new watery medium. For the kayaker, these prosthetics make us whole; the assembled sense of a body constrained by torso-tugging wetsuit and hip-hugging boat gives a sense of protection from the bombast of the sea, as well as the freedom to be buoyed by it. As a consequence of this cyborgian engagement, kayakers are able to feel the sea's motion on and through our extended bodies, but we are nevertheless insulated from its temperature. This is a huge benefit when seeking to maximise the length of time you can stay in the sea without suffering from hypothermia, as well as extending your ability to catch a higher number of waves. Through the use of paddles, kayakers are also advantaged by being able to generate more power when crossing the surf zone to 'out the back' beyond where the waves are breaking. As a consequence, kayakers are able to catch more waves per unit of energy expended. However, not all surf-kayaks are the same. Surf-skis for example, are flat(-ter) boats on which you sit, strapped in, often around your waist or over your thighs. Surf-skis are thus the closest technology to surfboards. When on a surf-ski it is as if you are sitting on a narrow, precarious tray. As a consequence, a surf-ski is liable to tip when stationary, but will glide effortlessly when propelled by the sea's momentum (or your paddling) (see centralcoasttoday, 2008, http://www.youtube.com/watch?v=VClP4BclJic for an example). Sit-on-top kayaks, by contrast, have more depth. Often made from air-blown plastic, sit-on-tops offer stability to the surf-kayaker when stationary or at slow speeds. However, this stability involves a trade-off in this craft's ability to reach high speeds and prime manoeuvrability in fast water. Both craft are easy to 'bail out' from when they do capsize – it is not necessary to be able to 'Eskimo roll' a surf-ski or sit-on-top kayak (see Anderson, 2013b, http://youtu.be/rYSNxll_L1Y) – and as a consequence both appeal to the occasional surf-kayaker or those who lack confidence in their 'bomb-proof roll' in large surf.

Surf-kayaking is, therefore, different from surfboarding due to the different position of the surfer's body in relation to the water, their different source of propulsion, and the different degrees of marginality each enjoy with regard to the mainstream. Due to these differences, surf-kayakers also often 'read' the sea differently from other surfers too. All surfers may read the sea from the shore as if they were discerningly analysing a text (Barthes, 1973). All surfers note where other water people are in the sea and where the waves are breaking. They will note how many waves are in a set and which are biggest. Surfers turn and note shore-side landmarks that will prove useful orientation points when they look back from the sea, and take mental notes of obstacles or rips in the water that may help or hinder their progress 'out back'. With my kayak, however, I look again at the water. Where are the easy routes through the surf, where are the quiet and noisy sections? Which routes will I take due to my ability to paddle, knowing boardriders do not share this ability? Then, I look across the bay to see where the waves are breaking. Where are there whole parliaments of surfers waiting for waves, and dutifully obeying the cultural etiquettes of who rides which breakers?

(see Anderson, forthcoming). I look beyond these hotspots for less populated zones. In short, I look for the sea less travelled.

Then I enter my craft. Clothed in shorts, rash vest, wetsuit socks, snug in a neoprene wetsuit and corseted by a dry-suit top and buoyancy aid,[8] there is a familiar comfort in settling inside my kayak cockpit. A mix of security and excitement, entangled with a tingle of apprehension and, if I'm honest, a hint of fear. The waves seen from a standing position seem negotiable, from a sitting position they appear daunting. You stretch the neoprene spray-skirt over the cockpit, making a waterproof fit. A push from the hands as you balance the paddle across the hull, and you're away; released from the terrestrial shore, buoyant, grabbing for the paddle to propel a course through the soup.

The first splash of waves jolts you. The cold assault slaps you as the incoming swell breaks your bow and collides with your skin and eyes (see for example, Anderson, 2013c, http://youtu.be/MaJpPSwNNF0). You shake it off, smiling, sadistically glad for the intense shock, but certain that if you do not recover and prepare yourself quickly the next one will demolish and drag you back to shore. In a kayak, riding up waves is often as fun as riding back with them. Where surfers may duck dive under advancing waves, kayakers ride them like a ramp, careering over the top, taking air for a moment as the wave passes beneath, then landing with a happy thwack on the leeside of the rise (see Anderson, 2013d, http://youtu. be/YLZTPK4XBTg). I remember Wilson capturing this feeling well:

> *I felt sparks of exhilaration beginning to kindle ... the entire front half would lift and crash downward as the kayak regained full contact with the water, and a quivering thump would run through my whole body. The surface of the sea was level with my hips, while the whole length of my legs, encased within the kayak, lay below water level. The result, part of the unique experience of the kayak, was to feel curiously part of the ceaseless motion of the sea's surface. (Wilson, 2008, p. 28–9)*

Then you turn. Wait. Just be. There, outside the breaking waves, it is possible to find breathing space. From the crowds, from your job, from the stresses of everyday life. From other water people if you're lucky too. Just you and the ocean. Watching the colours change. Perhaps the sun will glint in magic ripples. Perhaps rain will fall, littering the whale-grey water with a symmetry of splashes. Then, the waves come (see Anderson, 2013e, http://youtu.be/JiMSVpW0Aks).

I attempt to gather pace, timing my speed to coincide with the rising waves – if I'm too slow the wave will pass without me, too fast and I'll shoot ahead and miss

---

8   The need for all this kit, especially in cold-water surfing areas, also renders surf-kayaking less accessible and thus less popular.

the crest. It comes, it's upon me. I lean back, feeling for the drive. The boat rises, and with a pivot of my hips I can turn it easily along the lip, riding sideways and forwards towards the shore. Clean, fast. Hips pivot back, the boats wants to stay, but bracing my paddle it reluctantly straightens and instantly remembers the fun it can have being driven arrow-straight.

The sea as viewed from kayak level can be an exciting but also an intimidating place. All surf-kayakers are aware of the inevitability of rolling – of the need to test their capsize skill, find it fit for purpose, or find a way to survive an encounter with a breaking wave (or maybe two). For all surfers, whatever their craft, the sea is sometimes just too big to ride. Surfboarding legend Greg Noll, recounts his experience of a 'wipe out' with a 25-foot wave in Makaha Point, Hawai'i.

> Finally a set came thundering down … I started down the front of the wave and my board began to howl like a goddamn jet. I flew down the face, past the lip of the wave, and when I got to the bottom … I looked ahead and saw the sonofabitch starting to break in a section that stretched a block and a half in front of me. The wave threw out a sheet of water over my head and engulfed me. Then for a split second the whole scene froze forever in my mind. There I was, in that liquid green room … I had been in and out of this room many times. Only this time the room was bigger, more frightening, with the thunderous roar of the ocean bouncing off its walls. I realized that I wasn't going to go flying out the other end into daylight. This time I was afraid there might be no way out.

> My board flew out from under me. I hit the water going so fast that it was like hitting concrete. I skidded on my back and looked up just as tons of white water exploded over me. It pounded me under. It thrashed and rolled me beneath the surface until my lungs burned and there was so much pressure that I felt my eardrums were going to burst. Just as I thought I would pass out, the white water finally began to dissipate and the turbulence released me. I made it to the surface, gulped for air and quickly looked outside. There was another monster heading my way. (Cited in Booth, 2001, p. 12)

Conclusion

For us water people, 'the sea has a profound effect on who we are, what we are, and how we live' (Wilson, 2008, p. 52).

As I have highlighted, there are many ways to surf the littoral zone. In this chapter I have introduced a range of different means through which surfers encounter the surface swell, and the differences these technologies have for the tactile and relational world produced through these encounters. I have highlighted how the range of surfing technology enables each individual water person to choose the best means through which we can access our own place on the surfed wave. Through these different technologies, surfers attempt to gain temporary ownership of a place that is both collective (that is, it is possible for anyone to experience) but also intensely personal. As Kampion the boardrider narrates: 'The only place he had to call his own – outside of the front seat of his truck – was the arching face of an incoming wave' (2004, p. 44) and Wilson the kayak-surfer describes: 'The great swell-waves still pile in upon Scottish shores from the wide Atlantic; the tides scour and swish through the island narrows ... the kayak is still the best way I know of to make it my own' (2008, p. v).

In this sense, the place of the littoral zone is, for us water people, a place where we belong. It is here that we engage in the surface of things and find in the thrill and risk of the surf zone everything we need. In this marginal zone we find a fluid world that is constantly changing, but in the psychological wait for the 'perfect wave' (Anderson, 2007), then the physical encounter of the surface swell, we find a somewhere in which 'time seems to stop, a place to which we can return, a place whose wholeness and integrity confirms our own' (Tuan, 2004, pp. 45, 47–8).

References

Abbey, E., 1992. *Desert Solitaire: A Season in the Wilderness*. London: Robin Clark.

Abse, D., 2009. At Ogmore-by-Sea this August evening. In: O. Sheers, ed., *A Poet's Guide to Britain*. London: Penguin, p. 290.

Anderson, J., 2009. Transient convergence and relational sensibility: Beyond the modern constitution of nature. *Emotion, Space, & Society*, 2, pp. 120–27.

———— 2012. Relational places: The surfed wave as assemblage and convergence. *Environment and Planning D: Society and Space*, 30, pp. 570–87.

———— 2013a. Cathedrals of the surf zone: Regulating access to a space of spirituality. *Social and Cultural Geographies*, 14(8), pp. 954–72.

———— 2013b. Roll. Available at: http://youtu.be/rYSNxl1_L1Y [accessed June 2013].

———— 2013c. Paddle out stills. Available at: http://youtu.be/MaJpPSwNNF0 [accessed June 2013].

———— 2013d. Paddle out rhossil. Available at: http://youtu.be/YLZTPK4XBTg [accessed June 2013].

———— 2013e. Kayak wave. Available at: http://youtu.be/JiMSVpW0Aks [accessed June 2013].

———— 2014a. What I talk about when I talk about kayaking. In: J. Anderson and K. Peters, eds, *Water Worlds: Human Geographies of the Ocean*. Farnham: Ashgate, pp. 103–18.

———— 2014b. Exploring the space between words and meaning: Knowing the relational sensibility of surf spaces. *Emotion, Space & Society*, 10, pp. 27–34.

———— forthcoming. Surfing between the local and the global: Identifying spatial divisions in surfing practice. *Transactions of the Institute of British Geographers*, doi: 10.1111/tran.12018.

Bakhtin, M., 1994. The dialogic imagination: Four essays. In: P. Morris, ed., *The Bakhtin Reader: Selected Writings of Bakhtin, Medvedev, Voloshino*. London: Arnold, pp. 74–80.

Barilotti, S., 2002. Lost horizons: Surf colonialism in the 21st century. *Surfers Journal*, 11, pp. 88–95.

Barthes, R., 1973. *Mythologies*. London: Paladin.

Bodysurf, n.d. Bodysurf net home page. Available at: http://bodysurf.net/ [accessed May 2013].

Booth, D., 2001. *Australian Beach Cultures: The History of Sun, Sand, and Surf*. London: Frank Cass.

Capp, F., 2004. *That Oceanic Feeling*. London: Aurum.

Centralcoasttoday, 2008. Wave skiing. Available at: http://www.youtube.com/watch?v=VClP4BclJic [accessed May 2013].

CoastlineTobi, 2013. Full length video of Garrett McNamara giant wave Nazaré – 28.01.2013. Available at: http://www.youtube.com/watch?v=iC76The-FMU [accessed May 2013].

Csikszentmihalyi, M., 1990. *Flow: The Psychology of Optimal Experience*. New York: Harper and Row.

dawnrboucher, 2011. Big wave tow in surfing at Jaws Maui January 20 2011. Available at: http://www.youtube.com/watch?v=EulFrt1rpPA [accessed May 2013].

Duane, D., 1996. *Caught Inside: A Surfer's Year on the Californian Coast*. New York: North Point Press.

Edensor, T., 2010. Walking in rhythms: Place, regulation, style and the flow of experience. *Visual Studies*, 25(1), pp. 69–79.

Emerson, R.W., 1994. *Self Reliance and Other Essays*. New York: Dover Publications.

Finisterre, 2012. Coldwater surfing. *Surfers Path*, Sep/Oct, p. 4.

Fordham, M., 2008. *The Book of Surfing: The Killer Guide*. London: Bantam Press.

Fordham, M., Carlson, A., Monzani, C., Brazier, L., Vega Borrego, S., Tait, M. and Pietrasik, A., 2013. California road trip: Surfing the perfect wave – video. Available at: http://www.guardian.co.uk/travel/video/2013/jun/06/california-road-trip-surfing-culture-video [accessed June 2013].

GoProCamera, 2010. GoPro HD HERO camera: Teahupoo barrels with Kailani Jabour. Available at: http://www.youtube.com/watch?v=4T2AG5fIfsc [accessed May 2013].

Gosch, J., 2008. *Bustin' Down the Door*. New York: Screen Media Films.

Howdynews, 2009. Caught inside. Available at: http://www.youtube.com/watch?v=nAlAI6UOHoo [accessed May 2013].

Jones, M., 2009. Phase space: Geography, relational thinking, and beyond. *Progress in Human Geography*, 33(4), pp. 1–20.

Kampion, D., 2004. *The Lost Coats: Stories from the Surf*. Salt Lake City: Gibbs Smith Publisher.

Lewis, N., 2000. The climbing body, nature and the experience of modernity. *Body & Society*, 6, pp. 58–80.

London, J., 2004. A royal sport – except from The Cruise of the Snark. In: M. Warshaw, ed., *Zero Break: An Illustrated Collection of Surf Writing*. Orlando: Harcourt, pp. 1777–2004.

Maffesoli, M., 1996. *The Time of the Tribes*. London: Sage.

Mattos, B., 2004. *Kayak Surfing*. Bangor: Pesda Press.

McCabe, S., 2004. *Littoral Documents*. Charlottetown, Prince Edward Island: Confederation Centre Art Gallery.

Minhinnick, R. 1999. *Selected Poems*. Manchester: Carcanet.

Montero, A., 2009. Surf rage. Available at: http://www.youtube.com/watch?v= CcyFwnftALQ [accessed July 2013].

Pollett, N., 2013. Uber slo mo Hawaii. Available at: http://www.carvemag. com/2013/03/uber-slo-mo-hawaii/#.Ubc7JufFV5Z [accessed May 2013].

Price, P., 2013. Place. In: N.C. Johnson, R.H. Schein and J. Winders, eds, *The Wiley-Blackwell Companion to Cultural Geography*. Oxford: Wiley Blackwell, pp. 118–29.

Sanford, A.W., 2007. Pinned on Karma Rock: Whitewater kayaking as religious experience. *Journal of the American Academy of Religion*, 75(4), pp. 875–95.

Sheers, O., 2009. *A Poet's Guide to Britain*. London: Penguin.

Sheller, M. and Urry, J., 2006. The new mobilities paradigm. *Environment and Planning A*, 38, pp. 207–26.

Taylor, B., 2007a. Focus introduction. Aquatic nature religion. *Journal of the American Academy of Religion*, 75(4), pp. 863–74.

――― 2007b. Surfing into spirituality and a new, aquatic nature religion. *Journal of the American Academy of Religion*, 75(4), pp. 923–51.

――― 2007c. The new aquatic nature religion. *Drift*, 1(03), pp. 14–23.

――― 2008. Sea spirituality, surfing, and aquatic nature religion. In: S. Shaw and A. Francis, eds, *Deep Blue: Critical Reflections on Nature, Religion and Water*. London: Equinox, pp. 213–33.

Taylor, K., 2005. *Returned to Water: Surf Stories and Adventures*. San Diego: Dimdim Publishing.

ThreeSixty, n.d. ThreeSixty home page. Available at: http://www.threesixtymag. co.uk/ [accessed May 2013].

Tuan, Y. F., 2004. Sense of place: Its relationship to self and time. In: T. Mels, ed., *Reanimating Places*. Farnham, UK and Burlington, VT: Ashgate, pp. 45–56.

Wade, A., 2007. *Surf Nation: In Search of the Fast Left and Hollow Rights of Britain and Ireland*. London: Simon & Schuster.

Warshaw, M. ed., 2004. *Zero Break: An Illustrated Collection of Surf Writing 1777–2004*. Orlando: Harcourt.

Whitman, W., 1855. *Leaves of Grass*. Nashville: American Renaissance.

Wilson, B., 2008. *Dances with Waves*. Ullapool: Two Ravens Press.

Winton, T., 2008. *Breath*. London: Picador.

Chapter 5

Sailing across the Cook Strait

Robyn Zink

The Cook Strait separates the North and South Islands of New Zealand, and connects the Tasman Sea to the Pacific Ocean. Boats have traversed the Strait since Māori arrived in New Zealand, as the Cook Strait links the two main islands and is a rich food source. British explorer Captain James Cook first sailed through the Strait, which now bears his name, in 1770. It is characterised by a deep, steep-sided canyon that runs north/south through the Strait, which is 14 nautical miles wide at its narrowest point. Both wind and water are squeezed through the Strait by the land masses of the North and South Island.

In the mid-1990s I was living in the Marlborough Sounds, which is sheltered from the Cook Strait by Arapawa Island and the mainland of the South Island. The Sounds is a boating paradise and I had Valarie May, a 32-foot Herreshoff yacht built of kauri. She had beautiful lines and creaked and groaned in the way wooden boats do. The sound of a wooden boat moving through the water is a soft 'thuck', a sound of settling in where wood and water are working together.

Tory Channel bisects Arapawa Island and the mainland and provides the shortest route between the Marlborough Sounds and Wellington, New Zealand's capital city at the bottom of the North Island. We were on our way to Wellington; we being Valarie May, myself and my partner. I cannot remember if there was any specific reason for going to Wellington. Maybe we just wanted to get a fill of the city, hang out in some cafés, go to movies and bookshops, and be surrounded by the buzz of people and buildings.

According to Wikipedia, the Cook Strait is considered one of the most dangerous and unpredictable waters in the world (http://en.wikipedia.org/wiki/Cook_Strait). I do not know if this is the case but, because of the topography of the Strait and the fact that it connects two major bodies of water, the tidal currents are strong and there are overflows and rips. And the wind can howl through the Cook Strait. The combination of wind and tidal flows can make for challenging and dangerous sea conditions. Peat (2010, p. 59) describes the Cook Strait as 'a natural dynamo, a place where tides, currents, vortices and winds interact in a hurly-burly of natural forces'. But we had good weather and tidal information and we were not sailing to a timetable so there was no need to put ourselves in a situation where we were going to meet that hurly-burly.

The weather was looking perfect – a 15-knot north-westerly was predicted and the tide was good to be leaving the entrance to Tory Channel at midnight.

Tory Channel is nine nautical miles long. It is a narrow waterway with numerous deep bays on either side. The water is crystal clear and the strong currents in the channel showcase the long and elegant tendrils of bull kelp at each of the rocky points to perfection. Just before the entrance, Tory Channel does a sharp right turn and it feels as if you are sailing into a deep bay and then, at the last minute, you catch a glimpse of the Cook Strait. A line of rocks extend off the southern entrance toward the middle of the channel. At night all you can see is the white phosphorescence of the waves crashing over the rocks and you can hear the thunder of the water. It really does feel as if there is nowhere to go. Then the leading lights come into view and, once those are lined up, the passage into the Cook Strait is clear. As Valarie May noses out into the Cook Strait, she picks up the swell and starts to settle into the rhythm of the wind and the sea.

On this night we have a full moon. It is a perfect wind for Valarie May, a 15-knot broad reach and a gentle, long rolling swell that allows her to relax into her stride. The sails are full and shining in the moonlight and the boat is slipping through the water leaving behind a beautiful trail of phosphorescence. All is quiet except for the wind in the rigging and the boat moving through the water. The occasional ghost of a seagull glides by as the wind and tide take us toward the North Island. Everything is working perfectly – everything 'feels right'.

'Feeling Right'

I have had numerous experiences like this on the sea, where everything feels right and it is one of the things that bring me back to boats and to the sea. There are many things that draw me to boats and the sea, and most of these I can explain quite easily. They include the challenge of working with a boat, the sea and the weather to set a course and reach a destination, the sense of space and beauty of the water, the birds and the sky, the sense of mastery that comes with learning how to use tools and understanding the fundamentals of a diesel engine. However, there is something about the 'feels right' moments that is central to pulling me back to the sea, which is more difficult to explain. It is something more than an ephemeral moment of pleasure, though it is that as well. Something about this feeling is important to understanding myself as a human being. In this chapter I set out to explore this feeling, why and how it is important.

Narratives of Freedom and Escape

Narratives of freedom and escape are common in outdoor adventure literature. People go into the wilderness to discover their true selves, to be free of the oppressive strictures that society puts on them or to get closer to a more 'natural' human nature. The mountains or, in this case, the sea, speak for themselves and speak to us in a way that is untainted by human beings or social convention. Or so the story goes (for example, see Cronon, 1996; Lynch and Moore, 2004). I must have read enough feminist theory in my teens to have some inkling that things were not as simple as the sea speaking for itself. Certainly the mountains and the sea seemed to say very similar things to the things I was hearing in other parts of my life, particularly when it came to gender.

The true self that is being sought by going into the wildness is premised on a

> rational cognitive subject [which] is a deep-seated presupposition of many stands of philosophy. In this picture, the subject gathers sensory information in order to learn about the features of the world; processes that information into representations of those features; calculates the best course of action in the world given the relation of those represented features of the world and the desires it has (whether the subject is thought to be able to change those desires through rational deliberation or not); and then commands its body and related instruments to best realize those desires given the features of the world it has represented to itself. (Protevi, 2009, p. 3)

Within this vision of how a subject functions, the relationship between the subject and the world it inhabits is one of separation, rather than one of interdependence. This is exemplified by the risk narratives that are used to explain motivations and desire for going into the outdoors, as the rational cognitive subject gathers information and then commands their body to realise their objectives or desires (Boyes and O'Hare, 2011).

More recently there has been a phenomenological turn in outdoor writing in recognition that outdoor experiences are more than fodder for rational, cognitive processes. Wattchow and Brown (2011, p. 72) make the point that 'the sensing body is a pathway to embodied knowing that is currently under-utilised in outdoor education practice'. Amongst others they draw on the work of Merleau-Ponty who 'asserted that we should consider the world of experience prior to our worlds of abstract meanings' (Wattchow and Brown, 2011, p. 73). Perhaps I lack imagination but it has never been clear to me how to put the world of experience before that of abstract meaning-making. Focusing on sensation, on how something feels, is one thing. I can dive into the ocean, lie on my back and revel in the sensation of being held and caressed by the water. But I am not a blank slate. I come into that experience with a whole bundle of abstract meaning-making, including the complex relationship that I have with this body I call mine. Maybe that is why I cannot hear what the sea has to say when it speaks for itself.

Merleau-Ponty's work does take experience seriously, locating it midway between the mind and body but, as Foucault found, phenomenology is problematic because of the way it brings a particular reflexive gaze to bear upon experience, in order to grasp the meaning of experience. Foucault stated that 'phenomenology attempts to recapture the meaning of everyday experience in order to rediscover the sense in which the subject that I am is indeed responsible, in its transcendental functions, for founding that experience together with its meanings' (Foucault, 2002,

p. 241). As he states so clearly here, even though phenomenology takes experience seriously, the subject who has experiences is no different from the rational, cognitive subject of so many strands of Western philosophy. Phenomenology might give me licence to describe the bodily sensations that I experience when it feels right, but this licence comes with the requirement to then grasp meaning and represent that meaning in quite specific ways, reinstating 'I' as the progenitor of that experience. Claiming responsibility for creating moments that 'feel right' finds a comfortable home in narratives of freedom and escape that so powerfully inform outdoor experiences, however I felt there was more to moments where everything feels right than I was able to express through this particular story.

Finding Foucault

It was not until I came across Foucault's work that I gained some conceptual tools and language that enabled me to begin to unpick the narratives of freedom and escape and understand some of the normalising practices at work that give those narratives their power. My work has thus far focused on understanding practice 'with the aim of grasping the conditions that make these acceptable at a given moment ...' (Foucault, 2002, p. 225). But I am not interested in grasping the conditions that make sailing across the Cook Strait acceptable as something to do. Rather I follow Blencowe (2012) in a project of positive critique. Positive critique sets out to describe how knowledge, discourse, institutions and practices become intelligible and the work this does in forming social practices 'rather than denouncing them on the grounds of their destructiveness, irrationality or fallacy' (Blencowe, 2012, p. 7). At the risk of sounding like I am dropping into a theory of flow, an experience that is engrossing and intrinsically rewarding (Csikszentmihalyi and Csikszentmihalyi, 1999), those moments where it feels right seem to me to be about connection. I turn to positive critique because it is about the 'production of things, pleasures, affects and capacities' (Blencowe, 2012, p. 6).

Foucault and Experience

Foucault's work complicates the relationship between experience, knowledge and the subject. While he describes the body of his work in a range of ways throughout his career, one description of his overall project was to uncover how human beings have come to understand themselves across time (Foucault, 2000). This is useful here. He argues that with modernity came the obligation to seek the 'truth' about oneself (Foucault, 1997). The desire to remove oneself to a wilderness that is construed as free of social and cultural influences begins to make some sense because one can then seek a truth about oneself through experience that is apparently untainted by the social, cultural or the historical. The subject turns to itself. Foucault (2005) states that this turn to the self, the view that it is possible to know the truth about oneself, is one of the most powerful technologies of the self the West has known.

Foucault had a very different quest in his own work. He did not want to find the truth about himself. Rather he wanted to become something other than himself. His was a project of de-centring the subject. He was calling 'into question the category of the subject, its supremacy, its foundational function' (Foucault, 2002, p. 247). Rather than seeking experiences, he was interested in limit-experience, that which 'wrenches the subject from itself' (p. 241). For Foucault, writing books was a limit-experience, as the aim was a transformation of the relationship with himself and with knowledge. Writing books was a way of constructing himself and of experiencing the world in which we live, so that he would come out of it transformed into someone other than who he had been before the experience (Foucault, 2002).

Thompson (2010) describes limit-experiences as reaching the borders of subjectivity, whereas the phenomenological subject sets out to bring a reflective gaze to bear on an experience to grasp its meaning. The phenomenological subject, indeed the subject of most Western philosophy *has* experience, from which they derive meaning and in effect bring it under control. In this sense I can reflect on the experience I have of the sea and extract meaning from that experience. It may well be partial but the relationship I have with myself has not changed, though my knowledge of the objects of this experience and the meaning it has for me may have shifted. In contrast to a Foucauldian perspective, I do not 'have' an experience; rather the self emerges from experiences and is something that is continually in the making or in process. In other words, the self is not something that can be found if enough reflection is brought to bear on the task and the shackles of social forces can be loosened sufficiently. Had Foucault chosen to go to sea, it would not have been because of the opportunity this might offer to uncover the truth about himself, rather he might have gone because it offered an opportunity to become someone other than he was before he set out on the voyage.

Sailing across the Cook Strait that night, where everything was working, where everything felt right, seems at first glance a long way from a limit-experience where the subject is wrenched from itself. Nonetheless, this experience is not mine in the sense that I am responsible for it, yet I sense it is about the 'production of things, pleasures, affects and capacities' (Blencowie, 2012). To explore this further I turn to the work of Deleuze (1992), and Deleuze and Guattari (1987) because they use philosophy to go beyond what life is to what it might become (Colebrook, 2002).

Deleuze, Desire and Affect

Deleuze also described his work in various ways but one aim was to challenge us to think differently 'in order to avoid the notion that "we" have a fixed identify or being that we then engage with through ideas' (Colebrook, 2002, p. xvi).

Like Foucault's work, Deleuze's work is a practical philosophy in that he is interested in the relationship between practice and theory and how each forms and shapes the other. Deleuze argues the world is in a constant state of flux that does not harbour a foundation or starting-point, but is always in motion: 'our relation to the world is dynamic ... Life itself is constant change and creation' (Colebrook, 2002, p. 51).

As with Foucault, Deleuze was trying to complicate the relationship between the subject, knowledge and power. Foucault saw power as positive and productive. Power produces knowledge, pleasure, subjects (Foucault, 1995). How I understand myself as a sailor is produced through relations of power, rather than being something essential or inherent to myself. Deleuze takes this further with the concept of desire. Desire is a productive and creative energy. Desire does not compensate for a lack or for something that is missing as per psychoanalytical theory. Deleuze would not reduce my sailing endeavours to a form of penis envy. Nor is desire a force located with the individual. Desire is a social force. It does not reside with an individual but circulates to produce what we know about the world and how we interact and connect with that world. Desire operates as flows. 'What something *is* is its flow of desire, and such forces produce diverging and multiple relations' (Colebrook, 2002, p. xv [original emphasis]). Different flows of desire produce different relations. Whereas a self-generated subject is presumed to navigate their way across experiences in a relatively stable and consistent way, Deleuze argues that bodies are produced through certain desiring relations and different sets of relations produces different bodies. Robyn the woman, the sailor, the human, come into being because of the flows of desire and the ways those flows produce diverging and multiple relations. The body in this sense is not a single entity but is always coming into being through relationships. The 'I' who is variously a woman, a sailor, a Kiwi, a human being, is not a single 'I' that transcends all of these positions or identities. These terms are not imposed on my body as there is not a real or true self to be found. The only way I can come to understand myself is in relation to the world in which I live, or in relation to the flows of desire that are circulating.

Deleuze saw our dependence on identity as destructive because it keeps us wedded to a self-generated subject that moves through experiences. In this sense I am essentially the same, the grounding being, irrespective of the relationships into which I enter. I reflect on experience to extract meaning and knowledge. When asked to explain myself, typically this requires me to articulate what sailing means to me, what being on the sea means to me. In effect it requires me to map out an identity. Deleuze was not interested in what things mean, he was interested in what they can do, that is, what relationships, desires and flows are at work and what bodies come into being through relationships with other bodies. I am drawn to this way of thinking about a moment that feels right because of the primacy of relationship and connection over meaning. Deleuze's work offers some conceptual tools and language to explore relationship and connection without reducing it to meaning.

When Deleuze and Guattari (1987) talk about the body they are not referring to a corporeal body that is anterior to experience, or occupying a privileged space in relation to the other elements that compose experience. For Deleuze a body can be anything. 'It can be an animal, a body of sounds, a mind or an idea; it can be a linguistic corpus, a social body, a collectivity' (Deleuze, 1992, p. 629). Bodies are not defined by their form, function, organs, substance nor by a subject (p. 269). The question for Deleuze and Guattari is always what can a body do? not what it is. Rather than give a physical description of my body or details of who I am, the focus shifts to what this body can do and what it can do in relation to the other bodies it connects with. Sailing across the Cook Strait is not about me, or my corporeal body and my boat. It is about wind/body/boat/sea/movement as an assemblage coming into being in relationship with each other.

A 15-knot nor'wester and a tidal flow rushing toward Wellington smooth the sea, Valarie May slides through the water, picked up by the tide and sails filled with a steady breeze, free hand in my pocket to keep warm, water pushing against the rudder, connecting to the tiller, extending the tiller to the hand and arm. Bodies are not bound up as single entities but they come into being through relationships with other bodies and through assemblages (Deleuze and Guattari, 1987).

An assemblage 'groups together an infinity of particles entering into an infinity of more or less interconnected relationships' (Deleuze and Guattari, 1987, p. 254). Deleuze and Guattari do not distinguish between the animate and the inanimate, or the artificial and the natural. I, or my body, do not take primacy over Valarie May, nor am I of a different character, because I am animate and she is inanimate, just as the sea and Valarie May are not differentiated by the artificial/ natural divide. It is the relationship between the elements that is important, not the elements themselves. Through assemblages, Deleuze and Guattari are trying to deal with the messiness and multiplicity of reality and the fact that reality is constantly changing. Assemblage draws attention to relating rather than knowing. Some aspects of assemblages are not dissimilar from flow (Csikszentmihalyi and Csikszentmihalyi, 1999). For example, where there is a heightened awareness that merges with action and a loss of ego, as these are also about relating to the world. Where the two concepts dramatically diverge is that in flow, people are described as having a sense of control and that the experience is goal-orientated. Although flow allows for a loss of ego and 'produces a person enriched by new achievements and stronger confidence' (Csikszentmihalyi and Csikszentmihalyi, 1999, p. 155), the subject of flow remains the self-generated subjects who command their bodies to realise their desires. Assemblages do not have a goal orientation, they are a means to imagine more flexible boundaries; a move to relating rather than knowing.

Deleuze and Guattari (1987) turn to Spinoza to map the relationships in assemblages through the cartography of longitude and latitude. This is a cartography familiar to sailors but the way they use this cartography tells a very different story from the story a chart tells a sailor. Longitude maps the 'particle aggregates belonging to that body in a given relation' (p. 256). At a given moment, the assemblage of sea/body/boat/movement is amongst the particle aggregates that are in relation to that body. The focus shifts from identifying the parts of the experience, or the subject and the object, to exploring what comes into being through relationships of speed and slowness. Longitude maps the 'extensive parts falling under a relation' (p. 257). This maps the capacity of a body to act, given the relationships that form that body. Some of the relationships at work forming this body include the sailor, who is captain of the ship, making decisions based on the information at hand to sail Valarie May toward Wellington; a middle-class woman who can afford a boat and the leisure time required to pursue adventure activities; a woman who navigates the gender politics of outdoor adventure and more specifically of the boating environment, which is a masculine space in New Zealand; and a rational cognitive subject who gathers information and makes decisions. Deleuze and Guattari are not suggesting these forms do not exist. By mapping longitude they are mapping what is actual, but this actuality emerges from the flows of desire rather than originating from the subject itself. They are trying to get behind the object to the relationships that form the object and in this they are mapping the capacity of a body to act.

The latitude in this cartography corresponds to the degree of power or the ability of a body to affect other bodies or be affected by other bodies. Affect is the modulation[1] that occurs when bodies collide or come into contact. Affect is distinct from feelings. Hickey-Moody (2013) describes affects as being 'in between feelings and changes to what you can do ...' (p. 79). It refers to changes in bodily capacity and describes a body's capacity to form relations with other bodies or elements and the nature of those relationships. 'The intensive [affect] is first encountered as the actual knocked off its tracks' (Portevi, 2009, p. 11). It is where something shifts between the actual and the environment, and the resultant shift in flows of desire moves 'toward thresholds where their [extensive relations] behaviour might change' (p. 11). This is what Deleuze (1992) refers to as deterritorialisation or becoming.

If I were to talk to another sailor about this trip across the Cook Strait, I might describe how I calculated tide and ascertained weather, how I charted a course, determined the sail combination, and these actions resulted in a perfect broad reach across the Strait. The wind, the water, the boat become a backdrop to my desires and commands. I am (re)instated as a deciding subject against a nature that merely is. However, taking the lead from Deleuze and Guattari, I might describe this moment through affects and what a body can do as follows: the wind filling the sails, ruffling the water and the fringes of my hood, the moonlight reflecting on the water and sails, the water pushing against the rudder onto the tiller and hand as we move through the water, being cocooned by wet weather gear, gumboots on feet, hood over head, sitting with feet braced against the lee side of the cockpit, rocking with the movement of the boat, marked by a trail of phosphoresce.

---

1 I follow Hickey-Moody (2013) in the use of modulation, rather than change or variation as used by Deleuze and Guattari, to avoid the sense that change or variation are somehow pre-mediated or pre-determined or are part of working to an end or larger goal.

The elements come into a different relationship with each other when describing what this body or assemblage can do. I am an element in the assemblage and what I do is in relation to the other elements, rather than being separate from those elements. Thinking through affect opens the possibility for loosening the borders of identity where behaviour might change, or for becoming.

Deleuze and Politics

Deleuze argues that asking what something can do is a more productive way of engaging with the world than pursing meaning and representation because it loosens the borders of identity. Representation, on the other hand, limits thought as rules and dogma are imposed on thought (Colebrook, 2002). It becomes a question of how individuals enter into composition with each other, that is, how they connect and their capacity to affect and be affected (Deleuze, 1992). Whereas the narratives of freedom and escape have me going to sea so I can come to a deeper and clearer understanding of myself, freeing myself from the shackles of social constraint, Deleuze is more interested in the connections that are made, the bodies that emerge through those connections and the ability of those bodies to enter into composition with other bodies. Rather than being set free from social constraint, affect enmeshes bodies in the social world.

Any claims of being responsible for creating moments that 'feel right' that I might make are enmeshed in the social world I inhabit because it is this social world that gives those claims their points of connection. In part, claiming responsibility for moments that 'feel right' is given legitimacy through narratives of freedom and escape and through technologies of the self that require me to know the 'truth' about myself. In this sense 'affect is inherently political: bodies are part of an ecosocial matrix of other bodies, affecting them and being affected by them' (Protvei, 2009, p. 50). Deleuze (1992, p. 628) argues that 'a thing is never separable from its relations with the world'. A body must be ordered to some extent to be able to make connections with other bodies and it is a body's relations with the world that order that body. My body is ordered by the ecosocial matrix that includes being human, gender, race, class, physical ability to name but a few elements of the matrix. It is this ordering that allows me to make the connections that I make with other bodies and other bodies to connect with me. Unlike structuralists, who begin with a subject who orders and categorises the world from which difference is established, Deleuze starts with difference. Order is produced out of difference. However, Deleuze (1992) argued that entering into composition with other bodies is not about taking control of other bodies, or being taken control of by other bodies. I do not get captured by the social or cultural. Rather, entering into composition with others is about sociabilities and communities. Subjects 'develop by being patterned by the society in which they are found' (Protevi, 2009, p. 96). The sociabilities and communities in which I am located are the means by which I enter into composition with other bodies. It is the means by which I come to understand not only myself but others. Or as Protevi puts it, 'we are what we can do with others', including inorganic, organic and virtual others.

Many people have traversed the Cook Strait before I did, and while we share commonalities such as experiencing the movement of the wind, the water and the boat, the connections we make with these are not necessarily the same. A sailor on the Endeavour with Captain James Cook would have been unlikely to be infused with the romantic notions of the ocean that I have been. They were, after all, sailing into the unknown, an ocean inhabited by monsters, in search of Terra Australis Incognita. Whereas I was sailing across the Cook Strait that, while being described as 'a natural dynamo, a place where tides, currents, vortices and winds interact in a hurly-burly of natural forces' (Peat, 2010, p. 59), has also been charted and ordered through weather and tide forecasts. What a sailor can do with others today is very different from what a sailor could do with others in Cook's time.

Affect is political because an encounter can enhance or decrease a body's power to act and form further connections. Deleuze and Guattari are seeking ways for bodies to retain the ability to experiment and be creative in their ability to connect to other bodies. That is, the 'ability to make connections that are not reproductive' (Protevi, 2009, p. 110). Deleuze and Guattari posit that meaning and identity limit the experimental creativity of the organism. The hunt for meaning shifts the focus onto objects instead of relationships or flows of desire and identity seeks to anchor my responsibility for an encounter, rather than 'participating in an encounter that surpasses our ability to identify our contribution to it' (Protevi, 2009, p. 103). Deleuze and Guattari acknowledge that bodies still have to make choices but 'now it is a question of knowing whether relations (and which ones?) can compound directly to form a new, more "extensive" relation, or whether capacities can compound directly to constitute a more "intensive" capacity or power' (Delueze, 1992, p. 628).

As we left the Tory Channel to head into the Cook Strait my partner went below to go to sleep, quipping I was a much better sailor so there was no point in his being there. This encounter increased my capacity to act, or to form compositions with other bodies, as he left me to get on with it. By staying on deck because he was worried, I might not have been strong enough to deal with eventualities or trust my ability to handle Valarie May. We would have entered into an encounter that reproduced those gender relations that instate boating as a masculine space, diminishing my ability to act or to enter into composition with other bodies.

Delueze argues that the question is 'how individuals enter into composition with one another in order to form a higher individual … How can a being take another being into its world, while preserving or respecting the other's own relations and world?' (Deleuze, 1992, p. 628). As Deleuze says, many things change when you define bodies and thoughts as capacities for affecting and being affected. The wind, the sea and Valarie May are no longer backdrops for my actions. Counting affects tells us of the relationships between elements, and it these relations, the capacity to affect and be affected 'that defines a body in its individuality' (p. 625). By this Deleuze is not referring to some sort of end state but rather the way in which bodies, or assemblages, come into composition with each other. The wind, the moon, the tide, the boat, the sailor enter into composition with each other, and the modulations that occur when these bodies come into contact define the individuality of that body in composition at that moment.

'Feels Right'

Deleuze and Guattari's work provides a way to think about that moment where everything feels right that does not reduce it to the sum of its parts, nor does it (re)instate me as a self-generated, responsible subject who 'has' an experience. I am not required to grasp meaning or to represent that meaning. Claiming responsibility for when things feel right is seductive because it demonstrates my mastery of the situation: the boat, the sea, the wind and, of course, myself. Affect offers two things as I think with that moment where sailing across the Cook Strait feels right. First it challenges the narrative of freedom that so powerfully informs our understanding of outdoor adventure today. Freedom is not seen as the result of the isolated decision of self-present agents who can rise above or beyond social conditioning. Deleuze argues freedom is 'the power to affirm all those powers beyond ourselves which only an expanded perception can approach' (Colebrook, 2002, p. xl). Affect as a modulation works to loosen the borders of identity and expand perception. That moment when everything feels right is a point that enhances the capacity of a body, of 'this' body, to act, and its capacity to form assemblages with other bodies and to become something other.

Second, affect provides a different way of relating to the world and of conceptualising those relationships with the world, particularly in relation to what is commonly termed as the non-human or more-than-human world. Deleuze 'does not accept the distinction between a human life that is free and responsible for its own becoming, and a nature which is merely "in-itself" and determined' (Colebrook, 2002, p. xlii). Many things change when bodies are defined through their affective capacities. All of the elements of an assemblage are on the same plane. The wind, the sea and Valarie May are not backdrops to my sailing abilities. Nor does affective capacity lend itself to anthropomorphising the wind, the sea and Valarie May. Deleuze argues that nature is no less a response to the forces that confront and cross it than humans are; in effect its forces 'decide' us all, including the organic, the inorganic and the virtual. The question is how bodies enter into composition with one another and if this composition augments or diminishes the capacities of the bodies to connect with other bodies.

Moments when things feel right draw me back to the sea. The sea is a place where that feeling occurs in a way it does not anywhere else. Maybe what draws me back is that the assemblages that form at sea work to loosen the borders of identity and expand both perception and the capacity to enter into relationships with other bodies in new and interesting ways. I go to sea to because it affords opportunities to be in relationships that 'feel right'.

References

Blencowe, C., 2012. *Biopolitical Experience: Foucault, Power and Positive Critique*. Hampshire: Palgrave Macmillan.

Boyes, M. and O'Hare, D., 2011. Examining naturalistic decision making in outdoor adventure contexts by computer simulation. *The Australian Journal of Outdoor Education*, 15(1), pp. 24–36.

Colebrook, C., 2002. *Understanding Deleuze*. Crows Nest, NSW: Allen & Unwin.

Cronon, W., 1996. The trouble with wilderness: Or, going back to the wrong nature. *Environmental History*, 1(1), pp. 7–28.

Csikszentmihalyi, M. and Csikszentmihalyi, I., 1999. Adventure and the flow experience. In: J.C. Miles and S. Priest, eds, *Adventure Programming*. State College, Pennsylvania: Venture Publishing. pp. 153–8.

Deleuze, G., 1992. Ethology: Spinoza and us. In: J. Crary and S. Kwinter, eds, *Incorporations: Zone 6*. New York: Zone, pp. 625–33.

Deleuze, G. and Guattari, F., 1987. *A Thousand Plateaus: Capitalism and Schizophrenia*. Translated from French by B. Massumi. Minneapolis: University of Minnesota Press.

Foucault, M., 1995. Truth and power. In: D. Tallack, ed., *Critical Theory: A Reader*. London: Harvester Wheatsheaf, pp. 66–77.

——— 1997. Subjectivity and truth. In: S. Lortinger, ed., *The Politics of Truth*. New York: Semiotext(e), pp. 171–98.

——— 2000. Technologies of the self. Translated from French by R. Hurley. In: P. Rabinow, ed., *Essential Works of Foucault 1954–1984: Ethics, Subjectivity and Truth (Vol. 1)*. London: Penguin Books, pp. 223–51.

——— 2002. Questions of method. In: J.D. Faubion, ed., *Essential Works of Foucault: Power (Vol. 3)*. London: Penguin books, pp. 223–38.

——— 2002. Interview with Michel Foucault. In: J.D. Faubion, ed., *Essential Works of Foucault: Power (Vol. 3)*. London: Penguin books, pp. 239–97.

——— 2005. The hermeneutics of the subject. Lectures at the College De France 1981–1982. Translated by G. Burchell. New York: Picador.

Hickey-Moody, A., 2013. Affect as method: Feelings, aesthetics and affective pedagogy. In: R. Coleman and J. Ringrose, eds, *Deleuze and Research Methodologies*. Edinburgh: Edinburgh University Press, pp. 79–95.

Lynch, P. and Moore, K., 2004. Adventures in paradox. *Australian Journal of Outdoor Education*, 8(2), pp. 3–12.

Peat, N., 2010. *The Tasman: Biography of an Ocean*. North Shore, NZ: Penguin Books.

Protevi, J., 2009. *Political Affect: Connecting the Social and the Somatic*. Minneapolis: University of Minnesota Press.

Thompson, C., 2010. Education and/or displacement? A pedagogical inquiry into Foucault's 'limit-experience'. *Educational Philosophy and Theory*, 42(3), pp. 361–77.

Wattchow, B. and Brown, M., 2011. *A Pedagogy of Place: Outdoor Education for a Changing World*. Monash University: Monash University Publishing.

Chapter 6
Being a Brown Bodyboarder

Mihi Nemani

I walk backwards into the water at Piha beach, board under arm and shiver a little from the slight chill in the water. The water from the rip pulls against my legs so I turn and launch myself belly first onto the board and allow the rapidly moving water in the rip pull me out to sea. As I near the pack I get a few curious and concerned looks from some surfers and nervously note that no other females or bodyboarders are in the water. As usual, the majority are white surfers; I see a couple of brown short-board surfers and assume one is Māori from his tamoko (Māori tattoo). For a moment, I feel a bit self-conscious, but then remind myself that I've surfed all around the world so don't need to feel intimidated by this pack of surfers. I ignore their stares by keeping my head down, and take up a respectable position behind the leaders in the pack. And then, we wait.

Looking out to the horizon, I see a swell moving towards us. I start kicking slowly in the direction of the rolling mounds. Other surfers also start paddling towards the swell. The first wave gets closer and three surfers ahead of me who are in position to catch the wave turn and paddle. The surfer closest to the whitewash gets right of way, stands up and zooms past as I duck dive under the wave to move out of his way. The next wave arrives and again three surfers turn and paddle. The surfer closest to the whitewash gets the wave. Suddenly, the surfer who had the wave falls off his board while attempting a manoeuvre, and I find myself in the perfect position to catch the remainder of his wave. I quickly turn and paddle with all my strength to get up to speed. The surge of the wave lifts me up and, with one final power kick, I launch myself onto the face of the wave and feel the momentum and power of the wave propel me forward. I quickly glance to the right and, seeing I have right of way, point the nose of my board towards the middle of the steep mountain of water ahead of me. I yell 'Yup' to call off a couple of surfers who were also paddling for the wave. This wave is mine.

I see a vertical section ahead of me that looks like it's going to start pitching powerfully. Instinctively, I angle the nose of my board down and accelerate to the bottom of the wave. My stomach gets butterflies from the sudden drop, and with anticipation and excitement I scoop upwards from the bottom and head up the steep face straight towards the breaking section. As I hit the surging water, I push off and extend my arms towards the shore, simultaneously rotating and look over my left shoulder. The force of the water pitching, coupled with the momentum and speed of my bottom turn, throws my entire body out of the water and, as time slows, I'm launched high up into the air. I hear someone yell 'Woooo hooooo' as I complete a full loop and land heavily on my board back onto the face of the wave. Ahead of me a line of surfers are paddling to get out of my way; I note some are smiling, another has his arms up in the air cheering for my manoeuvre.

With a huge grin on my face I pull off the wave and begin the triumphant paddle back to the line-up. As I pull at the water with my hands, I make sure I keep my head down slightly. I arrive back at the pack and begin to renegotiate my place in the line-up. 'Nice wave', says one surfer. 'What was that move?' asks another, I get a head nod and eyebrow raise from others. 'Uh, it's called a roll', I reply and casually take my spot in the line up again. I no longer feel conscious of my brown, female body lying on this body-board. With our eyes toward the horizon, we wait together.

This experience was one of many that led me to question the sport of wave riding and the meanings it holds for me. During my many years sitting in the waves watching and observing others surfing, along with my post-surf reflections, I began to wonder: How do others read my brown surfing body? How do I negotiate space within this space dominated by white, male stand-up surfers? While I am able to access waves and negotiate space amongst my wave-riding peers, why am I so often the only female bodyboarder, and almost always the only brown female bodyboarder? It was only through engaging with the sociological literature on lifestyle sport, gender, culture and ethnicity during my postgraduate studies, that I started to develop an awareness of the minority position that others associated with my outward appearance.

To begin this reflexive account of my experiences in the surf it is important to understand the perspective from which this chapter is written. Hence, my history with the surf will be outlined along with insights relating to Māori and Samoan ways of being. I have found Bourdieu's theoretical concepts of habitus, field and capital useful to understand and analyse operations of power in the surf field relating to gender and ethnicity, so have used them to unveil how I negotiate space from what could be deemed a triple minority position: being brown in a white environment, being female in a male-dominated sport, and being a bodyboarder in an environment that is subjugated by stand-up short-board surfers. In this chapter, I will show that my engagement with and in the sea has shaped who I am in ways that traverse identities that 'are marginalized and stigmatized by the larger culture' (Denzin, 2002, p. 486).

A Life of Surfing

I was drawn to the water from an early age where summers were spent in Punuruku and Oakura with my father's family from the Nga ti Wai Hapu (a New Zealand Māori tribe from the far north) where we would fish, dive and swim. An older cousin introduced me to wave riding as he lived fewer than 500 metres from the beach and had an array of bodyboards, knee-boards and surfboards. My love of riding waves became an addiction and my years completing undergraduate studies on the island of Oahu in Hawaii were shaped around surf conditions and numerous surf trips to the outer islands. While I dabbled in stand-up short-board and long-board surfing, the humble bodyboard became my choice of wave-riding instrument due to the type of waves that could be ridden, variety of manoeuvres that could be performed, and culture associated with those who bodyboard.

As my wave-riding skills improved, I entered the competition arena and won several New Zealand titles, which provided opportunities to compete at World Surfing Games events in California, Ecuador and Portugal. These experiences, combined with encouragement from my husband and family, prompted me to enter the World Women's Bodyboarding Tour where I won three world amateur titles. Competing in the tour involved travelling the world and, as a result, I had the opportunity to surf at world renowned breaks coveted by many surfers including Teahupoo (Tahiti) and Pipeline (Hawaii).

Eager to give back to my sport in New Zealand, I became associated with Surfing New Zealand (SNZ) and Bodyboard Surfing New Zealand (BBSNZ) where I assisted in formalising processes for the competitive side of bodyboarding. During this time I gained surf qualifications including Association of Surfing Professionals (ASP) and International Bodyboarding Association (IBA) judging certifications, and a Level 1 Surf Coaching certificate. I also helped organise and facilitate numerous bodyboarding competitions, managed and coached New Zealand bodyboarding teams at international competitions, and introduced hundreds of individuals to bodyboarding through coaching clinics.

Over the past two decades I have had multifaceted experiences in the sport of bodyboarding that influenced my identity, and in turn affected how I feel about wave riding. Some of the aspects that influenced and affected me related to issues of ethnicity and lifestyle sport culture, such as discrimination from stand-up surfers based on the type of surf craft I had chosen to ride. Over time I became increasingly interested in learning about the cultural dimensions of bodyboarding, for example, power relations on the water and who has access to waves. I felt it was important to find my own voice among those who had previously investigated surf culture, so was motivated to reflect on my experiences rather than being told of the experiences of others. Thus, to help the reader understand my perspective as a Māori Samoan woman I have presented a reflexive account of Māori and Samoan ways in terms of how they shape my worldview.

Māori and Samoan Ways

As an indigenous female researcher I do not occupy one space but rather three simultaneously: the academic, the Samoan, and the Māori. The academic in me wants to ensure that what I write is 'correct' and to make sure that I follow the 'rules of engagement' when writing. However, there are other stronger impulses that compel me to search for deeper meaning, to pull away from what I know as an academic and delve into my lived experiences as a Māori Samoan woman who bodyboards. I feel aligned to the position expressed by Smith (1999): 'People now live in a world which is fragmented with multiple and shifting identities, that the oppressed and the colonized are so deeply implicated in their own oppressions' (p. 97). The perspective from which I have experienced the social world, a combination of Samoan, Māori and European worldviews, has not been extensively investigated in sociology, and so I often feel like I am exploring new ground without a road map. Despite this, there are a few academics who have helped shape my views of who I am and why I am able negotiate space in different social settings.

Some aspects of Kaupapa Māori (a theoretical model used when researching things Māori) have been helpful to inform my understanding of my own experiences of being Māori and experiencing Māori ways (Bishop, 1999; Smith, 2012). One particular statement that resonated with me was provided by Rolleston, who explains:

> Kaupapa Māori can only be truly understood by a person whose wairua, or essence, is Māori. Kaupapa Māori does not require the person to be fluent in Te Reo Māori or an expert in Tikanga Māori although it is fundamentally about Te Reo Māori and Tikanga Māori. It is a knowing, a feeling deep within oneself … It is about whanau, hapu and iwi … It is a profound understanding of *being* Māori. (Rolleston, 2011, p. 6)

I came to understand that my lived experiences as a Māori gave me the right to feel Māori despite not speaking the language and knowing or understanding all the customs associated with Māori culture. Further, my early childhood experiences with my Māori relatives connected me to the ocean, through gathering sea food and enjoying the waves.

Samoan ways of being are also part of my story and, while it would be easy to clump my 'being Samoan' under a Pacific Island umbrella, it is important that readers understand what 'Pacific Islander' means. Pacific Islander is a term that is used to identify people whose ancestry originates from one of the many Pacific Islands (McFall-McCaffery, 2010). As such, each culture, language and customs practiced differ from one group to the next (McFall-McCaffery, 2010). It is important to acknowledge that individuals 'whose knowing is derived from Western origins are unlikely to have values and lived realities that allow understanding of issues pertaining to knowledge and ways of being … [from] …

Samoa, Tonga, Fiji, Tuvalu or the other Pacific nations' (Vaioleti, 2006, p. 22). I do not wish to delve in depth into the diverse nuances of each ethnic culture. However, each culture, which is frequently clumped into the term 'Pacific Islander', is very different and each needs to be identified as such.

In addition to the unique differences within and across Pacific Island cultures, the acknowledgement of Western influences upon urbanised Pacific Island ethnic groups also needs to be taken into consideration as they are part of my story. Samoans born and raised in Samoa have different ways compared to Samoans born and raised in New Zealand. Also, Samoans born and raised in New Zealand have different ways compared to Samoans raised in America. It is, therefore, important to note that 'being' Samoan can hold different meanings depending on where you were raised (Keddell, 2006; Schaaf, 2006). Being a New Zealand-born Samoan means that I can mingle with and gain insider status among Samoan people who were also raised in New Zealand. Although I do not speak Samoan, I practise and embrace Samoan ways. One of the most endearing aspects of being Samoan is the humorous, friendly disposition coupled with loud laughter and lots of food. Samoans are very generous and will sometimes give more than they can afford to, a characteristic I have experienced in my extended Samoan family. Many Samoans are humble and, from experience, are sometimes misjudged and taken for granted due to their quiet nature when among those who do not have Samoan ancestry.

Having multiple worldviews has provided me with a unique perspective in society. Being Samoan Māori enables me to draw upon ways of being and knowing from each ethnicity and, as a result, I am able to gain insider status when amongst Māori or Samoans. I am able to enjoy both cultures and have experienced the similarities and differences between the two. Perhaps one of the greatest benefits I have experienced is that I do not feel obligated to be either Māori or Samoan and so I am not bound by the diverse, but at times restrictive, traditions and ways of being that are inherent in each. While this may seem like a negative statement, it means that I am able to use a mixed approach to my worldview and how I operate in society. As a result, I acknowledge and accept that there are many ways of viewing the world. I also believe that my worldview explains why I am able to engage and adapt in different social environments.

While occupying multiple worldviews holds benefits, there are also disadvantages. Smith (2012) points out that 'For some indigenous students one of the first issues to be confronted is their own identities as indigenous' (p. 137). This statement strongly resonates with me as my own identity was one of the major issues I faced as I was growing up. When I was younger, not knowing nor practising the language and culture of Māori or Samoan made me feel like an outsider with my extended family and people who related strongly to either the Māori or Samoan culture. There are assumptions within Māori and Samoan cultures where if you are Māori, you speak and understand all things Māori, or if you are Samoan you should speak the language and live by the cultural values. In 2012 I attended a Māori research symposium at which Charles Royal (2012) explained that 'Te Reo is important because it is the pathway into the Tangata Whenua World View' (personal conference notes, 2012). This view of the importance of language extends to the Samoan culture. I have had numerous experiences where I have identified myself as Samoan or Māori, and individuals have spoken to me in Te Reo (Māori language) or Samoan. However, when I explain that I do not speak Māori or Samoan there is often a change in their countenance, and I felt they relook at me through pitying eyes. I have often heard my Samoan relatives refer to me as being 'fia palagi' (white) (Keddell, 2006) or 'Maoli' (Māori), thus identifying that I was culturally different from them.

Throughout my life I have had many experiences where cultural differences have influenced the way I am treated. For example, in my career as an educator, I have often been asked to give a karakia (prayer) at meetings where the majority of individuals were New Zealand European. While I personally have no qualms about performing this ritual, the fact that I was asked without prior knowledge of my religious affiliations signals a cultural difference between myself and others who were not approached. In my experience, there is an assumption that 'brown' individuals are religious so know how to pray. Royal (2012) notes that the opportunity exists to form a 'New lens encompassing new solutions and possibilities for our people' (personal conference notes). So, while I present my story through Samoan and Māori worldviews, I acknowledge that my Westernised ways play a large part in how I negotiate my way through society thus inadvertently creating a new lens.

Habitus, Field and Capital

Pierre Bourdieu's theoretical framework of habitus, field and capital has helped me to understand my lived experiences in the surfing field by providing insight into how I am able to negotiate space in a predominantly white, male environment. Houston (2002) explains that 'The interrelationship between habitus, field and capital helps explain how culture affects people, and how they reproduce their taken for granted worlds' (p. 159). Reay (2004) provides additional clarification on how the concepts are related when stating that 'it is through the workings of habitus that practice (agency) is linked with capital and field (structure)' (p. 432). Although these statements of how habitus, capital and field are linked seem confusing at first glance, the following overview will define and clarify how I use them to share my story.

Habitus

Habitus is defined as 'our "cultural unconscious" or "mental habits" or "internalised master dispositions" which lead to particular perceptions and actions' (Houston, 2002, p. 157). Habitus is not just the way we think and the way we do things, it is our entire being in terms of how we dress, speak or act. These practices learned from a young age from parents, family, teachers and peer groups, are repeated over and over and as a result, these embodied practices become common-sense and thus often difficult for many of us to critically reflect upon. In other words, habitus refers to the socialising structures that explain why a person acts a certain way in different social environments (Reay, 2004). In reference to social structuring, Bourdieu (1984) explains that 'The habitus is not only a structuring structure, which organizes practices and the perception of practices, but also a structured structure' (1984, p. 170). Hence, habitus can be viewed from many perspectives.

Surfing culture has been presented from the perspective of short-board stand-up surfers through the work of Ford and Brown (2006), Stranger (2011), and Olive, McCuaig and Phillips (2013). However, the perspective of bodyboarders has until recently been neglected (Waitt and Clifton, 2012). Reay (2004) points out that 'there is a need to expand habitus to explore how gender and racial differences are linked to circumstances that can occur within and across cultures' (Reay, 2004, p. 436). Therefore, since gender and ethnicity inform my habitus, it is common-sense to also include them in this chapter and how they influence my experiences in the surf field.

Field

Bourdieu (1985) describes social spaces 'as a field of forces, i.e. as a set of objective power relations that impose themselves on all who enter the field' (p. 724). Within fields, members of the group consciously or subconsciously vie for position through the accumulation of power or capital (Bourdieu, 1984). The fields that exist in organised sport, such as rugby, come with a pre-determined set of rules that are based on the play of the game. However, it is not the set rules of the sport that field investigates, but rather the underlying negotiations and perceptions between players and team members that establish the unspoken rules that structure hierarchy within the group and allocate status, respect and power to some participants based on their performances on and off the sports field. It is important to note that field is more than just a social space. It includes the social interactions and perceptions of individuals along with the rules that are operating within that space, as well as the struggles for power and respect from others in the group.

In surfing culture, there are 'structures (surfing associations, etc.), rules, knowledge, practices and crucially *people*, as it is *within* and *through* people that surfing knowledge and practice are brought together, "lived", given value and ultimately transmitted to other people' (Ford and Brown, 2006, p. 127). The waves are a social space where hierarchies are played out among wave riders, whether they are on the same or different types of surf craft. Ford and Brown (2006) discuss levels in the surf field when explaining, 'The field of surfing therefore, is comprised of a number of sub-fields, all of which give value to the practised, surfed body in subtly different ways and these manifest themselves through surfing styles' (Ford and Brown, 2006, p. 128). Although in the context of this statement,

Ford and Brown (2006) were scrutinising the differences between competitive and soul surfers, it also relates to riders of different surf craft such as bodyboarders.

Capital

A third key concept of Bourdieu's framework is capital. Houston (2002) explains that, while field represents a struggle for power and hierarchal positioning, capital is characterised where 'the outcome of the struggle will be determined by the amount of capital (or resources) possessed by competing actors in a given field' (p. 158). Therefore, in various social fields, hierarchies are determined by what an individual has accumulated in terms of capital. It is important to note that different fields privilege different forms of capital. For example, in an educational setting, a person would hold more capital depending on the level of education he or she has attained. Hence, a person who has a Master's degree would have more capital and, therefore, higher status than another who has completed a Bachelor's degree. However, if the same two people surfed, and the person who completed the Bachelor's degree had a higher level of skill, then in the surfing field, this individual would have more capital. Thus, the rules of field and types of capital in each field change accordingly.

In the surfing field, the form of capital that is most highly respected is physical capital. In this case, it relates to displaying high levels of ability and, in some circumstances, putting oneself at risk. Physical capital, therefore, equates to the size and type of wave being ridden, along with the risk involved on the wave (Ford and Brown, 2006). This also relates to one's ability to manage fear in dangerous situations. Manoeuvres are also linked to physical capital and individuals who are able to execute technical manoeuvres with style, will gain the respect of their peers, which in itself is a valued form of capital in surfing culture. Hence, the bigger the wave and the more critical the ride or manoeuvres, the more capital gained from one's surfing peers. Ford and Brown (2006) explicate that 'The precise degree of *value* or physical capital that a surfer athlete, soul surfer or any other kind of surfer may possess will differ in relation to the various subsectors of the field of surfing they occupy and the current value of these subsectors' (p. 127). In regard to the subsectors or subfields in surfing, such as long-boarding or bodyboarding, Ford and Brown (2006) stress that each holds a different distinct form of capital, which is a reflection of the habitus of that particular style of wave riding.

The Surfing Field: Hierarchies in the Waves

In surf culture, identities are constantly undergoing scrutiny and hierarchal power battles are being negotiated in and out of the surf. Preston-Whyte (2002) points out that 'surfing space is constructed through the mediation of social practices and social processes' (p. 308). Due to the varied spaces and social practices that can be investigated in surf culture, it is important to understand that the field in focus for this chapter is the surf zone, that is, the space between the ocean and shore where the waves break. In this section, I will discuss the hierarchal interactions that exist in the surf zone, and how power is distributed between bodyboarders and stand-up surfers.

Surf Craft Hierarchies

A number of scholars have investigated the hierarchal structures in the surf relating to the type of surf craft being used. Ford and Brown (2006) identify young, male, short-board riders as having the most status and respect in the surfing field, with female surfers, older surfers, long-boarders, bodyboarders and surf-ski riders typically holding positions of less respect. Stranger (2011) also discusses the hierarchal relations between the various types of wave riders and similar to Ford and Brown, places young, male, short-board riders as being at the top of the pyramid in the surf followed by bodyboarders and long-boarders. It is important to note that Ford and Brown (2006) and Stranger (2011) approach their research from a position of male academics who also surf short-boards, which may explain why they have provided little room for the voices or experiences of wave riders other than young, male short-board surfers.

Hierarchies and power relations between bodyboarders and short-board surfers are ever present, and status in the surf is often dependent on physical capital and ability to negotiate space. Waitt and Warren (2008) explain that 'Each time a surfer enters the ocean they begin a complex process of negotiation through their bodies to configure and stabilise their subjectivity through making connections with the surf conditions and people' (p. 360). Despite the negotiating that takes place, Stranger (2011) states that 'The short board is the dominant surf craft and is used for high performance, high energy surfing' (p. 72). This belief is a commonly accepted norm in and outside of the surf. On the other hand, bodyboarders are often seen as the cause of overcrowding at surf breaks due to the ease with which bodyboarding can be performed by novice water goers (Stranger, 2011). Despite the initial introduction of bodyboarding being negative, Stranger (2011) highlights the competent bodyboarding community and gives a glimpse into how some bodyboarders negotiate space in the surf in some areas of Australia. For example, he explains that in some areas of Australia where there are more bodyboarders than surfers, bodyboarders dominate the break. He explains that 'for some bodyboarders, surfboard riding is seen as a step up in the surfing hierarchy, while for others their group solidarity and conflict with surfboard riders has provided the basis for a separate status structure' (Stranger, 2011, p. 75).

While some of the perspectives presented by Stranger (2011) resonate with me and I appreciate that he acknowledges bodyboarders in his book, I argue that some of the points mentioned do not offer a true reflection of bodyboarding culture and, in so doing, misrepresent the complexities within the sport. For example, I am particularly concerned by Stranger's (2011) assertion that 'It is rare to find core bodyboarders over the age of 25. By this age they have either stopped surfing altogether, adopted a 'recreational' pattern, or made the transition to surfboard riding' (p. 75). Stranger does not include interviews with bodyboarders in his extensive ethnographic study of Australian surf culture, thus such statements are based on assumptions that I find very problematic. Indeed, in the international competitive bodyboarding arena many of the male and female participants are over 25 years old. In fact, of the riders listed in the 2012 Top 10 Bodyboarders on the Men's World Tour only two are under 25 and the oldest, Mike Stewart, who is viewed as the king of bodyboarding, is nearly 50 (Taylor, 2012). In New Zealand the majority of core participants are also over 25 years old.

For many short-board surfers and experienced bodyboarders, frustration toward novice bodyboarders is based on their getting in the way or dropping in. Stranger (2011) elucidates this point when explaining that many novice bodyboarders 'don't learn the etiquette of surfing before venturing out to compete for waves' (p. 73). Due to the behaviour of many novice bodyboarders, core bodyboarders are sometimes treated with very little respect when they paddle out to surf among stand-up short-board and long-board surfers. To address this perception, core bodyboarders employ a variety of strategies to negotiate space and gain respect. A method I sometimes use involves paddling with power and speed with my chest off the board but my head level. It is almost like a proud peacock paddle where I display confidence while paddling into the line-up. I will then make sure I catch a wave and perform a manoeuvre to prove to everyone in the water that I am not a 'kook' ('a derogatory surfing term for someone who lacks surfing skills' (Waitt and Clifton, 2012, p. 7)) and that I know what I am doing.

Despite the lack of research into bodyboarding as part of surf culture, scholars who have investigated surf cultural hierarchies perpetuate the notion that short-board stand-up surfing is the dominant method of wave riding (Stranger, 2011; Waitt and Clifton, 2012; Waitt and Warren, 2008). Among my bodyboarding peers this view is also accepted when viewing surf culture in general and, from experience, is commonly accepted in mainstream society. However, the interactions in the surf between bodyboarders and surfers play out differently as I will later discuss.

Gendered Hierarchies

It is clear from surfing literature (Booth, 2001; Ford and Brown, 2006; Stranger, 2011; Waitt, 2008) that hierarchies in the surfing field extend to gender. Historically, sport has been considered a male domain where females are often marginalised, based on the ideologies that participants need to portray physical strength, skill and ability to be successful (Coakley, 1994; Messner, 1990). As of late, these ideologies have been contested by feminist scholars and activists as well as female participants, who seek to redefine sport according to their own experiences (Birrell and Cole, 1994). It has been argued that lifestyle sports, such as surfing and bodyboarding, offer new spaces for different gender relations (Thorpe, 2011; Wheaton and Tomlinson, 1998). Due to lifestyle sports such as surfing, being less structured, where participation is by choice and in spaces that are not controlled by referees and umpires, there are arguably more opportunities for women to re-shape and define terms of participation. However, it is thought by some that 'Sport is so thoroughly masculinised that it seems unlikely that it can be reclaimed to serve women's interests' (Birrell and Cole, 1994, p. 48).

In surf culture, the perceptions of hierarchies relating to surf craft and gender place the female bodyboarder at the bottom of the pyramid and indeed, based on my experiences in and outside the surf, I feel that I have often been treated as such. However, despite this perception, opportunities for me to gain respect in the surf field exist because of my physical abilities and bravery in the surf. Despite these abilities, because I do not stand up, I am often still marginalised. For example, I have caught waves that surfers were afraid to catch, or performed manoeuvres that have impressed the surfers in the water (much like the opening narrative) and, as a result, I was given respect and access to waves. However, in these instances, the power did not shift to me, rather a mutual respect was given from the males in the surf and as a result, access to waves ensued. It was as if I had been granted a privilege that they were able to confer. What is important to note is that, despite the physical prowess and courage I portrayed, I was still confined to the rules set by men in the surf field. Hence, to understand why I continue to participate in bodyboarding, it becomes important to understand the reasons I surf. Olive et al. (2013) agree that understanding why individuals participate in surfing is important when stating that 'it is the everyday experiences and relationships of surfers in the waves that remain the most powerful in how women understand and experience surfing and surfing culture at an individual level' (p. 15). For me, I love the thrill of harnessing Mother Nature by catching and riding waves. I believe that the bigger the wave or manoeuvre, the greater the thrill (to an extent of course). I find that being in the surf and enjoying the speed and power of the waves is fun, enthralling and highly addictive. I feel free from the social constructs of the land and, with my added confidence and ability, I know that there is a space for me in an ocean of males.

Getting Barrelled: Bodyboarders' Claim to Capital in the Surf

Regardless of the surf craft being used, one of the most exhilarating experiences for serious wave riders involves riding big waves and getting barrelled or, in non-surf speak, being entirely covered in a tunnel of water while riding a wave. The thrill of paddling into a mountain of water, speeding down a steep slope and being propelled into a barrel or tube is something that can only be truly appreciated through the embodied experience of a wave rider. Highly committed and proficient surfers and bodyboarders will conduct extensive research and go to great lengths to search for and access waves that can provide the best opportunities for 'getting barrelled'. Waitt and Clifton (2012) explain that 'Riding inside a hollow barrel or tube as part of a breaking wave is the ultimate thrill for both short-boarders and bodyboarders' (p. 7). Drawing upon Bourdieu's concept of capital, the longer one rides inside a big barrel, the more status, respect and thus capital gained. If the rider exits the barrel without the curtain of the wave breaking even more respect is gained. Booth (2007) also points out that 'Among surfers competition for prestige [capital] involves displays of physical prowess and courage in big waves' (p. 321). Put simply, demonstrations of physical ability via a well-executed barrel are a form of power within the surf field.

When riding a bodyboard in a prone position, a rider is able to enter a barrel more easily than a stand-up surfer. Stranger (2011) acknowledges this position and explains that for bodyboarders, there is 'different potential inherent in the board, such as taking off on very steep waves, tucking into smaller tubes and performing a range of different manoeuvres' (p. 74). As a result of the versatility of the bodyboard, there are specific types of surf breaks that favour bodyboarders over surfers. These types of surf breaks have waves that are very steep, break quickly and are sometimes shallow (Stranger, 2011; Waitt and Clifton, 2012). Thus at surf breaks with these characteristics, bodyboarders have more access and, therefore, more capital. Indeed, it is in the potential for accessing barrels and big, powerful or heavy surf in shallow areas that bodyboarders can gain access to waves that most stand-up surfers are unable to access. Over the years, I have experienced and seen respect given from stand-up surfers to bodyboarders who have caught a wave where they have been barrelled and in the larger, shallow dangerous surf. The awe or disbelief of putting oneself in potential danger is perhaps an aspect that bodyboarders find thrilling. There is a sense of bravado from 'charging' onto big waves that others, particularly males, are afraid to catch and it is this respect that I claim and enjoy while stamping my mark and claiming my space in the surf.

Bodyboarding Habitus

From my many experiences with surf culture, the mainstream perspective is that bodyboarding is an activity that requires less skill and is thus less deserving of respect. Many of my bodyboarding friends express frustration at such opinions but few attempt to challenge the assumptions underpinning the basic structure of the surf field. Understanding this stance is an embodied feature of being a bodyboarder and is one that those who do not bodyboard may not understand. I recall an experience when I was bodyboarding at Piha and was approached by a male stand up surfer who said, 'You're pretty good on that thing, when are you going to get a surfboard?' Unbeknown to him I had just won my second world amateur bodyboarding title. My reply was, 'I don't want to surf on a surfboard; I love bodyboarding'. The surprised look on his face suggested that he had never thought that anyone would just want to bodyboard, let alone love it.

Although the perceptions of short-board surfers toward bodyboarders have been investigated by some scholars (Stranger, 2011; Waitt and Warren, 2008), the perceptions of bodyboarders towards surfers and perceptions of themselves as bodyboarders is an area that is yet to be investigated. Bourdieu (1984) explains 'The perception of the social world is itself the product of internalization' (p. 170).

From my extensive national and international experience with bodyboarding over the past 23 years, I would describe the bodyboarding community as inclusive, friendly and, at times, eccentric. Some bodyboarding brands even embrace the 'outcast' identity with names like 'No Friends' and 'Rejected'. Waitt and Clifton (2012) provide similar perspectives when stating that bodyboarders view themselves as 'oppositional – transgressing cultural norms in the surf and their everyday lives' (p. 8). These 'odd ball' non-mainstream characteristics embraced by bodyboarders signify differences in taste and perception where it is almost cooler to be different. A slogan used at the 2005 Australasian National Titles was 'Stand out, not up', thus signifying to the stand-up short-board surfing community that to be outstanding one does not necessarily have to stand. Given my mixed ethnic background and feelings of not fitting entirely into Māori or Samoan culture, this aspect of embracing difference in the culture of bodyboarding gave me a place where I felt I belonged.

Being a Brown Bodyboarder

Some of the earliest recorded accounts of wave riding in New Zealand included stories about Māori men, women and children riding waves using a variety of objects, such as boards (referred to as kopapa), logs, canoes and even bags of kelp during the early 1900s (Beattie, 1919; Best, 1924). With such a rich history in aquatic activities, it saddens me that during my travels to surfing beaches throughout New Zealand, I have meet so few Māori and Pacific Island bodyboarders. Such observations are not unique to New Zealand. International research shows that the sport of surfing is very white-dominated (Ford and Brown, 2006; Stranger, 2011). In this section I aim to shed light on embodied aspects relating to being brown, including some of the assumptions associated with brownness and bodyboarding.

Re-Appropriating 'Brown'

Skin colour is an identifiable characteristic that is often related to ethnicity and, as such, is a feature that needs to be explained, clarified and contextualised. In particular, the word 'brown' needs to be discussed as it is a term used by Māori and Pacific people in New Zealand. The word 'brown' has been used in the media (Edmunds, 2013; Neville, 2010), books (Grainger, 2008) and scholarly articles (Fitzpatrick, 2011; Grainger, Falcous and Newman, 2012; Kukutai, 2007; McKinley, 2005) to differentiate Māori and Pacific Island people from the dominant ethnic group Pākehā (New Zealand European), who are described as being white. 'Brown' is also used in Fitzpatrick's (2011) work, where the youth 'refer to themselves and other Māori and Pacific peoples as "brown", rather than black, as in the USA' (p. 3).

While the use of 'brown' is used flippantly to discuss skin colour and differentiate one ethnic group from the other, the terms also refer to embodied characteristics related to the ethnic cultures they describe. Bourdieu (1984) is useful here, particularly when he explains 'that bodily properties [such as skin colour] are perceived through social systems of classification which are not independent of the distribution of these properties among the social classes' (p. 193). The term 'brown' for me means more than just the colour of skin, it includes a way of thinking, understanding and behaving. It is an innate sense of being that is understood by those who are brown. In every day conversation my family, friends, colleagues and students use the word 'brown' to describe how they perceive particular individuals and how their actions portray embodied characteristics of 'brownness'. For example, I often refer to one of my New Zealand European colleagues as being 'brown' because of the way he embodies brownness. Not only has he learned how to make flowers and bags using harakeke (flax), he goes out of his way to assist students in their learning and would give the shirt off his back to help someone. These qualities, plus a myriad of others, resonate with what it means to be brown.

Having a mixed Māori Samoan ethnicity and brown skin comes with a set of assumptions that are sometimes imposed on me in and out of the surf. One assumption is that Māori and Pacific Island people are more suited to particular types of sport (Edwards, 2007). From experiences working in the sport and education industries and through stereotypes portrayed in the media, it is assumed that Māori and Pacific people are better at team sports rather than individual sports. An experience where this assumption was manifest occurred when I was guest presenting Pacific Island perspectives to a group of students at Waikato University. At the start of the lecture I gave the students the opportunity to guess my ethnicity and which sport I was successful at internationally. A large majority of the class guessed correctly that I was Māori (possibly due to my Māori name) and some guessed that I also had Samoan ancestry. However, the majority of students assumed that I played rugby or touch rugby and some thought that I played netball. Nobody guessed that I was a bodyboarder or that I even surfed.

Another assumption in New Zealand society is that Māori or Pacific Island people are not very good at swimming. Indeed, the *Auckland Regional Drowning Statistics* (WSNZ, 2011) show that Pacific people have the second highest drowning rate after New Zealand Europeans. Due to this assumption, there have been numerous occasions where the lifeguards have advised me to stay between the flags for my own safety when walking towards the surf carrying my board and fins. While I understand that they are just doing their job, it becomes clear that they are singling me out when they do not approach white individuals carrying surfboards. I have come to accept that because the majority of 'brown' individuals in the surf at Piha are between the flags or need to get rescued, I will always be questioned about my ability to paddle out to catch waves with the short-board surfers.

Brown Bodyboarder

In bodyboarding and 'brown' circles there tends to be a sense of camaraderie stemming from common experiences of being marginalised in the surf field and in society. Indeed, when I see another brown person or bodyboarder in the surf, there is a sense of understanding and respect for what it took to be in that position. Going against societal norms is no easy feat and Bourdieu is useful to help understand this position. He points out that, with people who have similar tastes, there are ways of knowing, understanding and appreciating the nuances associated with that practise (Bourdieu, 1984). Thus, knowing the feeling of being marginalised in the surf, by being brown or by being a bodyboarder, is one that helps me feel united with individuals who have similar experiences.

My mixed ethnic upbringing has played a major role in being comfortable about going against societal norms, as I do not feel confined or obligated to join mainstream ways of being. I am Māori, yet I do not feel confined or obligated to practise Māori traditions. I am also Samoan, but I do not feel confined or obligated to practise Samoan traditions. I feel I can move freely in both worlds, which is why I believe I have the confidence to make my own space in the surf field. One of the most enthralling aspects I enjoy is being different. I am in no means your typical 'girly-girl'. I do not choose to wear make-up or dresses and my favourite clothing is surf shorts and a t-shirt. My idea of fun involves elements of risk most females fear. I do not know how to play rugby or netball, although many of my friends do. I embrace the fact that I am brown, that I am female and that I bodyboard. There is nothing stereotypical about who I am and what I represent. The surf enables me to express myself freely, to show that yes, I am different but I belong here.

Last Wave

Aching legs kick powerfully and heavy arms pull strongly against the water. The surge of the wave equals my efforts and I position myself on my board, chest high, leaning onto my elbow as I catch my final wave of the day. This is going to be a good one I think to myself as I see the clear wall of water beckoning to me. Taking a high line near the breaking lip, I powerfully carve back towards the whitewash behind me and intuitively push myself up high onto the board, knees on opposite corners, crossing my legs and looking over my shoulder as I spin around like a spinning top 360 degrees until the foamy whitewash is once again behind me. I see a watery section ahead that looks as though it's going to barrel so I stall by digging my flippers into the water and angling my board towards the centre of the wall. As expected the barrel forms and within milliseconds I'm entirely enclosed in a tunnel of water. I remain calm although my heart is beating fast and I make slight adjustments with my board as my flippers act like a rudder to ensure I stay in the barrel as long as possible. The opening of the tunnel is an arm's length away and I see the curtain of the wave begin to close. To speed ahead and make it out, I lean forward, make a sharp but strong bottom turn and kick hard. I feel the spit from the barrel as it launches me out, hair shooting forward and covering my face and I jubilantly turn my board towards land and allow the power from the foamy whitewash push me towards the shore.

I meander my way past a few novice stand-up surfers floundering in the whitewash and use the last dregs of the wave to kick slowly to the shallows. Flipping onto my back I sit watching the surf, elated with my final wave while peeling off fins and fin socks. I stand and rinse them off while watching another wave then gather my board under arm and hang fins off my wrist as I slowly walk backwards up onto the beach, eyes still fixated on the surf. Five hours surfing is enough I tell myself, as I watch another perfect wave rolling in resisting the urge to paddle back out for more. 'Excuse me, but you need to make sure you stay between the flags. It's very dangerous out here, lots of people drown.' I get a little startled from the voice and turn around to see that a lifeguard had walked up behind me to deliver his message. I look to my left and see that I am about 10 metres away from the flags. 'Sweet az', I reply looking at him squarely in the eyes. Then I shrug my shoulders and walk up the beach with eyes watching and judging my brown body carrying my bodyboard.

References

Beattie, H., 1919. Traditions and legends collected from the natives of Murihiku (Southland, New Zealand). *The Journal of the Polynesian Society*, 28(XI), pp. 212–25.

Best, E., 1924. *The Māori as He Was: A Brief Account of Māori Life as it Was in Pre-European Days*. Government: Wellington.

Birrell, S. and Cole, C.L., eds, 1994. *Women, Sport, and Culture*. Champaign, IL: Human Kinetics.

Bishop, R., 1999. Kaupapa Māori research: An indigenous approach to creating knowledge. In: N. Robertson, ed., *Māori and Psychology: Research and Practice – The Proceedings of a Symposium Sponsored by the Māori and Psychology Research Unit*. Hamilton: Māori and Psychology Research Unit, pp. 1–6.

Booth, D., 2001. From bikinis to boardshorts: Wahines and the paradoxes of surfing culture. *Journal of Sport History*, 28(1), pp. 3–22.

——— 2007. Surfing. In: D. Booth and H. Thorpe, eds, *Berkshire Encyclopedia of Extreme Sports*. Great Barrington, MA: Berkshire, pp. 317–23.

Bourdieu, P., 1984. *Distinction: A Social Critique of the Judgment of Taste*. Translated by R. Nice. London, England: Harvard University Press.

——— 1985. The social space and the genesis of groups. *Theory and Society*, 14(6), pp. 723–44.

Coakley, J., 1994. Gender: Is equity the only issue? *Sport in Society: Issues and Controversies*, 5, pp. 208–38.

Denzin, N.K., 2002. Confronting ethnography's crisis of representation: Review symposium: Crisis in representation. *Journal of Contemporary Ethnography*, 31(4), pp. 482–90.

Edmunds, S., 2013. We're not racist, but … *New Zealand Herald*, 28 April 2013. Available at: http://www.nzherald.co.nz/ [accessed 19 September 2013].

Edwards, M. ed., 2007. *Sport and Identity in Aotearoa/New Zealand* (2nd ed.). Auckland, New Zealand: Thomson.

Fitzpatrick, K., 2011. Brown bodies, racialisation and physical education. *Sport, Education and Society*, 18(2), pp. 135–53.

Ford, N. and Brown, D., 2006. *Surfing and Social Theory: Experience, Embodiment and Narrative of the Dream Glide*. New York: Routledge.

Grainger, A.D., 2008. *The Browning of the All Blacks: Pacific Peoples, Rugby, and the Cultural Politics of Identity in New Zealand*. PhD, University of Maryland, College Park, MD.

Grainger, A.D., Falcous, M. and Newman, J.I., 2012. Postcolonial anxieties and the browning of New Zealand rugby. *The Contemporary Pacific*, 24(2), pp. 267–95.

Houston, S., 2002. Reflecting on habitus, field and capital towards a culturally sensitive social work. *Journal of Social Work*, 2(2), pp. 149–67.

Keddell, E., 2006. Pavlova and pineapple pie: Selected identity influences on Samoan-Pakeha people in Aotearoa/New Zealand. *Kotuitui: New Zealand Journal of Social Sciences Online*, 1(1), pp. 45–63.

Kukutai, T.H., 2007. White mothers, brown children: Ethnic identification of Māori-European children in New Zealand. *Journal of Marriage and Family*, 69(5), pp. 1150–61.

McFall-McCaffery, J., 2010. Getting started with Pacific research: Finding resources and information on Pacific research models and methodologies. *Mai Review*, 1 (Library Workshop 8), pp. 1–5. Available at: http://ojs.review.mai. ac.nz/index.php/MR/article/view/332/367 [accessed 20 February 2013].

McKinley, E., 2005. Brown bodies, white coats: Postcolonialism, Māori women and science. *Discourse: Studies in the Cultural Politics of Education*, 26(4), pp. 481–96.

Messner, M., 1990. Boyhood, Organized Sports, and the Construction of Masculinities. *Journal of Contemporary Ethnography*, 18(4), pp. 416–44.

Neville, A., 2010. Rugby 'browning' talked about but 'darkie' wrong word to use. *New Zealand Herald*, 30 May 2010. Available at: http://www.nzherald. co.nz/nz/news/article.cfm?c_id=1&objectid=10648410 [accessed 20 February 2013].

Olive, R., McCuaig, L. and Phillips, M.G., 2013. Women's recreational surfing: A patronising experience. *Sport, Education and Society*, pp. 1–19.

Preston-Whyte, R., 2002. Constructions of surfing space at Durban, South Africa. *Tourism Geographies*, 4(3), pp. 307–28.

Reay, D., 2004. 'It's all becoming a habitus': Beyond the habitual use of habitus in educational research. *British Journal of Sociology of Education*, 25(4), pp. 431–44.

Rolleston, A., 2011. *Guidelines for Health Research with Māori*. Tauranga, New Zealand: Western Bay of Plenty Primary Health Organisation.

Royal, C., 2012. Opening address. Paper presented at: Nga Pae O Te Maramatanga: Enhancing Māori Distinctiveness Research Symposium. Rotorua, New Zealand, 14–15 May 2012.

Schaaf, M., 2006. Elite Pacific male rugby players' perceptions and experiences of professional rugby. *Junctures: The Journal for Thematic Dialogue*, 7, pp. 41–54.

Smith, L., 1999. *Decolonizing Methodologies: Research and Indigenous Peoples*. London, England: Zed Books.

———— 2012. *Decolonizing Methodologies: Research and Indigenous Peoples* (2nd ed.). London, England: Zed Books.

Stranger, M., 2011. *Surfing Life: Surface, Substructure and the Commodification of the Sublime*. Farnham, UK and Burlington, VT: Ashgate.

Taylor, G., 2012. International Bodyboarding Association. Available at: http://ibaworldtour.com/ [accessed 1 September 2012].

Thorpe, H., 2011. *Snowboarding Bodies in Theory and Practice*. Houndmills, UK: Palgrave Macmillan.

Vaioleti, T.M., 2006. Talanoa Research Methodology: A Developing Position on Pacific Research. *Waikato Journal of Education*, 12, pp. 21–34.

Waitt, G., 2008. 'Killing waves': Surfing, space and gender. *Social and Cultural Geography*, 9(1), pp. 75–94.

Waitt, G. and Clifton, D., 2012. 'Stand out, not up': Bodyboarders, gendered hierarchies and negotiating the dynamics of pride/shame. *Leisure Studies*, doi: 10.1080/02614367.2012.684397.

Waitt, G. and Warren, A., 2008. 'Talking shit over a brew after a good session with your mates': Surfing, space and masculinity. *Australian Geographer*, 39(3), pp. 353–65.

Wheaton, B. and Tomlinson, A., 1998. The changing gender order in sport? The case of windsurfing subcultures. *Journal of Sport and Social Issues*, 22(3), pp. 252–74.

WSNZ, 2011. Regional Drowning Fact Sheet Auckland. Available at: http://www.watersafety.org.nz [accessed 16 March 2013].

Chapter 7
Sailing with Gregory Bateson

Peter Reason

Like many small boys of my generation, my enthusiasm for sailing came originally from my avid reading of Arthur Ransome's *Swallows and Amazons* series. The accounts of the Walker and Blackett children's imaginative adventures in the English Lake District and Broads were accompanied by vivid and completely realistic accounts of sailing small dinghies. Ransome's description of the gybe that led to Swallow crashing into a rock in Swallowdale is both technically accurate and deeply evocative. Reading these books gave me an illusion I could already sail – an illusion that was destroyed the first time I got into a sailing dinghy and capsized it before I had left the jetty. So I took lessons and over the years learned to handle a sailing dinghy more or less competently.

I started sailing larger cruising yachts when my two sons were in their early teens. Fired up by Robert Bly's insistence on the importance of the relationship between fathers and sons (Bly, 1990), I chartered small yachts and took Ben and Matthew, along with other men friends, on increasingly ambitious sailing adventures in the English Channel. We learned a lot about how to live together and look after each other in challenging conditions. I bought my own yacht, Coral, just at the time when the boys were leaving university and getting into their independent lives and responsibilities, and were no longer available.

By this time, my sailing was taking on another dimension. I was increasingly concerned about the state of the planetary ecology. At the University of Bath I was developing undergraduate and Master's teaching programmes (Marshall, Coleman and Reason, 2011; Reason, 2001, 2007) and initiating and leading action research projects around sustainability issues (Reason et al., 2009). Intellectually, I was guided and influenced by Gaia theory (Harding, 2009), deep ecology (Naess, 1990) and above all by Gregory Bateson's particular brand of systemic thinking (Bateson, 1972, 1979; Bateson and Bateson, 1987). He has been one of my intellectual heroes since I first read *Steps to an Ecology of Mind* (Bateson, 1972) in the early 1970s and struggled to understand what he was saying. It took me years to appreciate his work. Bateson pointed out that human beings and human society are embedded in the general systemic structure of the natural world, which, he argued, was self-organising and self-transcending, qualities he saw as essentially those of mind. However, the Western perspective abrogates the notion of mind to the human and separates it from the natural world, which it sees as mechanical and mindless, leading to what Bateson has called 'pathologies of epistemology' –

there is something fundamentally wrong with our ways of knowing. He wrote as early as 1969, well before the current 'environmental movement' developed: 'Epistemological error is all right, it's fine, up to the point at which you create around yourself a universe in which the error becomes immanent in the monstrous changes in the universe that you have created and now try to live in' (Bateson, 1972, p. 485).

The idea of epistemological error brought about by non-systemic thinking influenced my own teaching and research and that of my colleagues and students (see, for example, Marshall, 2004; Marshall et al., 2011). But increasingly it became part of the perspective through which I saw and experienced the world, including my sailing experiences.

Since I retired from academic life I have recast myself as a writer of eco-literature, exploring how to express Gaian and systemic ideas through creative writing, as in the following description of sailing through the Chenal du Four.

The Chenal du Four is the inner passage round the northwest corner of France, available to a small coasting boat wishing to avoid the longer and more exposed passage in the open Atlantic. The Chenal opens in the north between Le Four lighthouse on the mainland coast and Île d'Ouessant to the west. Le Four is familiar to many people from the photographic prints by Guillaume Pilsson showing a wave breaking right over it in a storm. Île d'Ouessant – the island traditionally known to British sailors contemptuous (or maybe incapable) of French pronunciation as Ushant – is off the northwestern corner of mainland Europe, the southern entrance to the English Channel, celebrated in the old sea song *Farewell and Adieu to You, Spanish Ladies*:

> We will rant and we'll roar like true British sailors,
> We'll range and we'll roam o'er all the salt sea.
> Until we strike soundings in the channel of old England;
> From Ushant to Scilly 'tis thirty-five leagues.

On the west side of the Chenal, south of Île d'Ouessant, a series of wild rocky outcrops and islands stretch down toward its southern end, where it opens onto the Rade de Brest between a dangerous expanse of underwater reefs and rocks called the Chausée de Pierres Noires and Point de St Matthieu on the mainland.

This is rightly called 'Finistère', the end of the land. Here, France thrusts out west into the Atlantic Ocean, diverting the tidal streams so that huge quantities of water flow twice each day in and out of the English Channel and the Bay of Biscay, forced through narrow channels between the rocks and islands. The currents here are strong and complex. At the northern entrance, where the Chenal is open to the North Atlantic, a huge swell can develop as water piled up by winds in the middle of the ocean rolls in toward the land. In the Chenal itself strong winds blowing against big tides can make the surface rough, but even in calm conditions the stream, swirling around the rocks and shallows under the water, creates strange ripples, eddies and overfalls that take hold of a small boat almost as a toy in a bathtub.

I was on route in Coral for Southern Brittany. The word 'yacht' may be misleading, possibly implying the grandeur and ostentation of hedge-fund traders and Russian oligarchs. Coral is a Rustler 31, small and rather elderly. She was built in the 1960s for offshore racing but is completely outclassed by more modern designs. I have sailed her all over the Western Channel for nearly 20 years, making passages to France, Spain, Ireland, often with my sons or with friends as crew, and sometimes on my own. With a heavy keel deep in the water, she is very seaworthy.

I started sailing seriously when my two sons were teenagers as a way of growing up together. Over the years, sailing has become a kind of pilgrimage for me, an encounter with the forces of the more than human world, with the rigorous beauty of the sea. I have noticed that, when asked to think of a place in the natural world that is special to them, most people think of a hillside or a woodland; for the more adventurous it may be a mountain peak. The special place for me is out of sight of land somewhere in the entrance to the English Channel, where the broad Atlantic Ocean with its waves, currents and weather systems, meets the constricted waters of the northwest European coast.

On this passage I was sailing with my young American friend Monica. We had crossed the channel from Plymouth two days previously and had made our way down the French coast to L'Aberw'rach to wait for favourable winds and tide. L'Aberw'rach is a small river estuary about 10 miles west of Le Four. Here the river emerges into the sea through narrow channels between rocks and underwater reefs. At high tide the estuary fills, so that many of the rocks are submerged while the others rise dramatically from the water. At low tide these same rocks are connected by long sandbanks, golden in sunshine or greyed out lines through mist and rain. Tidal streams flow across the estuary and can carry the boat sideways into the hazards. The safe passage is found by following leading lines, indicated by alignments of beacons built on rocks and on shore, or by a lighthouse with a distant church spire – that show where the channel is to be found.

In clear weather it is great fun to sail through close to the rocks, the depth sounder showing that the boat is in deep water; but with poor visibility it is easy to lose one's sense of direction. The Grand Chenal out of L'Aberw'rach is particularly alarming because Le Libenter, a long hidden reef, is shallow enough to be dangerous, but deep enough that the waves do not always break to mark where it lies.

The Chenal du Four itself is only passable in a yacht with a favourable tide, so ideally we need to time our arrival at Le Four just as the tide turns south. But the peculiar way the tides interact with the coastline means that a yacht leaving L'Aberw'rach to catch the favourable tide down the channel arrives at the northern entrance after half the south-going stream has gone. In addition, the whole of this coast is littered with outcrops of rocks, some visible, some lurking underwater and some reaching way offshore. A safe passage involves a long detour offshore or careful inshore pilotage. It is not easy to know when to set off to make the best of the conditions. Every evening we joined the anxious little crowd around la Capitainerie, where the weather maps for the following day were posted, and joined in discussions in broken 'franglais' as to when would be the best time to leave.

After a little wait we decided the perfect weather would never arrive and left L'Aberw'rach on a wet and windy morning. As Monica dropped the mooring line and we motored away from the buoy, cloud and fine rain descended on the river. Quickly the mist was so thick that all the leading lines were obscured. For a moment I was alarmed and tempted to turn back. But soon the weather cleared enough for us to get out safely along the Grande Chenal, past Le Libenter, out into the channel.

Once we were safely clear of the outlying rocks we turned westwards. I checked our course carefully, for a while clambering up and down between the cockpit, from where I could see landmarks and take compass bearings, and the pilot seat below, where I could check our position on the instruments and against our large-scale chart. I decided that with Coral sailing close to the fresh south-westerly breeze we would clear the hazards safely. We settled down for a long haul through the rain and mist.

One of the challenges of long shorthanded passages at sea is simply sailing the boat effectively while attending to navigation and other necessities and getting sufficient rest. The person at the helm will tire after a couple of hours at the most and lose concentration. So I have equipped Coral with Aries, a self-steering system bolted to the stern with a wind vane above and a paddle deep in the water below. The wind vane is set so it stands upright when the boat is on the correct course. When the boat wanders off course, the wind catches the side of the vane and blows it over and, through a clever system of gears, turns the paddle. The flow of water past the boat forces the paddle to one side and lines connected to the tiller move the rudder to correct the course. The wind vane returns upright and everything returns to its starting point – although in practice there is constant movement as small adjustments are made to respond to wind and waves. Aries works as a simple cybernetic system, encompassing all of what Gregory Bateson called 'criteria of mental process' (Bateson, 1979, p. 92). Information about the correct course flows in a circuit between the sails, the hull, the wind vane and the rudder, and the system is powered, not by electric power derived from fossil fuel, but by the movement of the boat through the water. I find it delightful that Aries works on the same principles as all natural ecological systems to maintain a dynamic balance around a zone of relative stability.

So with Aries taking care of the steering we could huddle under the sprayhood, half out of the rain. All the morning and into the afternoon we made a series of long tacks, far over toward Île d'Ouessant on a port tack and then back again toward the mainland on starboard. At the end of the port tack we could just see the high coastguard watchtower that dominates the eastern end of Ouessant, faintly standing up through the mist. At the end of the opposite starboard tack, Le Four and the mainland would emerge dimly, breaking surf on the rocks. Each time we tacked we headed back into a featureless sea, sailing on through shades of grey, lighter above in the mist and clouds, darker below in the water and waves.

On occasion our track crossed that of another yacht working up into the wind like us, and we felt mildly competitive – were we doing better than them? Were we holding a course closer to the wind? We were very scornful of the German yacht that had motored all the way from L'Aberw'rach. It had taken a more cautious route than we had, going further out to sea before turning south, so it passed us twice. But most of the time it felt desolate and lonely, as if we were sailing our tiny boat on and on to nowhere, across a sea with no boundaries.

The swell came out of the Atlantic, rolling hills of sea that we sailed up and down, and then up and down again, knocking our way through the shorter sharper waves set up by the wind and the tide. Several times Monica and I remarked to each other how well Coral was sailing, how hard we were pushing her, how she was moving through and over the waves so smoothly, as if to reassure ourselves that maybe we were actually getting somewhere. I read our position from the GPS and marked it on the chart. Yes, we were making progress, but in this grey mist it felt unreal. But in that unreality we were also strangely happy. We were warm and dry and not too uncomfortable. We were doing the best we could in the circumstances. Above all, we were sailing, and sailing well in unpleasant conditions. It was oddly rewarding.

After a while the cloud lifted a little and I could see a beacon tower some way in the distance. Consulting the pilot book and chart, I identified it as Le Faix on the Plateau de la Helle. Checking the tide times again, I realised that with these long tacks doubling the distance we had to travel, we would not make it through the Chenal before the tide turned against us. The wind had not, as I had hoped, veered westerly, allowing us to sail a direct course. We would have to use the engine and motor sail straight down the channel.

Motor sailing – with both engine and mainsail working together – and with the electric Autohelm taking over from Aries, we moved much faster and closer to the wind. The log showed that Coral was now making 6 knots through the water and the GPS that the tide was adding 2–3 knots to this. We raced south and would easily reach Pointe St Matthieu before the tide turned.

The whole sensation of moving through the water had changed: we were forcing our way into the wind rather than working with it. A mechanical wake of water stirred up by the propeller streamed out astern; the bows crashed directly into and through the waves rather than riding obliquely over them. No longer balanced against the wind, Coral sat level in the water yet pitched up and down as if irritated by the waves. And instead of the slap of the waves, the hum of the rigging and the wind in our ears, the steady roar and vibration of the twin cylinder diesel engine under our feet, running at almost maximum power, dominated everything.

Edward Abbey in *Desert Solitaire* wrote of turning on the generator outside his trailer in the middle of the slickrock desert in order to have light to write a letter. Unable to hear anything but the clatter of engine noise, he was 'shut off from the natural world, sealed up, encapsulated, in a box of artificial light and tyrannical noise', exchanging a 'great and unbounded world for a small, comparatively meagre one' (Abbey, 1968, p. 15).

It was not quite like that in the Chenal de Four. I was still standing in the open air in the cockpit, legs braced and balancing against the movement of the boat. I faced the wind, peering under the peak of my cap and over the top of the sprayhood, eyes narrowed to keep the fine rain from my eyes. I was looking out for buoys and beacons on our course down the Chenal, and indeed for other boats. We had to slow down to make way for a seaweed-harvesting barge, laden to the gunwales with the load of a day's work, as it crossed the channel on its way back to Lanildut, its home port and the centre of seaweed harvesting on this coast.

I was not shut off from the wider world but my relationship to it had changed, forcing my way *through* it rather than riding *with* it. To adjust my course, rather than physically pull the lines that adjust the Aries vane and winch in the sheets of the sails, I simply pushed a button on the Autohelm – 10° or 1°, port or starboard, as I chose – and the boat's heading changed. I had not actually changed the laws of physics, but I was using them in a different way, a way that gave me the illusion that I could cut straight through all the obstacles and go directly to my goal.

This reminded me of one of my favourite pieces of Bateson's writing, *Conscious Purpose Versus Nature* (Bateson, 1972). Bateson starts off by exploring how dynamic balance is maintained in natural ecosystems. An undisturbed woodland, for example, contains many different species. To survive, each must be capable of reproducing exponentially, as did the pet mice I kept as a small boy (we bought four and a year later had over 100, much to my mother's horror). The population of each species is maintained by a combination of interdependence and competition. Any species whose activities are unchecked will grow to dominate and overwhelm the ecosystem.

> In a balanced ecological system whose underpinnings are of this nature, it is very clear that any monkeying around with the system is likely to disrupt the equilibrium. Then the exponential curves will start to appear. Some plant will become a weed, some creatures will be exterminated, and the system as a balanced system is likely to fall to pieces. (Bateson, 1972, p. 431)

In contrast to this, human awareness and activity is ordered by conscious purpose: we see what we are interested in and go straight for what we want. Conscious purpose cuts across the complex dynamic balance of ecosystems. It has done so since Neolithic farmers began cutting down forest to create farmland. It is particularly destructive when linked with a powerful technology.

We humans have for a while overwhelmed our historic predators – infectious bacteria as much as sabre tooth tigers – and draw on the buried energy of millennia, as does my marine diesel, to go directly for what we want. Bateson is challenging: conscious purpose 'is a short cut device to enable you to get quickly at what you want' rather than act with wisdom. Wisdom is 'knowledge of the larger interactive system', which if disturbed may rapidly degenerate. A species 'unwise enough to quarrel with its ecology' will cause trouble for itself and other creatures, for 'lack of systemic wisdom is always punished', writes Bateson (1972, p. 434).

Having a reliable diesel on a yacht makes the kind of voyaging I do possible. Yet when I start the engine to push against the prevailing conditions, I always feel regret as well as relief. Here in the Chenal de Four we *could* have found a place to anchor and wait for the tide somewhere between the rocks off the French coast, but it would have been uncomfortable and delayed our progress. Using the engine to make the best of this failing tide, we would get through the Chenal and reach our planned destination after nightfall but still in time to pick up a mooring buoy and have some supper.

I was both pleased to be making progress and disturbed by the implications of what 'progress' meant. Just as Aries reminds me of the balancing feedback of ecological systems, starting the engine reminds me of the shadow of human ingenuity, which means that we live in a time of dangerous climate change, loss of species and degradation of ecosystems – the 'monstrous changes' that Bateson warned of in the 1960s.

We still had a way to go: 12 miles to Pointe Saint-Mattieu and then another 10 or so to Camaret. As the engine urged us forward we passed between the red and green buoys that mark the rocks at La Plâtresses and followed the channel down to the narrows off the port of Le Conquet. There the large red octagonal structure of La Grande Vinotièrre dominates the middle of the channel. The last time I came this way, the tide was running strongly past it, creating a standing wave upstream and a wake of disturbed water running 100 metres or so downstream. But this evening the stream had run its course and as we passed, the waters lapped quietly at its base.

We turned east round the Pointe Saint-Mattieu, with enough light to look through binoculars at the complex of beacons, lighthouses, radio towers and the old ruined abbey that stand high on the cliffs. We motored on across the Avant Goulet de Brest to Camaret. We could have sailed this last bit but the wind had dropped and, once the engine is running, there is always the temptation to keep it going and press on. As I expected, we arrived after dark but with enough light to find a vacant mooring buoy. Safely secured, we turned off the engine and in the delightful silence made a quick supper – pasta, pesto and Parmesan cheese again, it is all we could manage – and fell into our bunks.

In his account of Gregory Bateson's life and work, Noel Charlton points out that in the last 10 years of his life, Bateson was increasingly concerned about ways in which Western errors in epistemology were having a serious impact on the ecology of the planet (Charlton, 2008, chapter 5). He was also continuing to explore a theme he first developed in his early anthropological studies, linking the aesthetic and the beautiful in nature and in human art with the possibility of enlightened ways of being. Creative activity and appreciation of art is a means of recovering grace, the reintegration of the 'diverse parts of the mind' – especially those we (maybe wrongly) call the conscious and the unconscious. And he increasingly began to link these two themes, suggesting that aesthetic engagement is an essential part of a path toward ecological wisdom, for the appreciation of the systemic quality of the natural world is primarily an aesthetic, rather than an intellectual experience.

So my delight in the systemic qualities that allows Aries to work so well lies as much in my appreciation of its elegance as in my understanding of the feedback loops. My feeling that it was 'oddly rewarding' to tack to and fro across the entrance to the Chenal du Four arises from the graceful interaction of Coral with the wild tidal waters we were encountering and our sense of being embedded in our natural context. And the move away from this grace to the pounding against the waves, while (perhaps) rationally necessary, was aesthetically disturbing.

One of Gregory Bateson most quoted phrases is 'The most important task today is, perhaps, to learn to think in the new way' (1972, p. 462) – and of course he means not just thinking intellectually but in the whole manner of our engagement with our world. Sailing can, of course, be an over-heroic attempt to conquer the waves. I hope I have shown that it can also be a way of healing pathologies of epistemology and beginning to rediscover the experience of grace.

References

Abbey, E., 1968. *Desert Solitaire: A Season in the Wilderness*. New York: Random House.

Bateson, G., 1972. *Steps to an Ecology of Mind*. San Francisco: Chandler.

——— 1979. *Mind and Nature: A Necessary Unity*. New York: E.P. Dutton.

Bateson, G. and Bateson, M.C., 1987. *Angels Fear: An Investigation into the Nature and Meaning of the Sacred*. London: Rider.

Bly, R., ed., 1990. *Iron John: A Book About Men*. Reading, MA: Addison Wesley.

Charlton, N., 2008. *Understanding Gregory Bateson: Mind, Beauty and the Sacred Earth*. Albany, NY: SUNY Press.

Harding, S.P., 2009. *Animate Earth*. Foxhole, Dartington: Green Books.

Marshall, J., 2004. Living systemic thinking: Exploring quality in first person research. *Action Research*, 2(3), pp. 309–29.

Marshall, J., Coleman, G. and Reason, P., 2011. *Leadership for Sustainability: An Action Research Approach*. Sheffield: Greenleaf.

Naess, A., 1990. *Ecology Community and Lifestyle: Outline of an Ecosophy*. Translated by D. Rotherberg. Cambridge: Cambridge University Press.

Reason, P., 2001. Learning and change through action research. In: J. Henry, ed., *Creative Management*. London: Sage Publications, pp. 182–94.

Reason, P., 2007. Education for ecology: Science, aesthetics, spirit and ceremony. *Management Learning*, 38(1), pp. 27–44.

Reason, P., Coleman, G., Ballard, D., Williams, M., Gearty, M., Bond, C., et al., 2009. *Insider Voices: Human Dimensions of Low Carbon Technology*. Bath: Centre for Action Research in Professional Practice, University of Bath. Available at: http://people.bath.ac.uk/mnspwr [accessed March 2014].

Chapter 8

In the Middle of the Deep Blue Sea

Karen Barbour

In this chapter I draw on feminist and phenomenological perspectives as I write of my embodied knowing as a woman of the Pacific, moving back and forth from personal and family experiences, to offer socio-cultural commentary. Multiple stories of travelling the seas to these islands permeate contemporary life in Aotearoa, for both indigenous Māori and for many Pākehā as well (those of European ancestry like myself).[1] Through these autoethnographic narratives, I represent the way in which our experiences of personal and cultural identity have been shaped by the sea and contribute to ways of moving through the world. My central focus is on how their experiences voyaging on the Pacific Ocean contributed to the changing sense of cultural and personal identity for women in my family. Far from the homelands of European ancestors, a new sense of self and cultural identity has grown in relationship with these southern islands and the deep blue of the Pacific Ocean.

1951: Mary

The familiarity of life in Sunnybank, Scotland, was behind them now, and a new life lay ahead in New Zealand, a land of opportunity. Mary wasn't sure what that meant exactly, but she'd agreed when Bobby decided to apply for a post as glassblower at Victoria University of Wellington. Certainly there were not too many opportunities for them in post-war Scotland. Food rationing was still continuing and, with a growing family, this was a challenge for Mary. Apparently the climate was better in New Zealand. But not too much else was clear to her about what the family was to experience. Being posted to many places around England and Scotland during her army service was one thing; it was still an enormous wrench for Mary leaving her parents, brothers and sister, and her homeland of Scotland. Of course, Bobby had put aside all his doubts and was ready, with the spirit of adventure, for the challenges ahead; he'd already been on half a dozen trips across to Ireland. Having read Somerset Maugham's stories of travel through the Pacific, Bobby seemed confident in what the journey might offer them.

---

1   Pākehā – a Māori language word originally used to refer to people of predominantly European heritage. See discussion in Barbour (2011) and King (1999).

He also had relatives established in Central Otago who encouraged them to consider this post. It was his urge for better prospects that was really driving this family migration, Mary conceded.

Setting sail from Southampton on board the passenger ship *Rangitoto* with their boys Robert and James, it was clear to Mary that they were somewhat fortunate to have had the university arrange their travel and accommodation. Their family was booked on A Deck, with cabins simply furnished with wooden furniture, comfortable and spacious enough for the few possessions they had brought and two wee boys to play. Little Robert loved the bunk beds, and despite hitting his head on the sprinkler outlet above his bed, he resolutely claimed the top bunk. Some families were separated, fathers sharing cabins on D Deck with other men, while mothers and their children squeezed in together. Mary observed that the standard of accommodation did seem to fall from A Deck down to D Deck, despite cabins all being the same class. Some of the single women who were part of the assisted immigration programme were less fortunate, squeezed into a cabin with six other strangers. Mary was thankful for these small mercies and relieved the family was accommodated comfortably. However, the seasickness set in, compounded by what she suspected was morning sickness.[2] In her quiet, stoic way she endured the sickness and the sense of loss as they travelled across the grey cold Atlantic, further and further away from all she had known.

Mary and Bobby were seated for meals at the Chief Engineer's table and it was a relief for Mary that two other women seated with them had small children and another was heavily pregnant. They were doctors' wives returning to New Zealand after holidays at 'home'. With watchful eyes, Mary and the other women tended to the children first. The women complimented her on her boys' table manners and how well they used their knives and forks for such wee lads. After the children were finished and taken to the nursery, Mary ate politely through the nausea. Bobby was somewhat bored by the female company for meals, but he relished the chance to talk with the Chief Engineer about the *Rangitoto*, discussing the intricacies of engines, electrics and navigation methods at sea with much enthusiasm.

Early in the voyage, as they crossed the dark Atlantic Ocean, there was lots of entertainment in the form of life-boat drills and instructions for emergencies. Mary paid close attention, prepared for any eventuality and mindful of the boys. But Mary thought the best part of life on board was the nursery and play area, where she could relax with the boys as they played together with other children on the wooden decks, protected from the spray and wind by canvas tied onto the railings. Some days the children played at trains with their chairs all lined up in a row and, while they played, Mary carefully phrased questions to the other mothers about life in New Zealand, to prepare for what was coming. As the weather improved, a slide was constructed for the children and later, when the heat got unbearable, a makeshift paddling pool too. Some days she even let the boys sit naked to cool

---

2 Grandma later confirmed she was in the early stages of pregnancy on board the Rangitoto.

off – when other disapproving adults were not around of course. These hours in the nursery and walking around the decks were highlights, the play keeping the boys happy and the fresh sea air helping her constant nausea. Once the routine of life on board was established, all looked forward to each highlight in otherwise long days. Sometimes she and Bobby joined the other passengers on the upper deck, enjoying the glorious sunsets on the sea, but they did not attend the dances. As much as Mary might have wanted to attend, Bobby was not a dancer.

Refuelling at Curaçao was a highlight and, with boys firmly in her grasp, Mary and the family went ashore to walk around the wharf and small town of Willemstad. Tidy streets, buildings in brown, red and green paint and palms, shrubs and bright tropical flowers were a welcome relief after weeks of blue-grey ocean and sky. Bobby excitedly spotted a humming bird hovering in flowers. Laughing as they found the land rolling under their feet, the boys were equally surprised when they were soaked to the skin in a sudden tropical deluge! A strange new experience to be wet in the heat, and only short-lived as, by the time they returned to the *Rangitoto*, their clothes were quite dry.

Travelling through the Panama Canal, everyone thought the canal was an engineering marvel and both Bobby and the Chief Engineer offered much commentary on the construction of the canal and the efficiency of the locks. But the temperature was uncomfortably high, the humidity oppressive and everyone was relieved to reach the Pacific Ocean at last.

The first sightings of flying fish skimming across the sparkling surface of the blue Pacific entranced the boys, and later Mary pointed out porpoises diving in the distance. Crossing the equator was a highlight with a special social occasion. Certificates were presented to the boys from King Neptune, along with a ceremonial splashing of water. However, one day on the placid blue ocean became much like the other for Mary, marked by nausea and the boys' games in the nursery. Boredom set in for many as the *Rangitoto* travelled further southwest across the Pacific and the temperature began to drop. But Bobby was always able to find someone to regale with stories and Mary was constantly busy with the boys. The only challenge came in the last leg with some engine trouble in rough seas and cold winds not far off the east coast of New Zealand. Even sailing into Wellington harbour was uneventful, the family waking up on a bright frosty morning to discover they had arrived at last, having left Scotland far behind them. So it was at last that Mary and Bobby stood on the decks with two trunks, a hatbox, a handbag and the boys, searching for Cousin Gladys in the crowd on the Wellington dock. Stepping ashore onto solid ground, a new life had begun.[3]

_____

3   My Scottish paternal grandparents, Mary and Bobby, arrived in Wellington in August 1951 with my father, Robert, and uncle, Jimmy. Writing my grandmother's experiences was based on old photos of the children on board, my Aunt Sarah's recollections of her mother's stories, and brief transcripts from my grandmother's diary, as well as small excerpts from my grandfather's book about their decision to migrate (Barbour, 1993). Over cups of tea, my uncle Jim recalled more family stories and Aunty Chris checked dates and names in

≈ ≈ ≈

Aotearoa New Zealand was settled initially by Polynesian peoples sailing vast distances across Te Moana Nui a Kiwa (the Pacific Ocean) from their Pacific Island homes. In waves of successive voyages, many great waka haurua (traditional Polynesian double-hull sailing boats) arrived on these shores, centuries before Abel Tasman or Captain James Cook.[4] It was ngā iwi Māori (Māori tribes) as the tangata whenua (people of the land), who met the next wave of immigrants from Europe. In 1840, a treaty between representatives of the queen of England and some of the Rangatira (chiefs) of ngā iwi Māori set in motion a unique story of contact, conflict and eventually compensation for the harm caused in the 'land-grabbing' efforts of European settlers. Early in this story of contact and conflict, a treaty – Te Titiri o Waitangi (The Treaty of Waitangi) – was established between indigenous ngā iwi Māori and British colonialists (Orange, 1987). Dishonoured in its early years, the treaty nevertheless became a founding partnership document in the story of Aotearoa. As a founding document, the treaty continues to allow ngā iwi Māori to seek redress and reconciliation for injustices that occurred in the past and are presently occurring today.

In recent times, Aotearoa has been described as a colonial settlement country and these southern islands were further populated under subsequent governments through a number of deliberate programmes to bring people from Britain, Scotland and Ireland (Spoonley and Bedford, 2012). Under Te Tiriti o Waitangi, forms of assisted migration by boat began in the 1800s and continued until the 1970s – the three-month voyage eventually reducing to five weeks as technology improved (Brooking and Coleman, 2003; McCarthy, 2003; Richards, 2003; Spoonley and Bedford, 2012). In particular, 'Scotland possessed a long tradition of migration, indeed a culture of migration, and was almost always a net exporter of people ... This tendency continued well into the twentieth century' (Richards, 2003, p. 37). Scots became approximately 21 per cent of immigrants in Aotearoa in the nineteenth century (Brooking, 2003). Following World War II, more Polynesian peoples emigrated to these southern islands and, more recently, peoples from Asia

---

her genealogical files. On sending the draft version of this story around the family, small details were added from various family members. However, my grandmother herself spoke and wrote very little about her experiences. I have tried to imagine what she might have felt. In addition, other women's stories of migration from the same era have informed my imaginings (Dean, 2010; Hutching, 1999; Ryan, 2010). (The Rangitoto was a New Zealand Shipping Company cargo-passenger liner with one class accommodation for 436 passengers and refrigerated cargo. Information and photos can be found at: http://www.ssmaritime.com/nzsc2.htm.)

    4   Settlement dates and stories of Aotearoa are varied. Some iwi (tribes) believe that it was the Polynesian sailor Kupe who first discovered our islands but accounts differ as to when settlement occurred – between 925 and 1300 AD (Irwin, 2006). Dutch explorer Abel Tasman found our islands in 1642 and Captain James Cook circumnavigated and charted the islands in 1769 (Howe, 2006).

(Liu, 2005). However, these recent migrations were more commonly undertaken through increasingly accessible air travel.

Paul Spoonley and Richard Bedford (2012) comment about immigrants from the United Kingdom arriving on boats from the mid-1800s onwards:

> What is intriguing about the New Zealand story was that immigrants chose a country that was almost as far from Britain as it was possible to get ... This often meant a difficult and long sea voyage, settling in a frontier society with little that was similar to Europe and little or no on-going contact with family left behind. In relation to modern voluntary migration, it is both intriguing and impressive that such a migration was contemplated, especially when the means of transport were far from comfortable or safe. (Spoonley and Bedford, 2012, p. 10)

Even in the early 1950s when my Scottish family immigrated voluntarily, the journey was long and tedious, although perhaps not as unsafe as for previous immigrants. They had few expectations of seeing the families they left behind and, as Tom Brooking comments, there was a sense of a 'Scottish desire to merge as quickly as possible into the new society' (2003, p. 11). Brooking argues further that 'Scots did help to make and shape New Zealand culture but in subtle and nuanced rather than obvious and spectacular ways; this seems a thoroughly Scottish kind of contribution' (2003, p. 59). Regardless of any general desire of Scottish immigrants to both merge into and contribute to shaping culture in Aotearoa, my grandmother Mary wrote 'home' to her family every week. My grandmother, like generations of female Scottish immigrants to Aotearoa before her, reluctantly left 'home', even though there were continuing economic challenges in Scotland (McLean, 2003). For me, the first of a new generation of the family born in Aotearoa, nostalgic stories of 'home' and of Scottish relatives were told and retold – an essential part of my grandparents' contribution to my upbringing. My grandfather introduced me to the poet Robbie Burns, the value of gardening and conservation, and the joys of 'grandfather clocks', and my grandmother to kippers, old china, Scottish naming traditions and Scottish songs she played on the organ. Clearly embedded with our family culture was the strong Scottish emphasis and value placed on education for myself and my sisters, along with these other remnants of cultural and literary traditions (Brooking, 2003). Most important to them, I sensed, was that I understood where they had come from and that I knew my family genealogy.

However, the stories my grandparents told were of a 'home' I did not know myself. When I finally undertook the Kiwi 'rite of passage' – the big overseas experience or 'OE' (Bell, 2002) – Scotland did not feel like home (Barbour, 2011). I did trace my genealogy as I travelled around Scotland, locating gravestones, the houses each of my grandparents were born in, and meeting the few distant relatives remaining. But I did not have a deep embodied sense of knowing Scotland as home. It was a land, a genealogy and a culture apart from me and my home was Aotearoa.

Until recently, I knew relatively little about the journey my grandparents took from Scotland or why, or about the Scottish culture of migration (Richards, 2003). I appreciate now that they chose to follow my grandfather's job offer and likely were influenced by a range of other factors. Angela McCarthy comments that often 'New Zealand was chosen because it was considered small and comfortable, friends or relatives were settled there, it was similar to the United Kingdom and it was cheap to get to' (2003, p. 124). What I did experience as a child, and continue to experience now, is the sense of distance; the literal distance across the oceans to the other side of the world, but even more so the distance between the traditions and cultures of Scotland and what I know of as my 'culture' in New Zealand. My sense of cultural identity was built out of a 'distant' cultural background and my personal identity built on a contingent and partial sense of belonging. And always the vast oceans between here and there.

1969: Mary Jean

St John, New Brunswick was a cold, grey and bleak backdrop as Mary Jean and Pat waited for their freighter, the *Wharanui*, to load. Icy streets led uphill from the harbour past grimy, derelict shops. There wasn't much to do. The two cousins watched *Winnie the Pooh* playing at the only movie theatre, a source of laughter in the days before the freighter loaded and ventured out to sea. They sailed at last on New Year's Day, leaving behind the great frozen land and heading south, down the east coast of the Canada and the United States. The small portholes of the freighter offered only glimpses of slate-grey water and sky, and fresh air came in short icy blasts from the hatch. Mary Jean and Pat struggled with the confinement and close company but began to adjust to the daily routine, centred on meals and *tiffin* (afternoon snacks) with the officers and three other passengers.

Mary Jean discarded the pills her father had recommended for seasickness. The steady thrumming of the freighter engines resonated through her body and the occasional sensations of the water under the solid cargo freighter were uncomfortable initially. These sensations became familiar as the days passed. Time was lost in solitary hours reading, punctuated by the humour of their small group of officers and passengers, and accented by social sing-a-longs. Mary Jean was reluctant at first to bring out her new guitar, still mastering the 12 strings and unsure about what people would want to sing.

About three days into the long voyage to New Zealand, the grey began to slowly change to blue – both the sea and the sky – as they slipped through the Caribbean and the Gulf of Mexico, heading for the Isthmus of Panama. For Mary Jean, her school history lessons came alive as she imagined their stop in Panama, remembering stories of the Spaniards seeking Aztec gold, the mules that dragged ocean liners up the canal and the men who dug out the holding lake and locks.

The day onshore in Panama shocked their senses. Already used to the quiet of the *Wharanui*, the noise, heat, crowds, colours and constant action assaulted

Mary Jean and Pat and with relief they found a cool, dark bar, one that Somerset Maugham must surely have visited and featured in his stories. The overhead fan and rum punch took their toll when the girls eventually emerged, hit by the glare and heat again, but they were anxious to make the ship before it left without them. Mary Jean did not want to get left behind. She knew it was still a long way to New Zealand and to the two-year teaching post she was to begin. Fortunately, given the heat, the journey through the remaining canal locks passed quickly.

And then the Pacific Ocean stretched out ahead of them, an unimaginably large expanse of shifting blue, green, jade and purple, with days of tropical sun and gentle rolling seas under the ship. Time stood still for the first time in Mary Jean's life, offering the opportunity for meaningful conversations and friendships to develop. Her personal anxiety gave way to enjoyment in the prevailing sense of humour on board, an outcome of life spent in the merchant navy. The days were full of banter and spontaneous comedy, like a form of subtle theatre sports. Music and books were shared and discussed. Gordon Lightfoot and Mary Jean's guitar met the Seekers on vinyl.

The days held enough hours to learn to play chess and capture the ship's architecture in watercolours. Mary Jean spent hours trying to paint the shifting shades of the sea and sky too, committing moments of the journey to paper and paint. Visits to the bridge offered lessons in navigation by the stars and sextant and, one evening, Mary Jean was shown an old chart still in use, originally drawn and signed by Captain James Cook!

It turned out that four weeks were not enough. On arrival in Auckland, Mary Jean's life quickened again to routines based on hourly changes – 30 teenagers per class, six classes per day, weekend sport and recovery, and then all over again. And the familiar anxiety. But that journey left a trace for Mary Jean – a lived experience of calmer, deep blue seas.[5]

ᕔ   ᕔ   ᕔ

Canada shares with Aotearoa colonial settlement stories of Scottish and Irish immigrants travelling by boat to far-off shores (Brooking and Coleman, 2003; Liu, 2005; Spoonley and Bedford, 2012). My mother's Scottish and Irish ancestors undertook the arduous voyage across the grey Atlantic Ocean to settle in Canada in the 1800s. Generations on, she also wanted to travel and, motivated by the opportunity to take up a teaching post in New Zealand, she ventured to the other

---

5 My mother, Mary Jean, initially recalled only snippets of her journey to New Zealand, arriving at the port of Auckland in February 1969 after four weeks onboard the *Wharanui*. But that sense of having time to herself was significant and, after discussions, she wrote a short story for me. I have edited her story to create the narrative above, aiming to reconstruct something of Mum's adventure as a recently qualified teacher eager to travel the world.

side of the world. Inspired by the novels of Somerset Maugham, she chose to travel by boat rather than by air and, in particular, by freighter rather than cruise ship. So instead of participating in a pattern of immigration as my grandmother did, my mother set off on her own adventure – one that shaped her sense of self and offered a respite from a conservative culture of work and achievement in those weeks on the sea.

Like my Scottish grandparents' stories, my mother's stories of 'home' were also of a place I did not know and people I have met only once or twice. Travelling around Canada visiting family members helped me appreciate the ways in which Scottish and Irish cultures and values had morphed into this particular contemporary Canadian extended family. But again I felt apart, distanced, missing the ever-changing weather, the rugged green landscape and the island experience of Aotearoa. And I felt lost, unable to sense the sea in the vastness of the frozen land.

1998: Karen

Unnervingly, the horizon is continually shifting, rising closer to the heavy dark clouds looming above me and then dropping down as we move through the grey-green trough of the wave. Gripping the cool of the metal under my fingers, legs spread wide for balance, I concentrate on trying to ride the momentum of the ocean, feeling the yacht lift, almost surfing down the swell, and then slow as it is pushed by the wind in the sail to the top of the next swell. Knowing we are dragging a drogue behind the yacht helps me feel a little more confident about our stability on the ocean, but I am still finding my sea legs. Eyes flicking from the storm sail to check our northerly heading on the compass and back to the unsteady horizon, I feel like I am hanging on to the helm more for personal confidence than any sure sense of command of our little yacht Sun Seeker. Glimmers of a sunset sneak through the mass of clouds, little moments of gold in a world otherwise grey and threatening. Thick locks of hair whip around my neck with an additional gust and I am glad for the small comfort of my fully zipped wet weather gear. We encounter rough seas and stormy weather en route to Fiji from Auckland – not quite what I had imagined when I eagerly accepted the offer to crew with friends on the Sun Seeker.

Little in my recent experiences of cruising in the blue-green Hauraki Gulf between islands over summer holidays had prepared me for stormy open seas of the Pacific Ocean – I barely knew the ropes. Forty-eight hours of sailing downwind in gusting 40-knot winds and accompanying big seas had thrown me metaphorically in the deep end. We had been sleeping as best we could between watches in damp layers of polypropylene, lurching against the canvas lee cloths we'd hung to stop us rolling out of the bunks. Below deck, two of my companions are currently trying to sleep in preparation for their night watches and my loyal friend, Ruth, knowing my lack of confidence on the helm, is attempting to prepare another cup of sweet tea and round of encouraging words. Aware of the additional pressure I am putting on the others by needing a companion for watches, I've been preparing most of our meals for the last four days, legs braced against the galley walls and struggling last night with nausea while trying to chop onions for our pasta meal. Eventually I'd been forced up for fresh air and threw up overboard. My companions were to follow me in 'feeding the fish' too – we'd barely kept down one square meal in two days, even with sea-sickness pills. The next meal might be crackers, cheese and tea for us all I suspected.

Two hours later I crawl into my bunk without eating, grateful as John takes his watch and the Sun Seeker sails determinedly through the dark. I have a few moments of imagining I am at home in my warm bed. But I know my desire for adventure and new experiences brought me here and there certainly is no option to be anywhere else right now. I can't get off the yacht after all. I am here in our 'three-mile wide puddle' as Diane describes it, sailing somewhat precariously in a 43-foot sloop in the vast Pacific Ocean.

I don't sleep much despite being tired and it's not long before I hear Diane reporting in by short wave radio with our position as arranged. Listening in the dark, far from anyone else in this lonely ocean, we hear that a big winter storm has just hit New Zealand. Diane discovers, as she marks our GPS reading on the chart and compares it to the faxed weather report, that we are just on the edge of the storm. So, no rest for us and no likely respite from the elements at all. Even though the little Sun Seeker is fitted with a wind vane and electronic self-steering mechanisms, at this point of sail and in these conditions, self-steering is no use at all. We must actively sail the yacht downwind, not just keep watch, and hope the weather doesn't get worse.

As day breaks the rain sets in, becoming torrential during my early watch, and all four of us are awake on deck, anxious as the wind pushes us, soaked and exhausted, towards nightfall. We shorten our daytime watches to three hours each and so the time for each person on the helm seems to roll on quickly with little rest in between. My respect for Diane's skill and enthusiasm as a helmswomen grows even more today. Slightly built and in her mid-50s, she stands determinedly as sporadic waves sweep over the stern and the rain constantly batters her throughout the afternoon watch. Short brown hair plastered over her forehead, she shouts thanks to me through the wet for the hot tea I manage to prepare, adding 'Just remember, this old girl is not called the Sun Seeker for nothing. She loves a good battle with the elements when there is cruising in the sun to follow. She's a hardy girl Karen!' I imagine the same is true of Diane herself – a fun-loving restaurant owner who lives for these annual winter voyages to the islands.

Sitting cramped with Ruth under the partial shelter of the cockpit, I now know for sure that I smell, and something unexpected and unifying seems to be happening to my hair underneath the soggy woollen hat I've barely removed since we left Little Barrier Island off the Auckland coast. I stop just short of being miserable, remembering my commitment to adventuring – surely this sort of challenge is what life is all about. Unbidden, my grandmother's voice echoes in my thoughts – 'these things were sent to try us dear'. It's little comfort.

Happily, the wind drops to 30 knots just before dark and we venture forward on deck with our safety lines to drop the storm sail and stow it before hoisting the mainsail, reefing in the main as a precaution in case the wind picks up again. We pull in the drogue too and, feeling a little more comfortable with the boat's movement, I assemble a more substantial meal of tuna and olives, potatoes and coleslaw for us all before my next turn on the helm. But so much for glasses of wine with dinner, leisurely fishing and watching sunsets in light clothing.

Filling me in on the marine radio updates, John tells me of the reports from other yachties and fishing boats between Auckland and Fiji, and it seems that we are the envy of others for our latitude and speed. 'Hey we're outrunning the storm', John says optimistically, seeming to revel in the ocean's challenge in a way I am not. Enduring would be a more apt description of my attitude and perhaps of Ruth too – coughing and sniffing with the remnants of a winter cold. At least she has done this voyage before with her brother, John, and his partner, Diane, and she knows the reward at the end. John and I chat cheerfully, even laughing together as we make it to a speedy 11 knots down a swell, the yacht more comfortable under John's guidance as he takes over the watch. He sends me below and I eventually catch a little sleep.

At the change of watch during the night I head up on deck to much calmer seas and lighter winds. With relief, I help Diane hoist the mainsail to its full height. We unfurl the headsail too, swinging it out on the opposite side of the mast from the headsail with a spar to keep our speed in the welcome lighter winds. 'This is called running with the jib to windward, or a "goosewing"' Diane explains and I make yet another mental note of new sailing terminology. Diane stays with me for half an hour, concludes with obvious relief that I can manage alone and leaves me to the helm.

And, wonder of wonders, in the dark before dawn, I do my first solo watch. As the skies clear and the clouds become wispier drifting below the stars, the half-moon even makes an appearance. I ride the swells, body responding to the motion with ease, and I find myself singing under my breath, repeating the chorus to a Kiwi song – 'anchor me ... anchor me ... in the middle of the deep blue sea ....'[6] As the dawn approaches, I reflect that maybe this isn't simply an endurance test after all.

Dawn breaks on smoother blue seas and much clearer skies, delighting me with a spectacular gold that sets the horizon alight and gilds the remaining clouds. Golden light touches the rippling water and reflects off the white of the hull and sails. A growing sense of elation builds in my belly and ripples through my body until I am smiling proudly at Ruth as she relieves me of my duties. With renewed enthusiasm I cook bacon, eggs, tomatoes and toast in the galley. Sharing breakfast

6   *Anchor Me* is a popular New Zealand song written in 1994 by The Muttonbirds. A new version was released in 2005 by Greenpeace, in recognition of the anniversary of the sinking of the Rainbow Warrior protest ship in Auckland Harbour in 1985 (King, 2003).

and my gratitude with my companions as we sit together on deck, our spirits all lift. I begin the process of putting the cabin to rights, collecting waterlogged wet gear to hang until we reach land, airing damp sleeping bags and mopping the water that inevitably sloshed down the hatch during the worst of the weather. I cajole medicine into Ruth, locate dry clothes for her and push her into a bunk at the end of her duties. Up on deck with John and Diane, we decide to let Ruth sleep and recover until we make landfall, agreeing to extend our watches to cover her. We even pull out some CDs and the music adds to our lightening moods. As evening approaches, John takes the opportunity to explain use of the sextant for navigation, surprising me with the accuracy of his measurements when we compare them to the GPS readings. Gazing up at the Southern Cross in the night sky, the last of my tension and worry eases. And so the remaining days and nights of sailing pass, with longer turns on the helm and smoother sailing.

Gazing out across the brilliant blue water early one morning, I suddenly think I spy land on the horizon. Yelling with excitement, I hear John scrambling for binoculars below and he rushes up on deck to check my sighting. 'Landfall!' he confirms. It is a miracle, I think, to have arrived where we intended in Fiji after travelling about 1,200 nautical miles across the Pacific.

And so it is, later in the day, that we sail quietly into Suva, past people fishing, tug boats and even a few surfers, and come alongside the dock. While we wait for John to gain clearance from Fiji Customs, we slowly restore order on the yacht and personal composure, in the warmth and sunlight. On changing out of smelly clothes and washing properly for the first time in days, I discover that my hair has matted unhelpfully under my damp woollen hat, and I reluctantly begin cutting out the worst of the knots. Shorter, my remaining hair curls around my face and I feel lighter and somehow renewed. Ruth makes it up on deck, much happier for the sleep and the medicine. She, Diane and I worry about whether the Customs inspectors will discover and confiscate our wine supplies – none of our carefully planned stores having been consumed on our voyage here. But we are cleared by the Customs Officer with a simple greeting from the dock and so we furl the sails and motor directly around the port to The Royal Suva Yacht Club.

Suva looks pretty idyllic and welcoming over the lines of wet clothing I peg securely to the rigging. Palm trees sway in the light evening breeze against lush green vegetation – a perfect contrast to the blue waters. Completing our tidying by stowing the storm sail in its bag, wrapping the main in its cover and unloading the dingy and oars, we make it ashore for a real dinner in the relative comfort of the yacht club. My mum's relieved voice echoes down the phone as I let her know we've arrived safely in Fiji. Not surprisingly, we sleep late into the next day, wakening on board Sun Seeker to discover that our trusty yacht has truly lived up to her name.[7]

---

7   Some years ago I began writing this account of a sailing trip from Auckland to Fiji that I took over 15 years ago. Using my journal notes, photos and recollections, I attempted to recapture my experiences. In developing the story further for this chapter, I have changed the names and details of the yacht and those on board with me.

Three Generations and More

In many obvious ways it is the sea that connects our three stories, the way our identities as individuals and as families are located in these stories of adventures on the sea, whether adventures relished, chosen or endured. I dived into an adventure, relishing the challenge of ocean, sailing with naïve optimism. I also had a nostalgic desire to make the return journey by boat across the Pacific that both my mother and grandmother had taken. I wanted to participate in the Pākehā cultural practice of 'the big OE', the journey back to the home of the ancestors (Bell, 2002).

My mother, in the spirit of the 1960s, chose her own adventure and found peace and calm for herself in that liminal time as she journeyed from one side of the world to the other. My grandmother, like countless women past, came to the islands of Aotearoa from so far across the ocean. Leaving behind everything she had known for the promise of new opportunities that her husband sought, she endured the voyage through grief and illness. Still further back in time, my partner's paternal great-great-grandmother sailed from Scotland into Dunedin harbour, making the journey on her own to join her family and her husband. There are few stories remembered now, but my partner recalls hearing that the sea was so rough in the harbour that the ship could not actually come in to dock for weeks. He recalls how his great-great-grandfather bravely rowed out in a dingy to fetch her. What that end to the difficulty of the journey from the United Kingdom must have been like for a woman on her own, I can only begin to imagine.

And many centuries ago, in their adventurous quest and search for new opportunities, the sons and daughters of Hawaiiki sailed further and further south across the Pacific until they discovered Aotearoa. My partner's and son's Polynesian ancestors sailed on a waka haurua (a traditional Polynesian voyaging sail boat) across Te Moana nui a Kiwa. One of the stories passed down was that of Muriwai, the elder sister of the captain of the Mataatua waka. It is said that, reaching their destination on the shore of a wide bay, the men on board went ashore to survey the land. It was Muriwai who was left to haul the Mataatua waka up onto the shore when the outgoing tide threatened to drag it back to sea.[8]

The descendants of Muriwai, like the descendants of all those on the migrating Polynesian waka, were here when Captain James Cook came ashore from the ship Endeavour. They witnessed, resisted, fought and (arguably) eventually made some sort of peace with those Tall Ships full of Europeans. In some ways then, all of us now come from people who have made journeys across the Pacific Ocean with similar intentions, similar dreams of adventure and desires to explore new places to call home.

---

8   Muriwai 'cried out, "Ka whakatāne au i ahau!" [I shall acquit myself like a man!]. She saved the canoe and immortalised her actions in the name of Whakatāne' (Walker, 2012, p. 2).

In collecting and writing these richly descriptive, personal and family stories, I participate in autoethnographic research, aiming firstly to engage readers in our embodied experiences of being in the middle of the deep blue sea. Our embodied ways of knowing foster understandings that are based in personal sensory experience, and, together with knowledge gained from many other sources, informs our subsequent experiences and choices throughout our lives (Barbour, 2011). Beyond sharing stories of lived experiences, autoethnography also offers a context for shifting from writing about personal experiences to writing reflexively and critically towards understanding wider socio-cultural issues (Ellis, 2004; Richardson, 2000, 2005). Writing critically, I connect my own personal and family stories to shared experiences and issues faced by immigrants and in the development of cultural identities. Dealing with grief and change, new geographical and social environments, cultural encounters with others, retaining, letting go or transforming social values and practices, finding a place to call home, articulating the emergence of new identities – I suggest these are shared processes experienced by immigrants seeking to understand their changing personal identity and sense of cultural belonging. For myself, part of an emerging culture of Pākehā New Zealanders, discussion about values, practices and identities involves engaging in understanding my Scottish and Canadian heritages as well as indigenous Māori ways of being (Barbour, 2011). Part of this process is the journey back to the home of my ancestors. In experiencing our differences from those in Scotland, Canada and elsewhere, our Pākehā cultural identities become clearer (Bell, 2002; Liu, 2005). These understandings come out of living, drawing on embodied ways of knowing in developing new ways of being and new relationships with the land, the sea and the peoples of Aotearoa.

Epilogue

Light dances off the waters of the Waitemata harbour, the bright blue green of the Pacific Ocean a perfect colour to highlight the stunning views in front of us. Today we join thousands of other people on the water and waterfront to farewell a remarkable fleet of Tall Ships from Europe, the Netherlands, Scotland, Australia and New Zealand. The steady breeze of this October morning fills the sails of the Tall Ships, recreational yachts and waka haurua – full too with the stories of our people today and of yesteryear. Having bought tickets to board a small tugboat, the William C. Daldy, for this special day, we sit together revelling in this moment in all its splendour – imagining the past, sharing family stories and our own experiences on boats. My mother, Mary, concludes, counting back through the years of service of this tugboat, that this would have been the little tug that brought the freighter, the Wharanui, into Auckland when she arrived in New Zealand after the long journey from Canada. Musing quietly she reflects that, 'After 45 years, a walk around the harbour, the sound of a ship's horn, the sight of a chart and sextant, the feel of the sea through the soles of my feet on board a boat ... even now time can slow down enough to lose myself to the Tall Ships and this tugboat'. Her comment rests within me as we lose ourselves in our own reflections.

Later, seated happily between my partner, my mother and I, our son asks many questions about boats, sails, ropes, ship horns and destinations, all leading to the inevitable question – 'Mama, can I go on one of those boats one day?' Catching the smiles between my mother and my partner, I reply, 'Yes, my love. Maybe when you are bigger you can sail one of those Tall Ships'. And my partner adds, 'pērā ana, ki oū tipuna'.[9]

References

Barbour, K.N., 2011. *Dancing Across the Page: Narrative and Embodied Ways of Knowing*. Bristol, UK: Intellect Books.

Barbour, R., 1993. *Farewell to Farming*. South Church, Durham: The Pentland Press.

Bell, C., 2002. The big 'OE': Young New Zealander travellers as secular pilgrims. *Tourist Studies*, 2(2), pp. 143–58.

Brooking, T., 2003. Sharing out the haggis: The special Scottish contribution to New Zealand history. In: T. Brooking and J. Coleman, eds, *The Heather and the Fern: Scottish Migration and New Zealand Settlement*. Dunedin, New Zealand: University of Otago Press, pp. 49–65.

Brooking, T. and Coleman, J., eds, 2003. *The Heather and the Fern: Scottish Migration and New Zealand Settlement*. Dunedin, New Zealand: University of Otago Press.

Dean, R.K., ed., 2010. *From the Other End of the World*. Hamilton, New Zealand: Print House.

Ellis, C., 2004. *Ethnographic I: A Methodological Novel about Autoethnography*. Walnut Creek, CA: AltaMira Press.

Howe, K.R., ed., 2006. *Vaka Moana. Voyages of the Ancestors – The Discovery and Settlement of the Pacific*. Auckland, New Zealand: David Bateman Ltd.

Hutching, M., 1999. *Long Journey for Sevenpence: Assisted Migration to New Zealand from the United Kingdom 1947–1975*. Wellington, New Zealand: Victoria University Press.

Irwin, G., 2006. Voyaging and settlement. In: K.R. Howe, ed., *Vaka Moana. Voyages of the Ancestors – The Discovery and Settlement of the Pacific*. Auckland, New Zealand: David Bateman Ltd, pp. 54–91.

King, M., 1999. *Being Pākehā Now: Reflections and Recollections of a White Native*. Auckland, New Zealand: Penguin Books.

——— 2003. *The Penguin History of New Zealand*. Auckland, New Zealand: Penguin.

---

9   In te reo Māori, my partner adds that our son can sail like his ancestors from both sides of his family, who sailed the Pacific Ocean before him.

Liu, J., 2005. History and identity: A system of checks and balances for Aotearoa/ New Zealand. In: J. Liu, T. McCreanor, T. McIntosh and T. Teaiwa, eds, *New Zealand Identities*. Wellington, New Zealand: Victoria University Press, pp. 1–19.

McCarthy, A., 2003. 'For spirit and adventure': Personal accounts of Scottish migration to New Zealand, 1921–1961. In: T. Brooking and J. Coleman, eds, *The Heather and the Fern: Scottish Migration and New Zealand Settlement*. Dunedin, New Zealand: University of Otago Press, pp. 117–32.

McLean, R., 2003. Reluctant leavers? Scottish women and emigration in the mid-nineteenth century. In: T. Brooking and J. Coleman, eds, *The Heather and the Fern: Scottish Migration and New Zealand Settlement*. Dunedin, New Zealand: University of Otago Press, pp. 103–32.

Orange, C., 1987. *The Treaty of Waitangi*. Wellington, New Zealand: Allen & Unwin.

Richards, E., 2003. The last of the clan and other Highland emigrants. In: T. Brooking and J. Coleman, eds, *The Heather and the Fern: Scottish Migration and New Zealand Settlement*. Dunedin, New Zealand: University of Otago Press, pp. 33–47.

Richardson, L., 2000. New writing practices in qualitative research. *Sociology of Sport Journal*, 17, pp. 5–20.

——— 2005. Writing: A method of inquiry. In: N.K. Denzin and Y.S. Lincoln, eds, *The Sage Handbook of Qualitative Research* (2nd ed.). Thousand Oaks, CA: Sage, pp. 959–78.

Ryan, S.H., 2010. *Voyage of the 'Captain Cook' 1952*. Napier, New Zealand: A Cunningham.

Spoonley, P. and Bedford, R., 2012. *Welcome to our World? Immigration and the Reshaping of New Zealand*. Auckland, New Zealand: Dunmore.

Walker, R., 2012. Te Whakatōhea – Ancestors. Available at: http://www.TeAra.govt.nz/en/te-whakatohea/page-2 [accessed 24 February 2014].

Chapter 9

Standing then Floating:
Searching for a Sense of Sea-Place
on the South Coast of Australia

Brian Wattchow

Proem

I was born within sight of the ocean, on the southern coast of Australia. The coast and sea have provided a sense of 'home' all of my life. Even when work, study and travel has left me landlocked for years, I could hear the surf pounding beyond the hard edge of the horizon and feel the distant pull of the tide. In writing this chapter I returned to the sea once again, to a small coastal park I have visited many times. One morning I sat in camp, opened my journal and began to write. Questions poured out onto the pages alongside raw descriptions of my immediate surrounds – a tidal stream of consciousness, if you like. After a while I could resist the pull of the nearby ocean no longer. I got up, walked down the narrow sandy track to the small sand dune at the top of the beach. Once there I paused for some time to take in the scene, to conduct the 'old business' of looking deeply at what lay before me. I then stripped off my clothes, pulled on a pair of bathers and walked across the beach to stand on the very brink of land and water. Once again I paused briefly to reflect upon deeper meanings of the coastal edge and the sea in Australian national identity. Finally, I entered the sea. I moved into the water, lay back and pushed off from land, until I was floating – immersed, suspended, buoyed up by the ocean – and waited. I waited for the boundaries of my skin to dissolve, for body, mind, narrative and sea to become osmotic. I waited for the oceanic feeling of connection. It was the first day of spring and the sea was still bone-achingly cold. This humble act, the first swim of the season, is an experience shared by almost every Australian. It has qualities that are physical and metaphorical, sensual and spiritual. It is a rite of passage. It involves departure, an act of faith and eventual return. It is an act of great symbolism that says: 'This is where I belong. I am home.' For it is the land's edge, which is constantly at play with the ocean's tides and surf, that provides a sense of place for many of us.

Watching

It is early morning, low tide. Sunlight begins to filter through the coastal banksias and tee-tree scrub that surrounds my campsite in Bear Gully, a small regional park on the south coast of Victoria, Australia. I have a steaming cup of coffee in my hands as I listen to the voice speaking through my small transistor radio. It is the weather forecaster from the local Royal Australian Air Force (RAAF) base in Sale, a large regional town about 100 kilometres away. 'There will be light winds, a few showers and daytime temperatures will reach a maximum of 14 degrees [Celsius]. It is currently zero in the hills.' The radio rests on a copy of William J. Dakin's (1952) classic and quintessential guide, Australian Seashores: A Guide for the Beach-Lover, the Naturalist, the Shore Fisherman, and the Student. It should be compulsory reading throughout the length and breadth of the land. It is funny how something as simple as a weather forecast, an old book and a mug of coffee can shape what one does and thinks in the day ahead. It is still early and cold. I pull my beanie, a tight-fitting woollen hat, down over my ears and feel the warmth stored in my down jacket. The cold has driven other campers away and I have the place to myself.

Clouds are gathering on the granite peaks of Wilson's Promontory – Bishop, Vereker, Singapore and Oberon – before tapering off to the east. The wind behind the clouds, a south-westerly, also pushes a line of steepening swells across and into Waratah Bay, a 30-kilometre sweep of light-coloured sand that connects Bear Gully to 'the Prom' via the narrow Yanakie Isthmus. Both cloud and swell are the result of persistent low-pressure systems that come, like spinning tops, out of the polar ice cap and Antarctic waters far to the south.

As I sip my coffee I ask myself: Why do I feel so at home on the south coast of Australia? Why do I come here in times of stress and fatigue to be revitalised? What draws me back, again and again? I know that I intuitively recognise the weather patterns, the geology, the fish and bird species and the plant life. They are all familiar to me. Such knowledge has been accrued over a lifetime of visitation and is lodged in every cell of my body. I have walked, paddled, swum, fished, camped and explored a great deal of the 5,000 km southern coastline, from Cape Hicks in the east to Cape Leeuwin in the west. But really, I know it best through deep encounters with particular places.

The Australian land historian William Lines (2001) suggests that this way of knowing the world is natural and available to us all.

> Our bodies and interactions with the world provide the basis for our everyday metaphysics, our sense of what is real. I learned about Australia through my body, through what I could sit on, touch, taste, see, breathe, smell and move

within. My surroundings gave me my reality. My corporeality incorporated the world's corporeality. (Lines, 2001, p. 65)

These places on the south coast of Australia are like family to me. I was born in the South Australian tuna fishing township of Port Lincoln. Yet much of my childhood was landlocked as my father moved between schools in the mid-north of South Australia. As a teacher and school principal, he and my mother would load my brother, sister and me into the car and hook on the caravan every school holiday period throughout my childhood. So, for six weeks every summer, I lived a coast-life at Port Elliot, south of Adelaide, where we children were simply let loose into the outside world and filled our days with swimming, surfing and playing games on the beach. We were also regular visitors during other holidays to Port Vincent on the Yorke Peninsula in winter – a time of woollen jackets, beanies, fishing and beachcombing. When I moved interstate and started work as an outdoor educator, I quickly sought out coastal locations in Victoria where I could run bushwalking, sea kayaking and snorkelling camps. The Nooramunga Marine Reserve, the wild coast west of Portland, Wilson's Promontory, and family holidays to the shack at Lake Tyers with my wife and our children all extended my ties to the southern coast as an adult.

The billy boils again and I resurface from my reflections. I toss in tealeaves and watch them instantly bleed their tannin stain into the hot water. They settle and I pour another brew – hot, milky and sweet. A cup of tea in a quiet campsite leads to deeper thoughts about the past. How would I tell someone my story of the coast and the sea? Does the narrative only come from those particular sites with which I am familiar? There is more to it, I am sure, than my own layered experiences of these coastal places. My sea story is more than the immediacy of my encounters with the sea and coast. I am also part of a larger narrative, a more confusing and complex story. Australian identity itself seems to somehow wax and wane between the inland and the edge, between the red desert and the blue sea. To reflect upon the meaning of the coastal edge and the sea immediately brings to mind issues to do with land and sea ownership, reconciliation between Indigenous inhabitants and European colonisers, and the different expectations of multi-ethnic groups. All stake various claims to the beach, the coast and the sea. There are serious environmental challenges as well. Urbanisation, climate change, rising sea levels, pollution, over-fishing, are all changing the southern coast and the seas that send waves crashing upon its shores.

But these reflections will have to wait. I grab a towel, my tea, and head for the beach. I find a sheltered spot that captures a small pool of sunlight at the top of the small dune that overlooks the beach and pause to take in the view. It is old work, watching the sea. I am scanning. Deep in my subconscious I am searching for a white sail, a flock of birds hunting a school of fish, a rogue wave, a fin. My gaze, as always, works its way to the horizon. The sea darkens through shades

*of green to a deep blue and eventually a horizon line as sharp as a ruler's edge.
Far south, beyond 'the Prom', I can see the outcropping islands of the Ansers and
the Glennies and the massive summit of Rhodondo Rock. A squall approaches
the islands from the west – dark grey cloud trailing a white curtain of rain. The
white-capped waves increase and gather into Waratah Bay.*

Whenever I stand here I am conscious of the great elemental forces of land, sea,
wind and fire. It is a story I have told my students on field trips here many times.
Around four billion years ago the early Earth cooled enough for the vast amounts
of moisture trapped in gaseous form to condense. So began the torrential rains that
produced the Earth's first great flood and formation of the proto-oceans. Minerals
dissolved into the water and others were added from vents in the new sea floors
where the continental plates continued to be torn apart. The saltwater seas formed.
The supercontinent of Pangaea fractured, leaving the Gondwana landmass in the
southern hemisphere. Then the continents of Gondwanaland began to separate
about 180 million years ago. The Indian landmass charged north to collide with
Asia. Australia, Africa and Antarctica continued to drift apart. Crucially, the land
bridge between South American and Antarctica collapsed. This meant that the
waters of the southern ocean were no longer forced northwards into the warmer
tropical seas. With no land barriers to block their passage, the ocean waters cooled
as they began their relentless journey, lapping the southern hemisphere. The
Antarctic polar icecap grew and became the great driver of climate and weather
in the south. This is the wind I feel as it blows in forcefully from the southwest.

The hard, coarse-grained pink and orange granites of the mountains and
islands I can see across the bay, which solidified from molten rock deep beneath
the Earth's surface, have withstood the battering of the southern swells from
pre-history to today. And right here, just metres in front of me, is the small, dark
basalt reef that marks the land-sea divide between Bear Gully and the waters of
Bass Strait. I scoop up a handful of sand and study the grains of clear quartz, the
fleshy colours of the feldspars, the black flecks of biotite and the white and brown
chips of seashells. They are all ground down, weathered and polished by the
action of the sea. The whole story is right here – the grinding action of continents
and the elemental forces of wind and wave against stone; the relentless action of
water shaping life. I live in the water hemisphere of the Earth where 70 per cent
of the surface area is ocean and I have been watching it all, absorbing it all, from
my vantage point on the south-facing Australian coastline since before I could
walk.

I return to the southern shores of the continent frequently, seeking comfort
on the edge of things. The edge is a place for both action and reflection. I am
standing now, still looking, still searching. I step from my pool of sunshine onto
the beach. The sand is hard and cold beneath my feet. My nerves are tingling with
anticipation. The sea is calling and as I enter the water the words of Australia's
great novelist of the coast, Tim Winton, briefly come back to me.

The pounding of the swell against the land's edge was so clear it seemed the sea was only a dune away. I didn't need a map to know where I was. In the atlas I lived in a dot, but with that breeze on my back I had a life and a place. (Winton, 1993, p. 10)

The late historian Frank Broeze argued that historians and writers in Australia have focused exclusively on the land, failing to recognise the significance of the nation's maritime heritage. His book, *Island Nation: A History of Australians and the Sea*, traces the 'profound, diverse and all-embracing influence of the sea on Australian society' (1998, p. 3). Broeze's focus is largely upon 'settler society', which in Australian history is the term used to depict those European colonisers who came and stayed, and their descendants. The term highlights that the culture and landscape that emerged largely resulted from the meeting of European ideas and practices with the foreign Australian landscape. Central to Broeze's argument is that the significance of sea and coast has largely been overlooked in accounts of settler history. Three important over-arching themes emerge in his book. First, the Australian coast was colonised by imperial Britain in an effort to control sea-space in the southern hemisphere as much as it was to provide a convenient dumping-ground for the Empire's convicts. Second, how Australia overcame its sense of isolation from the rest of the 'civilised world', or how it dealt with a felt sense of sea-distance if you like, has been crucial to the development of identity in modern Australia. Finally, how we live with the sea, through work, culture and lifestyle, on a daily basis has been equally important in shaping an Australian reality of the sea, the coast and the beach.

When I read Broeze's arguments I am not only interested in an historical account. It is way of understanding contemporary Australia, my Australia, and how it is changing. Border protection against 'asylum seekers', 'illegal refugees' or 'queue jumpers', as they are variously typecast in the media, continues to be a divisive political issue in current times (this notion of the border, the edge, the line that marks the coast and *makes* Australia is pivotal in defining the national imagination, and is a theme I shall return to later). Also, some would argue that settler Australians continue to look across the seas to Europe and North America as centres of cultural meaning rather than to our Asian and Pacific neighbours with whom we share our regional seas or, even closer to home, to Indigenous Australians. Even how we go to the beach for leisure and revitalisation is changing. The sectarian riots originating at Cronulla Beach in 2005, where 'white Aussie locals' clashed with other ethnic groups 'of middle-eastern appearance from Sydney's western suburbs', as they were portrayed by radio shock-jock Alan Jones, reminded all of us that the beach and coast have always been a contested space. Finally, perhaps we no longer feel comfortable lying on the hot sand, bronzing ourselves beneath the summer sun, haunted as we are by the modern spectre of melanoma. Max Dupain's iconic photograph of a youthful, muscular man, his skin still wet and glistening with seawater, now seems an innocent image from bygone days. Dupain captured the famous image, where we see only the man's head and shoulders from sand-level, at Culburra Beach in 1937, with the lip of a white wave just visible, poised behind the Sunbaker, frozen in the act of tipping upon the beach. The image of a youthful, masculine, carefree Australia – the image I grew up with – is changing. While Dupain's photograph may have said something to Australians at the time and possibly for decades to follow, it is impossible to view it as innocently now. Aspects of sexism, racism, Indigenous land rights and environmental despoliation are now layered upon these earlier images of the coast, the beach and the sea.

These realisations do not make me doubt the sea and coastal fringe I know and love, but they do bring layers of questions about my own experience of it as a child, a teenager and an adult that call for answers. The great elemental forces of nature still dominate, but where once the sea and my coast-life vacations meant simplicity, a sense of freedom and even gave a coherency in my life as our family relocated from town to town, I now have to consider how my own story fits within the larger, shifting cultural narrative.

Standing

I look out from the top of the steep beach at Bear Gully. It is strewn with washed-up sea grass and kelp. It shows the remainders of recent storms. The kelp has washed in from deeper waters. Its stem and fronds are thick, hide-like and deep brown in colour. I know it will darken and harden in the sun. The sea grass will have come from the sea grass meadow just a stone's throw from shore where the water is two to three metres deep. Out there the grasses will be vibrant green and swaying back and forth with the current, much like a field of prairie grass that pulses in the wind. The differences in colour between kelp and grass, brown and green, reflect the water depth at which the different plants grow and the quality of filtered sunlight they receive and rely upon to photosynthesise.

Not long ago I had returned to Bear Gully on one of my regular visits. I was more than a little mentally battered and bruised after a series of difficult meetings at work. I pulled on my snorkel gear and finned out to the small rocky outcrop about 100 metres offshore. Waves washed over the rocks and I watched the local fishes darting about between rock and seaweed as I rose and fell with the swell. Swimming back to shore I paused and floated over the sea grass beds.

> After the meeting,
> With its egos
> And betrayals,
> There's cold silence,
> Like a cloudless night in May,
> The giant emu staring down.
> So, I return to Bear Gully

And the forgiving sea.
Stones skim across its surface,
Dreams skate along
Like polar explorers gone,
Not leaving a mark.

But slice the surface
And there's a field of grass
Waving in the tide, and
A chorus of zebra fish
Rising and falling,
Rising and falling.

And at the very end of breath
An eagle ray appears in the blue room
Filled with pops and squeaks,
Catches a shaft of sun,
Beats its wings and
Rides the invisible current away.[1]

Through time and experience the coast, the beach and even the undersea world reveals itself to those who are prepared to immerse themselves into it and who will take the time to reflect upon the meaning of those experiences. Writing, either prose or poetry, about those experiences makes me tease out my feelings and thoughts in a more disciplined way. It makes me take notice of what I see and feel. It makes me begin the process of searching for connections between the immediate and the historical. Away from the glare of city lights and the heated exchanges of meetings and crowded schedules, I feel like I participate with a more elemental world. Snorkelling over the reef and sea grass meadow reminds me implicitly that my body provides my direct point of contact with reality. I might doubt the motivations of some people and even the accuracy of the historical record, but I never doubt the blue, cold certainty of the sea. Even the constellations and the dark spaces between the stars of the Milky Way in the night sky over Bear Gully, seen in this part of the world as a Giant Emu, feel strangely 'local' here. Surely deep space, like the sea for some, should feel like the distanced Other. But that is not what I feel when I am here, tucked away in my corner of the south coast. 'It's the connecting sensibility', writes historian Peter Read (2000, p. 200), 'that's what Aborigines are doing talking about the dreaming and the land.... Connect Connect Connect'. Perhaps that is what my coast-life story is about – feeling connected to the sea as a place, both in the moment and across its complicated history.

---

1 From Wattchow, B., 2010. *The Song of the Wounded River*. Port Adelaide: Ginninderra Press.

Even the coastline here has changed dramatically in the last 10,000 years. The melting icecaps and resulting sea level rises at the end of the most recent ice age, and the seasonal round of erosion and deposition, have produced the beach and coast I am standing on this morning. The beach here is probably no more than 6,000 years old, a time span within the reach of Indigenous cultural memory and stories from the Dreamtime. There are signs everywhere, for those who pause to read them, about Bear Gully's past. An old midden, the remains of the shellfish meals of an Indigenous clan, built up over centuries, can be found on the scrubby hill at the end of the beach. The reef's fissures and rock pools harbour thousands of different flora and fauna species – shellfish like mussels, winkles and welks; the wonderfully named snot sea cucumbers, brittle stars and sea urchins; hairy crabs, Neptune's necklace and sea lettuce; shrimps, small fishes and octopuses. They are all going about their daily business of survival – feeding, breeding and growing. I have to sit and wait and be very still to see them. The animals are hunting or being hunted, darting between food and shelter. Perhaps that is what I am doing – darting between experience and reflection, the moment and memory. I stand on the beach and scan its sands from east to west. Perhaps I am thinking about my own survival in the water. What perils lurk for me there? I noticed a new sign at Bear Gully when I arrived yesterday, one I had never seen before. It was placed conspicuously at the start of the narrow sandy track that runs from the camping area to the beach. It was one of those standardised land management signs that seem to have cropped up all along the coastline. It read:

MAITLAND BEACH

! WARNING

Strong currents
Unexpected large swells
Dangerous tides
Submerged objects
Unstable cliffs

THIS BEACH IS NOT PATROLLED

Thank God for small mercies – a beach that is not patrolled – like the beaches of my childhood, particularly those of the Yorke Peninsula where we roamed the foreshore beachcombing and collecting bait. Before reading the new sign, I had never known that the sand I was standing on was officially, at least to some cartographer in central office, named Maitland Beach. Who or what was 'Maitland'? The locals had always referred to it simply as Bear Gully. Admittedly 'bear' is a misnomer. No doubt the place is named after the koala 'bear', which is not a bear at all but a marsupial. But at least you can still spot the occasional koala in the local Manna Gums of the park. Maitland, however, is long gone. Out on the horizon I can see the top of a container ship. It is heading west, bound for the port of Melbourne. I stand on the beach, shivering, and think of the strange, complex and even contradictory meanings of the beach and the sea for Australians. I'm standing on the very edge now. The cold Indian Ocean is lapping against my toes.

I am fourth generation native-born Australian. My ancestors came across the seas from Europe in the late 1800s. I was raised in a house of books, music and paintings, where the distant echo of Britain and Europe could still be heard but where my experiences outside were distinctly Australian. Settler Australians, I think, have a profoundly paradoxical relationship with the sea. The deeper layers of cultural meanings for the sea, inherited from the Old World, still resonate. But they have been interpreted through new experiences as Australia materialised out of *terra incognita* – the unknown land – in the southern hemisphere. As an island continent, the outline of the coast provides a powerful symbol to Australians. To see that simple outline on a page – the bulging coastlines in the east and the west, the box-like Gulf of Carpentaria, the north pointer of Cape York, the huge bite taken out of the underbelly of the continent known, ironically perhaps, as the Great Australian Bight. Together they make up the 36,700 km of coastline 'or more than 120,000 km if estuaries and the 1,800 islands are included' (Huntsman, 2001, p. 5). From the perspective of trying to understand how Australians experience and relate to their seas, I think we misconstrue the idea of Australia when we think of it as a single continental landmass. Really, Australia is an archipelago of islands. There are over 50 substantial islands in Bass Strait alone between Victoria and Tasmania (the largest of Australia's islands), the stretch of water immediately before me from my vantage point at Bear Gully. I have paddled my sea kayak out to many of those islands and I explored small offshore islands as a child in South Australia. But my school atlas image of the continent – all red desert, except for the green east-coast fringe, and the whole landmass surrounded by the bluest of oceans – impacted upon my sense of 'Australianness' from a young age.

Australia, according to my old school atlas, included the territorial waters in the Indian Ocean (off the west and south coasts) and the South Pacific (east coast). Australian waters also included the Tasman Sea (south-east), Coral Sea (north-east), Arafura Sea (north) and the Timor Sea (north-west). The land mass was so huge that it took a double-spread page of the atlas, a space into which you could cram dozens of European countries. I was proud of the size of the land I lived in. And there were hints that the surrounding blue waters were more than just the names of seas and oceans. The South Equatorial Current in the north, the Antarctic Circumpolar Current in the south moved phenomenal bodies of water in the water hemisphere. And the Leeuwin Current, off the coast of Western Australia, and the East Australian Current, offshore of Queensland and New South Wales, could be seen dragging warm waters south to mix with the cold.

It took centuries for the coastline of Australia to emerge in the imagined void (for Europeans) of the southern hemisphere. From as early as 1606, Spanish and Dutch explorers began the process of charting the coast. There is evidence that the Portuguese encountered sections of the coast even earlier, in the 1500s.

But it was not until June 1803, when Matthew Flinders completed the first full chart of the coastline through his circumnavigation of the continent in the Investigator, that we can say that the image of Australia we now take for granted began to truly crystallise in human consciousness. I have stared at a copy of Flinders's map – it is a beautiful artefact – and I felt connected to Flinders's story from a young age. One of my father's school postings was to Quorn, a small town in the Flinders Ranges, and my brother studied at Flinders University. I still run snorkel camps at the small coastal village called Flinders.

Flinders completed his work only shortly before the French sailor Nicholas Baudin concluded his lap of the continent in Le Geographe. The French also had designs on exploring and, perhaps, colonising Australia (Hill, 2012). By amazing coincidence the two sailors met briefly in the duly named Encounter Bay close to Port Elliot – the holiday grounds and seas of my youth and, as a child, I could readily make a picture in my mind of their white-sailed boats bobbing offshore, out behind the breakers with the two captains exchanging 'tense pleasantries' on deck. The seas and lands of the southern hemisphere witnessed a sea-space race in the 1700 and early 1800s as the great geopolitical European powers sought to spread their dominion across the southern half of the globe. A gaping space in the European imagination, a *terra incognita*, emerged in fragments: first as New Holland, then as the bifurcated continent of New Holland/New South Wales, and finally as 'Australia' on Flinders's chart.

Thus the image of Australia, of a hard, dry land surrounded by a spacious blue sea – each one defining the other – is surprisingly recent. 'Our land is girt by sea ... for we are young and free' we now sing collectively in the national anthem, and 'the image of a blue-bordered island continent brings with it pleasurable thoughts of wave and sand, surf and rollers, reef and sea as a place of free expression' (Sharp, 2002, p. 7). But the line that girds Australians is simultaneously a symbol of freedom and a persistent echo, since the day of the colonist and the convict, that the sea is also our jailer. And I imagine that members of Indigenous communities throughout Australia find the sentiments of the anthem cringe worthy. As an Australian I know and feel, intimately and immediately, why Robert Hughes (1986) titled his epic history of the convict era *The Fatal Shore*.

As a young lad I sat at my desk in school, through the stifling summer heat, daydreaming of the sea. But I recognised that gaining a sense of the importance of past events was important – even if we did study more European than Australian history. I've paddled my sea kayak out through the heads at Botany Bay, riding the same swells and taking bearings off the same sandstone cliffs as those early European colonists. The first fleet of eight sail ships arrived in Botany Bay, New South Wales between 18 and 20 January 1788. The 1,044 passengers included convicts, free settlers, naval officers and their wives and children. The all-important re-supply ships, bringing fresh personnel and supplies, did not arrive until mid-1790. The months between were a time of severe hardship and starvation. Imagine the sea-gaze to the horizon of those early colonists, hoping against hope for a glimpse of a white sail that would bring precious food, materials and news from home. I was raised in a house that felt simultaneously British-European and Australian and I have come to realise that I have to live within this strange paradox.

For several weeks this last summer, I sea kayaked down the east coast of Tasmania and landed at Port Arthur, which was established as the principal penal settlement of that island state, known at the time as Van Diemen's Land. The unbroken cliffs and violent sea approaching Port Arthur, located on the isolated Tasman Peninsula, felt utterly forbidding. The view and feeling from the pitching deck of a convict sail ship as it rounded Cape Pillar and Tasman Island, sailed on past West Arthur Head and the Isle of the Dead, and in to dock at Port Arthur, must have been one of abject placelessness. The Australian sea gaze, even my own, conjures contradictory images of freedom and internment – of land-bound prisoners surrounded by impassable walls of water.

The Australian writer Robert Drewe has suggested that 'Literature academics, though they rarely ventured there, favoured the dry, asexual, pragmatic myth of the bush and the inland desert' (1994, p. 6). They distrusted and denied the 'sensual intelligence' (Drewe, 1994, p. 6) – how we engage physically and bodily with the places where we actually live. Thus as a culture, we hover between the mythic landscape of the interior and the epic, primordial space of the ocean. As Tim Winton has commented, 'Australians are surrounded by ocean and ambushed from behind by desert – a war of mystery on two fronts' (Winton, 1993, p. 21).

As a people, settler Australians, have by and large, clung to the coastal rind of the continent. That is where we have built our homes. Now, as a culture, we have turned our attention to that edge in a search for meaning. For most of us it is the place where we actually live our lives. When we go to the beach to swim and surf, or simply lie beneath that melanoma-inducing sun, as we do in our millions, we have perfected a ritualised escapism from the increasingly crowded confusion of Australia's coastal cities, with their ever-burgeoning suburbs, and the endless heat and apparent barrenness of the inland that haunts us. Yet, we also fear the rip and the undertow, and we think the great white shark is gliding back and forth, waiting for us in that blue water, just beyond those beautiful breaking waves. With the Australian sea before us we are gripped by both fascination and fear. In his book *The Coast Dwellers: A Radical Reappraisal of Australian Identity*, Drew argued for a re-alignment with the coast in the Australian consciousness.

> Whatever is meant by Australia as an idea, it is no longer centered in the interior empty heartland, rather, it is outside on the rind around the periphery of the continent. The persistent imagery of a dead center will have to be replaced by the living edge if Australians are ever to come to terms with where they actually live. (Drew, 1994, p. 41)

Can we learn to live where we live, on the coastal fringe with the sea before us? Can we imagine that edge, that mixture of sea and land, as a sea-place? Can the fatal shore become a sacred home? There are promising signs. We carry our babies down to the sea's edge in summer and sit them in the small waves – as my mother did with me, as I did with my own daughters – a secular, saltwater baptism. But the challenges of learning to live meaningfully in places on the continent's edge are immense, for place is about collective, cultural attachment to the particular, in both body and mind, while the sea remains a potent symbol of the universal, and persists in cultural memory as a largely unknowable space that surrounds the huge, red continental land mass. The line that divides sea and land is also the line that defines the national and, to a significant extent at least, my identity.

Floating

I am standing now, balancing on the very edge of land and sea, as the first small wave washes across my feet. I begin to walk into the bone-chilling water to cross the line that separates land and sea. In 30 centimetres of water I can see and feel the ribbing in the sand. Sand and weed washes back and forth in the small wavelets. I am walking out to sea through a break in Bear Gulley's basalt reef. It is a small gap in the continuous line of the rocky coast – a portal.

Deeper, my calves and knees submerge – it is cold, really astonishingly cold. A small wave pushes water up to my waist. I tighten up. Quadriceps, the large thigh muscles, go rigid. I am chest-deep now and my breathing is disrupted. Focus. Breathe instead of gasp. Lie back, hands sculling to keep position, feet pointing out to sea. The shock of cold is like electricity. My heartbeat is racing. My extremities whiten. Blood is rushing back into my body's core. My body knows how to protect itself – how to preserve its heat. I am consciously attempting to calm my racing heart, to accept the coldness of the water.

Still sculling I can see the grey sky and clouds wheeling overhead. My horizon is only a few metres away. A small wave, no higher than 50 centimetres, curls in out of Bass Strait. I watch it steepen and its lip begin to feather. I think briefly of the long journey it has made across the waters to meet me here. It will break over me, so I submerge and listen to it roll over, a few centimetres above my face.

Underwater my hearing becomes unidirectional, a product of how sound waves travel in water compared to air. There is no wind and, save for the subtle sound of the wave and the action of water against rock and sand, it is strangely quiet. Opening my eyes I can see the silver world of air above me. I know it is within reach but I am happy to float here for a while, suspended in a state of neutral buoyancy. I am not bobbing like a cork or sinking like a stone. For a brief moment I am just part of the load of sand and weed suspended in the salt water, being pushed back and forth. Where is the eagle ray, I wonder, that I saw here on my snorkel dive a year ago? Does the shark cruise back and forth out beyond the little basalt island? Is a rogue wave building somewhere out in the Indian Ocean? Will the white sails crest the horizon soon? Are the great continents still drifting apart and rock and shell being broken and polished by the relentless action of the sea as I hover here in the water column?

I am sensation and memory. I am simultaneously here, suspended in the sea just offshore of Bear Gully, staring up at the bubble of air that circles the Earth, and I am a small boy once again diving beneath the wave towering overhead in the surf at Port Elliot. I can sense salmon, mullet and garfish schooling in the waters beyond my fingertips and I am a memory dangling its baited hook for them from the weathered timbers of the Port Vincent jetty. I am reaching beyond the limits of my skin, out into the sea and at the same moment I feel the ocean pouring into the cells of my body ...

But the cold returns and defeats me. My feet touch down on the hard sand. I use the small waves to make my way back to the shore. As I emerge from the water I clench my fists and bury them under my armpits and I hunch over as I climb the beach. I am in the cold water survival position – on land. I am empty of thoughts. I am at the very edge of pure sensation. My skin is pinking as I feel the first flush of heat return to my extremities. Walking up the beach I have the strange sensation that I can sense the full sweep of coastline east to Cape Howe and west to Cape Leeuwin. I am alive and streaming full of sand and wave, bird and fish, shell and weed and the long harmonic note of wind on stone. But by the time I reach camp I am shaking as I light the small stove to boil some water for a warmth-reviving brew. While the water heats, I dry myself off and throw on some clothes. I feel the bite of cotton on skin and the luxurious, soft comfort of wool. When the brew is ready, I fill my cup and return to the beach.

The sea gives me a sense of certainty and stability. But living on the edge, I also must embrace my marginality. As Huntsman (2001, p. 173) says, 'the beach never *is*, [it] is always *becoming*'. This idea correlates with notions of place and sense of place. Place scholars like Ed Relph (1976) and Yi Fu Tuan (1977) have long argued that place is best understood as a phenomenon. A place is always emerging – always becoming. A place is simultaneously personal, cultural and natural. It has embodied, rational, ecological and historical dimensions. It has a basis in geo-physical reality but it also relies heavily upon the ideas, beliefs and even assumptions that govern how we see, interpret and act in particular locations. Thus human beings live in a reciprocal relationship with particular places on the Earth's surface – whether land or sea or both. We are changed by the places where we live, but we also change them. In short, we are co-participants within the phenomena of the unfolding evolution of places. As Relph writes: 'The word "place" is best applied to those fragments of human environments where meanings, activities, and a specific landscape are all implicated and enfolded by each other' (cited in Cameron, 2003, p. 173).

So it is for specific seascapes for some of us. The sea enfolds me. Though its waters are large enough to circle the globe and I am as small as a piece of weed or sand suspended inside the wave – we implicate each other. While many know this, or at least intuit it, for landscapes, it has been harder for settler Australians to accept this for sea places. As I have outlined earlier, the cultural obstacles in our imagining of the sea in Australia are significant and are compounded further by the history of ideas of the sea in Western literature that view the sea as Other. It is counter to the experience of exploration and charting of the coastline and our colonial history. And, perhaps, just as we non-Indigenous Australians were coming to grips with what we thought coast and sea places might mean to us as a nation, we have been reminded that they are highly contested sites where race, ethnic and even sub-cultural values clash. And, finally, in the place where our parents once let us play all day in the sun, we now shelter our own children beneath the shade of the beach umbrella and cover every square inch of their skin, that great conduit between them and the natural world, with synthetic fabric.

Rather than continuing to look across the seas for answers as to how more might feel the 'localness' of their sea places, I think it is time to look closer to home. Indigenous Australians, particularly those tribal communities in the north, have long had a refined sense of sea-place. In her book *Saltwater People: The Waves of Memory*, Nonie Sharp (2002) examines differences between Western and Indigenous ways of relating to and living with the sea. Her exploration of the knowledge systems and practices of saltwater peoples charts the characteristics required of a culture that lives in harmony with its seas. To paraphrase Sharp, we need to recognise our sea as sacred and full of spiritual meaning and a place that reaches far back into our ancestry. This attitude engenders feelings of respect and obligation. We need to learn to read the subtle signs and markings that carry meaning in our sea places. Not only the major signs like the turning of the seasons, the storm or the rise and fall of the tide, but also when the small crabs shed their exoskeletons in the rock pools, what we find amongst the weed drying at the top of the beach and what this tells us about the health of the bird flocks and fish schools. These signs will tell us about the well-being, or not, of the sea that sustains us. We need to learn the stories of local people and places, not just the grand narratives of history. We need to extend our sense of attachment from the land into the sea, with the same level of fascination for the particular – *this* reef, *this* seabed, *this* meadow of sea grasses waving in the current. In the same way that we have rights and responsibilities for tracts of land, so we should for stretches of the seas. Finally, we need to acknowledge our sea traditions, not as something fixed, but as a conversation, sometimes difficult, with the past that reaches into the present and on into the future. When these elements come together, we will have learned to be at home with our sea. Then we will be a saltwater people.

Back on the beach I take one last look around and notice subtle changes. There is more light now over the Yanakie Isthmus and I can see the creamy sand dunes in the distance. A Pacific Gull has arrived to work the reef, assessing the flotsam and jetsam for a feed. A flock of Crested Terns are resting on the rock island offshore. The rising tide brings waves that splash them a few times before they lift off and peel away on the wind. I cradle my warm cup of tea and watch as they glide west along the thin line of the coast. Their flight through the air traces a line between saltwater and land and that line is both forming and dissolving as I watch the waves wash back and forth over the sand.

> [The edge is where] everything is being rearranged and redefined. The edge is where things happen, where sudden discoveries illuminate hidden memories: where revelations and metamorphoses occur ... [It is] also the edge of the self where inside and outside meet. (Leer, 1985, p. 11)

References

Broeze, F., 1998. *Island Nation: A History of Australians and the Sea*. St Leonards, NSW: Allen and Unwin.

Cameron, J., 2003. Responding to place in a post-colonial era: An Australian perspective. In: W.M. Adams and M. Mulligan, eds, *Decolonizing Nature*. London: Earthscan, pp. 172–96.

Daikin, W., 1952. *Australian Sea Shores: A Guide for the Beach-Lover, the Naturalist, the Shore Fisherman, and the Student*. Sydney: Angus and Robertson.

Drew, P., 1994. *The Coast Dwellers: A Radical Reappraisal of Australian Identity*. Ringwood: Penguin Books Australia.

Drewe, R., 1993. *The Picador Book of the Beach*. Sydney: Picador.

Hill, D., 2012. *The Great Race: The Race between the English and the French to Complete the Map of Australia*. North Sydney: Random House.

Hughes, R., 1988. *The Fatal Shore: The Epic of Australia's Founding*. New York: Random House.

Huntsman, L., 2001. *Sand in Our Souls: The Beach in Australian History*. Carlton South: Melbourne University Press.

Leer, M., 1985. On the edge: Geography and imagination in the world of David Malouf. *Australian Literary Studies*, 12, pp. 3–21.

Lines, W., 2001. *Open Air Essays*. Sydney: New Holland Publishers.

Read, P., 2000. *Belonging: Australians, Place and Aboriginal Ownership*. Cambridge: Cambridge University Press.

Relph, E., 1976. *Place and Placelessness*. London: Pion Ltd.

Sharp, N., 2002. *Saltwater People: The Waves of Memory*. Crows Nest, NSW: Allen and Unwin.

Tuan, Y.F., 1977. *Space and Place: The Perspective of Experience*. Minneapolis: University of Minnesota Press.

Wattchow, B., 2010. *Song of the Wounded River*. Port Adelaide: Ginninderra Press.

Winton, T., 1993. *Land's Edge*. Sydney: Macmillan.

Chapter 10

In the Name of the Whale

Robbie Nicol

My Way of Travelling

A black bear crashed through the dense, ancient undergrowth of Canada's Meares Island, breaking free and then rising up on its hind legs. It just stood there, very close, and stared at me. On the same coastal trip bald eagles, from their high treetop perches, imperiously observed the comings and goings of an intricate seaway. In age-old ways the heavenly alignment of the Sun, Moon and Earth combined to accelerate seawater on the incoming tide through narrow gaps between the archipelago's many islands, before receding back in the direction from whence it came, to pause only briefly before the tidal cycle begins once more. The pulsating seawater reminded me of the red river of life that courses through my own arteries bringing with it life and renewal. This is no mere metaphor. In bringing these thoughts to the fore and expressing them through words, I am basking in the beauty of conceptual thought, memory and embodiment, and considering what happens when time and space manifest themselves in the present at the cutting edge of experience. On this particular trip, I had been a 'greenhorn' in bear country. Anxiety and excitement were never far away. Despite the gentle, soothing lapping of waves onto the nearby shore, I clearly remember lying in a tent unable to sleep because every 'innocent' noise seemed loud and menacing, not because of what it was but because of what it might have been.

On another occasion off Scotland's west coast there were the basking sharks so close that their large floppy dorsal fins were seen to sway from one side to the other as they sieved the sea for plankton. Then there was the spectacular sight of whales breaching, their enormous bulks momentarily suspended above the water before crashing down again. As I consider where the words and ideas for this chapter will come from, this opportunity to reflect infuses my being with memories of moonlit nights, 'rafts' of jellyfish clusters, glowing waves of phosphorescence, 'singing' sands, golden beaches, campfires, songs, stories, abundant wildlife, and sadly, rare and endangered species. All of these experiences on, in and of the sea have left a powerful imprint on who I am as a person and what I am trying to achieve with my life. Furthermore, they were all possible because of the most humble of waterborne craft – the sea kayak.

Synthetic products have largely replaced natural materials, and ergonomics in design may have improved performance and handling features, but essentially the sea kayak is the same now as it has always been – long and slender. It is designed for travelling long distances and it had to be fast for the indigenous peoples who first used them for hunting seals and walrus. Sometimes used for long open crossings, for the most part, I like to hug the coastline and occupy that narrow ribbon of space in the intertidal zone, extending to 1, maybe 2, kilometres offshore.

Having a shallow draught, and in capable hands, the kayak provides me with high degrees of manoeuvrability to explore this complex and varied interface between sea and land. Sea caves, geos, cliffs, skerries, and all sorts of nooks and crannies that are inaccessible to most other craft are discoverable in a sea kayak. With several watertight compartments, plenty of equipment and food can be stowed for the long journeys I enjoy.

In challenging conditions I can employ a myriad of subtle bodily movements and paddle strokes to keep the kayak moving forward and upright. Here I am not limiting myself to the idea that these are mere technical skills but opening myself to the possibility of new ways of thinking about bodily experience. Talking of the hand, Thrift stated

> it is not just an 'external' organ: it is so vital to human evolution that it seems quite likely that parts of the brain have developed in order to cope with its complexities rather than vice versa, thereby providing a sense of the world deep in the supposedly enclosed human body as new kinds of distance have opened up between organism and environment which need to be crossed. (Thrift, 2004, p. 597)

Kayaking Without a Snorkel!

Deep strokes on either side provide forward momentum. Wide and shallow strokes help to steer and compensate for the effects of the wind and waves that would otherwise interfere with the intended direction of travel. In trying to understand bodily movement the way Thrift (2004; 2006) describes, it is necessary to reconsider, or perhaps consider *prima facia*, notions of time and space, mind and world. Take for example what happens when I capsize. My first reaction is to roll the kayak back to an upright position.

Hold this image of a capsized kayak in your mind and imagine the sequence of events that preceded it. From an upright position something interferes with the kayak, normally a large curling wave, strong wind or counter tidal movement, and, in the blink of an eye, I find myself upside down with my upper body fully immersed. Before describing the sequence of events required to 'roll' the kayak, let's pause with that image of me suspended upside down but still confidently wedged in and secure. It is another world, a world to which I am not adapted to live or survive. If I open my eyes I will not be able to see properly. There will be some colours but their appearance will appear blurred. There will also be a change in temperature – it will be much colder, at least around 56° N latitude where I normally paddle. Sound too will be very different, muted somewhat.

There will be a change in noise levels, which in other circumstances might be quite peaceful. However, in unintended capsize situations, the qualities associated with peacefulness are rarely experienced as such. Smell will be largely absent, or at least reprioritised, not least because of the fear of what might happen if I should inhale through my nose. Water ingestion at this point is likely to lead to a panic attack. This is why my nose and mouth will be clenched tight as even the smallest ingress of water is a reminder that seawater is not particularly palatable.

If I were to remain in this position I would have several minutes before oxygen deficiency led to asphyxiation. There is a reality here that is unavoidable and one that is worth pondering beyond the specifics of this situation. Evolutionary processes do not work at the speed necessary to provide me with gills to breathe underwater in the short time available. This playful thought is a reminder that the survival of our own species depends on relatively stable environmental conditions. When environmental conditions change, every species has the same options: adaption or extinction. As a submerged kayaker, unless I act quickly, I too will perish. Luckily the 'rolling' of a kayak is a straightforward technical exercise, at least in easy conditions. From an upside-down position, all I need to do is bring the double-bladed paddle to one side of the kayak and push the paddleshaft upwards to break the surface of the water. The leading paddle blade is then skimmed wide and backwards in an arc and this motion provides stability for the kayak to rotate 180°, on its horizontal axis, and just as a log rolls, I can return myself to an upright position once again.

Kayaking With a Cargo of Ideas

The connection between being upside down in a kayak and our adaptability as a species may not be apparent at first but it is worth exploring. I have focused on the disorientation I experience when I capsize and the actions needed in order to survive. It is not such a great leap, at least conceptually, to see the connection between this and the challenge for humanity to survive and attempt to live on the planet sustainably.

As a paddler and education researcher, I have been intrigued by my relationship with the natural world and the paradoxes that are inherent in my own actions as I seek out a more sustainable lifestyle. The human–nature relationship has been a central focus for environmental philosophers, some of whom have presented very different ways of viewing the world. One of these standpoints is 'anthropocentrism', which is a paradigm based on human-centredness where nature is subordinated to human need (Guha, 2005). Objectifying nature in this way was, as Pratt, Howarth and Brady (2000) observe, a key feature of the agricultural revolution. It continued into modernity and then, as Hayward (1994) noted, became embedded in societal consciousness throughout industrialisation. At this point, urban lifestyles began to mask the fact that food grows in fields and not supermarkets and that trees come from forests and are not just wooden artefacts found in furniture shops.

As individuals, at least those of us living in industrialised countries, we are generally well informed about these consumer issues, but the more important argument is that, at a social and political level, we do not act as though we are (Ekins, 2000).

Those who suggest that the anthropocentric paradigm is the central problem of the ecological crisis would offer an eco-centric, or biocentric, paradigm as an alternative (see, for example, Sessions, 1995). One of the key features of this paradigm is the concept of value. Value is said to inhere in nature and its moral standing has been variously termed as 'other than human' (Devall and Sessions, 1985) or, more stridently, 'more than human' (Abram, 1997). Such a paradigm would celebrate co-operation with nature rather than competition. It would require a shift from dominating nature to finding equality within it, from reductionism to holism, from shallow ecology (problems we already know about) to deep ecology (a change of worldview) and from hierarchy to understanding humanity within the web of life (Sessions, 1995). The tendency to look at relationships is a key feature of ecocentric thinking, as is the ecocentrists' view that there is something inherently wrong with anthropocentrism because it is based on an ontological dualism that separates people from nature.

Well that is the theory (or part of the theory), but I think something important is missing and this may well prove to be crucial. When upside down in a kayak, my first thought is not about the intrinsic value of the water around me. The sea cares nothing about my human hopes and fears. My fragile individual existence can be plucked away in an instant, yet still I go kayaking, as others do. On many occasions I go paddling solo and no one else is available to render assistance but this is not the point. Despite the objective dangers, I find solo paddling provides me with the time to think.

On one occasion I was paddling alone in an estuary helped along by the ebbing tide. The waves within the shelter of the Firth of Tay were small and manageable to start with. Slowly though and almost imperceptibly the nature of the waves began to change. The small waves within the firth had been created by the same wind I could feel on my face. It was a local wind and like the waves it was gentle and benign. As the firth widened into the open sea, the waves changed in nature as they were dominated by swell waves originating way out in the North Sea perhaps three or four hundred miles from here. These particular swell waves had travelled in long parallel lines with relentless power to reach Scotland's east coast. Here they met shelving beaches, which caused them to accelerate and rear up into large curling waves and finally break onto the beach discharging their pent-up energy. The growing omnipresence of an 'angry' sea had made me nervous. With thoughts of my own mortality occupying a large part of my consciousness, I thought about life and existence.

It is not uncommon to think of evolution as a process whereby single-celled life evolved into multi-cellular life, and somewhere in the distant past, humans emerged with their superior intellect and outstripped other multi-cellular organisms to sit proudly at the pinnacle of evolution above all other forms of life.

This creation myth of dominance and superiority over nature is so deeply ingrained in our culture that we rarely pause to question it at the socio-cultural level (Bowers, 1993). However, with the prospect of humanity facing a crisis of survival at some time in the not too distant future, there is good reason to pause and question many of our unexamined assumptions (Evernden, 1985).

In some ways it is understandable that a species, which evolved in such amazing ways and developed the capacity for analytical thought, should come to think of itself as a superior life form. After all chimpanzees do not build aeroplanes, mycetopholids do not drive cars, and earthworms do not fly rockets to the moon (not yet at least). When viewed through the spectacles of human achievement, there is no doubt that evolution has endowed our own species with spectacular attributes.

Gentle Jim and How to 'Be' in the World

In conversation, my good friend Jim Cheney once told me he had grown tired of academic discourse and ivory towers. Jim's point was that people who argued from differing sides of a perspective (whether anthropocentrism, ecocentrism or some other form of 'ism') simply abstracted nature, providing objects and ideas to be fought over. 'Is such jousting not simply reducing nature regardless of one's perspective', we wondered? Jim worried that it had become more popular to *talk* about the human–nature relationship than experience it. Weary of such discourse and looking beyond abstraction, the important thing for Jim was how to 'be' in the world. Jim has helped me to see that there is a difference between being in the world and theorising about being in the world. Out here on the sea where every sense is stimulated and every bodily action is highly tuned, thoughts are no longer commodities of an abstract world and the feeling of presence, of self, of absence of others stimulates my being in ways that are not always explainable from a rationale perspective.

Weston (1999; 2003), amongst others, has much to say in challenging abstraction and he has argued convincingly that intrinsic value, where value is said to inhere in nature (a core aspect of much ecocentric thinking), is itself a contradiction because the logic of the argument suggests it has independent existence. Thus, if something can be characterised by its independence, it can then be argued to be separate. Weston shows how isolating what is of value from the valuer is somewhat ironic because this separation reinforces the very polarity that proponents of intrinsic value seek to overcome. Instead he suggests 'we should prefer a conception of values which ties them to their contexts and insists not on their separability but on their relatedness and interdependence' (Weston, 2003, p. 312).

This is where the problem lies in my opinion. It is not our individual and collective inability to find the correct paradigm that prevents us from acting sustainably. It is more to do with the abstract thinking around issues, where clever arguments are advanced to support one position and then appear to be cancelled out when contested by other clever arguments in support of another position. In searching for a solution I would like to suggest that ecocentrism may offer a vision of the sorts of values central to a sustainable society, but, and this is a big but, the philosophical arguments that support this position remain difficult for people to translate into their everyday lives. Furthermore, there is a real danger that ecocentrists will fall into the very trap that they are trying to avoid, simply because their ideas are conceived by people. Put more stridently, ecocentrism is an anthropocentric conception (at least at a theoretical level). Of this Weston (2003, p. 315) has said 'philosophy has too long failed to take seriously what it cannot itself fully articulate'. From what has been said so far, I would conclude that, whilst the world of ideas has been helpful in identifying the problems of environmental sustainability, abstract thinking on its own will not be sufficient in the search for environmental sustainability.

Fishing Hooks, Barbs and Cormorants

I was reminded of the truth of this on another occasion when I found a cormorant swimming but in an obvious state of distress. It had a barbed hook in its mouth attached to a float by a length of fishing line. It was dragging the float around the surface. I prepared myself with a knife, ready to capture the cormorant and cut the line. I could see no other way to help. Left in this situation I did not think it was ever going to be able to catch fish to eat and would most likely die from starvation. I also remember thinking that I might have had to use the knife for another purpose if I was unable to cut the line. However, the tragedy was not to end with a swift conclusion. The cormorant still had a lot of energy left and dived below the surface every time I got near. The 'chase' began to cause me distress because I knew that the pressure of diving would only make the hook bite deeper and inflict even more pain. In the end, I knew that there was no chance of my catching the bird and so I left it to its fate.

As I paddled on I was left with a great sense of sadness and helplessness that I had been unable to assist. This single incident has resulted in much introspection. I know, for example, that around the world right now there will likely be other cormorants with hooks in their mouths suffering as this one did. However, knowing this does not affect me anywhere near as much as the personal encounter. Furthermore, I know that come the next day, with the power of human healing, the distress I feel for this cormorant will be less than it was that day and less the day after, and so on.

From these observations I conclude two things. The first is that, for humans to better understand their interconnection with nature, they need to have direct encounters. The second is because the power of experience can wane over time, encounters of this type need to be repeated and become a regular part of peoples' lifestyles. This is why for me *direct* experiences of the sea are central to understanding the human–nature relationship. I think it is also what Jim meant when he said we need to 'be' in the world and not only to think about it. As the cormorant dies a slow lingering death does it really matter to the cormorant, or me for that matter, if I view this situation from an ecocentric rather than an anthropocentric viewpoint (or vice versa). Here I am in agreement with James that 'there is no reason why a proponent of ontological dualism (i.e. an anthropocentrist) must be motivated to act badly in her relations with natural things' (2009, p. 20).

In my reflections on worldviews I have come to understand the importance of recognising the distinction between ontology and epistemology. If ontology means to study the nature of existence and being, then epistemology becomes the way that this can be understood (see, for example, Curry, 2006). I would like to begin with a generalisation that seeks to identify a gap in the literature. Environmental philosophers have focused much more on ontology (e.g. concepts such as intrinsic value and dualisms) and less on epistemology. In so doing, they have developed a body of literature that outlines some of the problems but at such a level of abstraction that it is not always clear what actions need to be taken nor the motivating factors that might induce actions in the first place.

There is, however, another body of literature that I have found helpful. It is the educational philosophy of the pragmatists. Pragmatist philosophy emerged out of responses to the social challenges of the twentieth century and embraced the core themes of experience, reflection, democracy, community and activism. These themes have never been more important than they are now in the twenty-first century as we grapple with how to live sustainably on the planet, both now and in the future.

This body of scholarship is perhaps even more important for the twenty-first century than it was in the twentieth, as society seeks to respond to the ever greater challenges of sustainability and the concomitant need for social change. Of this philosophy Dewey has said 'I assume amid all uncertainties there is one permanent frame of reference: namely, the organic connection between education and personal experience … [but] … we need to understand what experience is' (1963, p. 25).

In another article I have argued that one of the problems with the abstraction necessary for grand theory can be its failure to recognise an individual's agency, power and motivation to act (Nicol, 2013). This, I believe, brings us closer to the search for solutions. In this respect I have found Donaldson's comments useful, where she argues 'we do not just sit and wait for the world to impinge upon us. We try actively to interpret it, to make sense of it. We grapple with it, we construe it intellectually, we represent it to ourselves' (Donaldson, 1978, p. 68).

I am not rejecting the world of ideas out of hand, just observing the need for a transition from the sorts of ontologies, where abstract thought is paramount, to epistemology and the need for people to work with these ideas in their everyday lives. Nor am I, in sociological terms, elevating agency over the need for structural solutions. I am simply considering what all of this means to me as a kayaker, who regularly finds himself upside down and disorientated in a world confused by the challenge of environmental sustainability, not really knowing what is best to do but at the same time recognising the need for urgent action. This is why I am a sea kayaker.

Looking for Vision amongst Seals

At the mouth of the Firth of Tay, where it empties into the North Sea, there is a narrow passage created by the sands of the north and south shores. Through this passage Atlantic salmon make their way towards their breeding grounds in the upper reaches of the River Tay and its tributaries. Common seals and Atlantic grey seals line north and south shores waiting to ambush the next run of salmon and sea trout. Here the familiar call of eider ducks fills the air with their gentle 'hoo hoo' calls. There are rafts of hundreds, maybe thousands of individuals and I watch as the swell lifts them up only for them to disappear into a trough before the next swell wave picks them up again. They are there because of food – mussel beds abound on the seabed and the eider ducks swallow them whole.

Further on and looking for somewhere to stop for a rest some seals waddle into the water leaving behind a pup on the beach. Small waders are everywhere scurrying around looking for insects. Curious about the abandoned seal pup I land some distance away and find my camera. As I creep closer its behaviour does not appear to be normal. There had been many pups this size all of which had escaped into the water. As I look seaward they are there with their mothers, heads above the water and watching my every move. Giving the pup on the sand a wide berth I approach it from the other side and see straight away what the problem is. Some defect at birth, or perhaps an injury, has left it blind in one eye. It looks well fed for the moment but I wonder what the future holds for it when it is weaned and has to be dependent on its own hunting prowess.

Seeing new life in this way I sympathised with 'the hand' that nature had dealt it. I remember feeling as though I should have helped. This though was very different from the feeling of distress for the cormorant. Although both were likely to starve to death in due course, I did not see the hand of my own species in the fate of the seal pup. Nature finds its own way of dealing with life and death, but it is the weight of the hand of my own kind as it interferes with that balance that is most alarming. The cormorant was symbolic of that concern.

On another day, I remember experiencing the effects of the sea upon me.

Wildlife is everywhere. There are seals, eiders, small waders and a group of around 20 curlews fly by. A pair of shelducks draws my attention and then the beauty of the starkly contrasting brilliant white and jet-black plumage of a gannet as it wheels and plunges into the sea. The noise of the sea is everywhere, restless with movements and sounds. When I taste the water it is salty, when I splash it over my face it feels cold and wet, why am I surprised? My whole being is infiltrated by its presence and I am left thinking that my own body is made up of water and salt. I am the sea and the sea is me – a biological reality but a metaphysical one too that connects me to the waterways of Meares Island several years ago.

These inner and outer, metaphysical and biological realities are deepened when I round Whiting Ness and encounter sharply contrasting geological features. Numerous faults and bedding planes are everywhere, and even within the Old Red Sandstone there are layers of variations. Some of the rock is made up of fine-grained sandstone sediment and some is from much larger conglomerate sediment. The sea has eaten away at the 'softer' sandstone and sculpted it into wonderfully varied shapes, leaving the coastline littered with caves and stacks. All along this coast there are stories written into this landscape and with my limited geological knowledge I could only wonder at this mesmerising collision of time and space. Clearly great forces were at work here to create such a convoluted land mass.

To find some respite from the gathering wind and complicated sea conditions, I had sneaked into the deep recess known as 'Dickmont's Den'. I say 'sneaked' because my inclination had been to pass by as the onshore wind and resulting clapotis had caused tricky wave conditions, but curiosity had gotten the better of me. The waves had been funnelling through the narrow entrance and as I paddled closer I was waiting for a rogue wave that might pick me up and propel me onto the rocks. However, I managed to pass through the funnel with little drama. Sheltered from the wind and waves towards the back of the Den, I found absolute tranquillity. This set the tone for the rest of the day as I sought shelter and explored the inner sanctum of one cave after another. The experience bordered on the sacred. The coastline here is full of the history of landscape formation. It is not surprising that the Scottish geologist, James Hutton, coined the term 'deep time' to communicate his ideas about the planet's vast age and the long history of life (Macfarlane, 2003).

Whale Wisdom

With my senses straining at the leash, infused by so much external stimulus, I find myself scanning the coastline for the next natural wonder. Peering into a recessed bay, I see something large lying high up on the beach. Drawing closer I see it is the carcass of a whale and stop for a better look. Approaching a dead and decomposing whale from downwind is not a clever thing to do. The stench is appalling; something I later described as sweet, sickly and forever memorable. I pace out its length and estimate it is 12 metres long. Not being able to identify it, I took a photograph which I later sent to the Hebridean Whale and Dolphin Trust. They told me that its very long flippers helped to confirm that it was a humpback whale. Not only were they able to identify its species but they knew what had happened to it. They told me that humpbacks were not that common in the North Sea. This one was first reported dead the month before. It had been floating near to the beach I found it on. When it had first been examined it showed signs of having been entangled in lines, probably creel lines, which appear to have been the cause of death.

Looking round the carcass I can see that it has been vandalised and mutilated. One rusty leg from an old chair is protruding from an eye socket and another from its anal passage. I feel anger at the perpetrators and a great degree of sadness for this once magnificent creature lying debased in death. Yet in some ways the anger is illogical and a little strange. It is illogical because at one level this is only a piece of rotting flesh. However, it is not death, nor the manner in which it came about, nor even what had happened to the carcass after the whale's death, that troubled me. It would be easy for me to look at the whale and find some theoretical explanation about what was wrong here and perhaps externalise the whole experience by looking for other people to blame. By doing this I would be looking in the wrong place for answers to what grieved me.

I remember, as a child, using an air rifle to shoot garden birds for 'fun'. On reflection, I did not have a highly developed values system to appreciate living things. Nowadays, when I recall these experiences I shudder, knowing that my actions were cruel and wanton. I could spend a lot of time theorising my past actions to come up with 'clever' arguments that would justify these actions (for example, I was only a child; I am a different person now). Worse perhaps, I could conveniently overlook this incident, and others like it, pretend they did not happen, ignore my feelings, and try not to think about them. However, one thing I cannot do is to theorise away the *feelings* I have for what happened. This, I think, reveals one of the major obstacles in our search for sustainable lifestyles. To my way of thinking, our clever minds are constantly trying to rationalise our behaviour and this is a natural function of our intellect. However, by *post hoc* rationalising our behaviour in this way, is there not a danger that we come to blame others and not ourselves for our actions or inaction? Each of us could say 'environmental degradation is not my fault' and then bask in the glow of a clear conscience.

When I looked at the vandalised whale before me and considered who was to blame, the first image I had was of a gang of youths on a Saturday afternoon with nothing better to do. However, as I began to think less about the actions of whoever did this, it suddenly dawned on me that the hurt I was experiencing was not just for the whale before me but also the hurt that I have caused and been part of in my own life. One of the central components of pragmatism, the relatedness between experiences, was unfolding before me and happening without much prompting. This incident had become part of something shaped by my previous experiences and honed in the present by the immediacy of their directness and power. In this manner there exists a 'psychical connector between the object and the individual; it is like a psychical bridge – it connects the consciousness with some otherwise ostensibly independent object' (Jonas, 2011, p. 115).

Some Final Thoughts and Feelings

The incidents with the cormorant, the seal pup and the whale, and my attempts to continually relate mind to world, are a reminder of the pragmatist view that experiences are not simply individual but social. Evernden has stated 'this tradition implies that it is misleading to speak of an isolated self surveying a world, for the person is from the start *in* the world, and consciousness is always *of* the world.

The world is the evidence we have of our own involvement' (1985, p. 59). From this I conclude that it may well not have been Robbie Nicol who forced a chair leg up the whale's anus and another into its eye socket but it was someone not unlike me, and certainly someone of my own kind.

Dewey has said that 'every experience is a moving force. Its value can be judged only on the ground of what it moves toward and into' (1963, p. 38). It is the complete and utter directness of experiences such as these that may just provide the inspiration for people to do something about their unsustainable relationship with the planet. Such experiences have powerful emotional rawness that are direct and compelling and can be harnessed as moral impulses (Nicol, 2013, 2014). Perhaps this type of engagement with the world offers the best hope of developing a 'moving force' toward and into sustainable living.

Furthermore, as Weston has stated 'pragmatists are not looking for knockdown arguments; we propose to concern ourselves with defending environmental values in other ways' (2003, p. 316). I am not advancing the case for anti-intellectualism, not least because conceptual knowledge will always remain a central feature of this challenge – how else can we begin to understand, for example, the science of climate change? (Nicol, 2014). What I am suggesting is the need to experiment with what happens when direct experiences of the sea are consciously informed by our conceptual knowledge of the world.

Ultimately, the search for those elusive 'knock down' arguments that finally define intrinsic value, or resolve ontological dualisms, will, in their abstraction, miss the point. Reflecting on the experiences I have shared in this chapter I wonder if the connection between subject and object is based less on value and more on the significance to the individual of what is experienced. This is an important distinction for Evernden because focusing more on significance and meaning 'disposes of the distance between the thinker and his [*sic*] object. And given this different point of departure, one is free to ask quite different questions' (1985, p. 59).

There may well be a strong connection between the individual experiences presented here and the challenges posed to society by the need to live sustainability. These experiences can unite mind and world only when they are considered as a pro-active search for meaning amongst the beauty and inspiration of the sea. This is precisely what Thrift meant when he asked the question 'What is an idea?' He goes on to state 'whatever an idea's exact content might be, it is also important to be able to understand the way in which an idea is framed because that framing has consequences' (2004, p. 583). Experiences and ideas are meaningful when considered as an active quest to find purpose in a contemporary world characterised by a changing atmosphere, degraded oceans, reduced biodiversity yet infinite beauty. They are related by Evernden's ideas around the meaning and significance of experiences for the individual, and Dewey's idea that in order to be meaningful experiences need to be social as well as individual and move towards something (in this case environmental sustainability).

But, it cannot end there. Just as narratives of self (mind) can lead to navel gazing so too can narratives of society (world). For pragmatists it is not sufficient to just live in the world. As Heron has pointed out 'we [he is referring to his work with Peter Reason] believe that what we learn about our world will be richer and deeper, if this descriptive knowledge is incidental to a primary intention to develop practical skills to change the world' (1996, p. 239).

The questions I have posed, and in some way sought to answer, have been framed from my perspective as a sea kayaker. However, if we are to pay more than just lip service to purposeful movement towards connecting mind with world, and world with mind, then significance and meaning must extend beyond the individual. More and more sea kayakers are joining the growing body of enthusiasts who look to seascapes for their recreation, health and well-being. This sector comprises individuals spanning all classes, all professions, all ages and genders. The point is that these people, through their familiarity with sea and landscapes, represent a mind/world link to many aspects of economic society where decisions are made about the production, distribution and consumption of goods and services. Those who search for meaning through direct engagement in the outdoors are already part of a social web contained within the web of life itself. This is why it is so important that those who 'play' in seascapes remind themselves of the relationship between people and sea places because once motivated they are in a position to do something about it across a broad range of societal functions (for example local and central government, industry, commerce, consumer practices and so on).

Perhaps this reintegration of thought and experience provides the most compelling motivation for those with a love of seascapes to engage in and promote sustainable living. Weston has said 'we learned the values of nature through experience and effort, through mistakes and mishaps, through poetry and stargazing, and, if we are lucky, a few inspired friends' (2003, p. 316).

I would like to leave the last word to one of my own inspired friends. Very soon after my visit to Meares Island, I met Jim Cheney for the first time. We have shared many conversations on and off the water since. Jim's gentle nature and philosophical pragmatism is always informed by a fiery passion for people, planet and justice. His manner is impish and always infused by curiosity and mischievousness. Since we first met, there has never been a time when I have contemplated anything important without wondering what Jim might have thought. As an 'inspired friend', it is fitting to close with Jim's invitation to all of us to go out and *be* in the world, in the way that he meant it.

The sea calls to me to 'be' in the world. By *being* in the world, I gain a fuller understanding of who I am and how I might live in a meaningful manner.

References

Abram, D., 1997. *The Spell of the Sensuous*. New York: Vintage.

Bowers, C.A., 1993. *Education, Cultural Myths and the Ecological Crisis*. Albany: State University of New York Press.

Curry, P., 2006. *Ecological Ethics*. Cambridge: Polity.

Dewey, J., 1963. *Experience and Education.* London: Collier-Macmillan.

Devall, B. and Sessions, G., 1985. *Deep Ecology: Living as if Nature Mattered.* Layton, Utah: Gibbs Smith.

Donaldson, M., 1978. *Children's Minds.* London: Fontana Press.

Ekins, P., 2000. *Economic Growth and Environmental Sustainability.* London: Routledge.

Evernden, N., 1985 *The Natural Alien.* Toronto: University of Toronto Press.

Guha, R., 2005. Radical American environmentalism and 'wilderness' preservation: A Third World critique. In: L. Kalof and T. Satterfield, eds, *Environmental Values.* London: Earthscan, pp. 102–12.

Hayward, T., 1994. *Ecological Thought.* Cambridge: Polity.

Heron, J., 1996. *Co-Operative Inquiry: Research into the Human Condition.* London: Sage.

James, S., 2009. *The Presence of Nature: A Study in Phenomenological and Environmental Philosophy.* Hampshire: Palgrave Macmillan.

Jonas, M.E., 2011. Dewey's conception of interest and its significance for teacher education. *Educational Philosophy and Theory*, 43(2), pp. 112–29.

Macfarlane, R., 2003. *Mountains of the Mind: A History of Fascination.* London: Granta Books.

Nicol, R., 2013. Returning to the richness of experience: Is autoethnography a useful approach for outdoor educators in promoting pro-environmental behaviour? *Journal of Adventure Education and Outdoor Learning*, 13(1), pp. 3–17.

———— 2014. Entering the fray: The role of outdoor education in providing nature-based experiences that matter. *Educational Philosophy and Theory*, 46(5), pp. 449–61.

Pratt, V., Howarth, J. and Brady, E., 2000. *Environment and Philosophy.* London: Routledge.

Reason, P., 2006. Choice and quality in action research practice. *Journal of Management Inquiry*, 15(2), pp. 187–203.

Sessions, G., ed., 1995. *Deep Ecology for the 21st Century.* London: Shambhala.

Thrift, N., 2004. Movement-space: The changing domain of thinking resulting from the development of new kinds of spatial awareness. *Economy and Society*, 33(4), pp. 582–604.

———— 2006. Special issue on problematizing global knowledge. *Theory, Culture and Society*, 23(2–3), pp. 139–46.

Weston, A., ed., 1999. *An Invitation to Environmental Philosophy.* New York: Oxford University Press.

———— 2003. Beyond intrinsic value: Pragmatism in environmental ethics. In: A. Light and Holmes Ralston III, eds, *Environmental Ethics: An Anthology.* Oxford: Blackwell, pp. 307–18.

Chapter 11

Unlikely Becomings:
Passion, Swimming and
Learning to Love the Sea

Karen Throsby

I have never lived by the sea and I loathe boats, succumbing to seasickness on all but the most fat and stable of ferries on the calmest of days. My early ocean memories are from family holidays, of paddling in the shallows, or bobbing with my older brother in an inflatable dinghy, tethered to the shore by a long nylon rope held by my dad – a security against the perils of being 'swept out to sea'. As we got older, we played, untethered now and confident swimmers, jumping and bodyboarding in the breaking waves on Woolacombe Sands, our parents' warnings to 'stay between the flags' ringing in our ears. The shoreline was our holiday playground, a contained zone of summer excitement between the dry safety of the beach and the dangerous emptiness of a sea into which careless children could be 'swept'.

Fast-forward to the dawn hours of 2 September 2010.

I have been swimming for five hours, heading straight out from the pebbly shore of Shakespeare Beach in the pitch dark of night, swimming in a spot-lit pool of light cast from the boat beside me. It is a comforting tether to safety – I remember my dad, ankle deep in water, holding the nylon rope. In the half-light of a beautiful dawn, when I breathe to the left, away from the boat, I see a pinkish sky and a scattering of feathery clouds. A breath to the right reveals the shadowy shapes of my crew, Peter and Sam, watching over me from the deck, each with a neon light stick strung around their necks so I know they are there, even in the dark. The lights look like two bright green exclamation marks – a surprised commentary on the extraordinary situation I find myself in. I have strayed very far from between the flags and my skin prickles with an adrenalin-flooded burst of excitement when the reality of what I am doing hits me through the comforting tap-tap-tap of hands on water: I am swimming the English Channel.

Introduction

The English Channel has an iconic status in the swimming community but is just one of many sites for the sport of marathon swimming, which can be broadly defined as the activity of swimming long distances in open water without assistance from propulsion, buoyancy or insulation. The term 'marathon swimming' technically encompasses all swims of 10 km or more but my usage here refers to the ultra-domain of the sport, as represented iconically by the English Channel, but also including other long swims that commonly take 10–20 (or more) hours to complete over distances of more than 20 miles. In a nostalgic nod to the conditions of the first successful English Channel crossing by Matthew Webb in 1875 (Mortimer, 2008), what have come to be known as 'Channel rules' are now standard for a host of marathon sea and freshwater swims. These conventions dictate that swims are conducted wearing only a regular non-buoyant, non-insulating costume, a single latex or silicone cap and a pair of goggles, and swimmers must swim from shore to shore without purposefully touching the accompanying boat or anyone on it. It is a truism, then, to say that marathon swimming is a niche sport and one that both demands and produces particular relationships with the sea.

This chapter focuses on my own 'unlikely becoming' from holiday dipper and pool swimmer to passionate marathon swimmer, and my evolving relationship with the sea. How can I understand my transition from someone so geographically and experientially alienated from the sea to a swimmer whose first thought on glimpsing a stretch of water is: 'I wonder what it would be like to swim that?' The chapter is not about *why* I am a marathon swimmer or the psychologies of motivation but rather *how* that process of becoming occurred. What had to happen for this landlocked middle-aged sociologist to become so intimately engaged with the sea? What social and embodied processes are enacted in that transition? And how does it contribute to my understanding of who I am?

To explain this process, and my own shifting engagement with the sea, this chapter draws on Howard Becker's classic writings on 'becoming a marihuana user' – a segment of his broader studies of outsider status and deviant behaviour (Becker, 1963). Becker argued that psychological accounts of marihuana use (as a need for fantasy or as an escape from individual problems) were inadequate and that it was necessary to account for the social processes through which a vague impulse or desire to try the drug was 'transformed into definite patterns of action' (1963, p. 42). In short, he was looking for 'the sequence of changes in attitude and experience which lead to the use of marihuana for pleasure' (p. 43). The element of pleasure is important here (and to my own analysis), since it emphasises 'the noncompulsive and casual character of the behavior' (p. 43). This is reflected in the significant variability of use over time by individuals – a fact that Becker argues problematises theories of individual predisposition (p. 44). This is also appealing in terms of thinking critically about marathon sea swimming – a status-bearing activity that is often accounted for both within and outside of the swimming community via discourses of innate individual qualities (courage, toughness, determination). As Reischer argues in the context of the exhausted completion of a running marathon, it becomes 'metonymic of one's life' (2001, p. 30). But these narratives of individually held, innate qualities fail to account for the specificity of marathon swimming selfhood and the profoundly social nature of the processes through which that specificity is acquired.

Becker's theory begins with the person who is already willing to try marihuana, perhaps by being around people who are already using the drug and through whom they can gain access to a supply (1963, p. 61). This individual

> knows others use marihuana to 'get high', but he [*sic*][1] does not know what this means in any concrete way. He is curious about the experience, ignorant of what it may turn out to be, and afraid it may be more than he has bargained for. (Becker, 1963, p. 46)

The same may be said of marathon sea swimming, which, for many people outside of the sport, is not only inconceivable but actively undesirable (for example, on the grounds of fear or disgust). In the absence of the willingness to try, it is unlikely that these individuals will ever enter into the process of becoming a marathon swimmer. However, for others, the willingness to try, or perhaps to imagine, marathon swimming is already present, however latently. In my own case, this arose out of a lifetime of pool swimming and, therefore, an existing identity as a 'swimmer'. The groundwork was further laid by some cautious 'dabbling' in open-water lake swimming, and in the process, some chance encounters with English Channel swimmers triggered me to act upon my willingness to try. This entry into the sport reflects a combination of what Stevenson (2002) describes as 'seekership' and 'recruitment' – common processes through which initial entry into an activity is achieved. Existing identities as endurance athletes or as charity challenge participants, for other participants in my research, created a similar openness to the possibilities of marathon swimming as a plausible new dimension to an existing identity. Some marathon swimmers had simply grown up around the sea or lived near one of the geographical centres (Unruh, 1980) of the social world of marathon swimming where the sport had become normalised via a critical mass of accomplished practitioners. The readiness to imagine the activity's inherent pleasures and the willingness to try, then, is a necessary foundation for becoming a marathon swimmer (or marihuana smoker), and following Becker, is the starting point for my discussion.

From this initial readiness to try, Becker proposes that users have to pass through three consecutive stages in order to convert this willingness to try into the ability to use marihuana for pleasure: (1) learning the technique; (2) learning to perceive the effects; and (3) learning to enjoy the effects. For Becker, then, rather than deviant motives (or predispositions) leading to deviant behaviour, 'deviant

---

[1]   For the sake of tidiness, I have not corrected Becker's generic use of the masculine pronoun throughout.

motives actually develop in the course of experience with deviant activity' (1963, p. 41). 'The explanation of each step', he argues, 'is thus part of the explanation of the resulting behavior' (p. 23). This chapter takes this three-step process as a framework for examining both my own unlikely becoming as a marathon swimmer and my concomitant changing relationship to the sea.

The fit, however, is not a perfect one and requires some qualification. Becker was writing about those whose behaviours placed individuals within subcultures branded as deviant, falling outside of the socially and legally enforced rules of a given society. Marathon swimming, on the other hand, is an activity which is not only legal but also aligns easily with the dominant neoliberal social values of self-discipline and efficacy as well as demonstrating care and control of the embodied self. Indeed, while Becker's marihuana smokers pursued their 'deviant' practices necessarily outside of public view, marathon swims are often actively publicised and openly celebrated.

Nevertheless, it is by no means a mainstream activity and, for many, the extremity of marathon swimming places it outside of the normatively expected investment in the self. As such, we can understand marathon swimming as a form of 'positive deviance' (Ewald and Jiobu, 1985; Hughes and Coakley, 1991) – a good thing taken too far. Firstly, marathon swimming is physically punishing and injury is a perpetual risk and fact of the activity (see also, Turner and Wainwright, 2003; Hockey, 2005; Willig, 2008; Hanold, 2010). Secondly, like many 'serious leisure' pursuits (Stebbins, 2007), marathon swimming is a 'greedy avocation' (Gillespie, Leffler and Lerner, 2002, p. 288) consuming time, financial resources and emotional energy in ways which, for some, signify a solipsistic over-investment in the self and a selfishly unbalanced life in relation to domestic and work commitments (Baldwin, 1999; Gillespie, Leffler and Lerner, 2002; Raisborough, 2006; Stalp, 2007; Dilley and Scraton, 2010). And finally, the sea itself is perceived by many as dangerously 'out of bounds' in comparison to the more familiar sanitised spaces of the swimming pool or domesticated beaches.[2] Marathon swimming, therefore, while lacking the overt deviance of illicit drug-taking, is an out-of-the-ordinary practice whose intensity and extensity positions it as always potentially (positively) deviant.

---

2   See, for example, beach safety campaigns that emphasise the importance of staying within lifeguarded zones, not going out of your depth and the power of tides and currents (RNLI, 2011, 2013). In making this point, I am not disputing either the importance of these safety rules or underestimating the potential dangers of the sea; indeed, marathon swimmers are among the most keenly aware of those risks and the sport is characterised by high levels of attention to swimmer and crew safety. Rather, I want to emphasise the common representation of the open sea as a place of danger.

Aquatic Sociology

In order to explore this positively deviant social world, in 2009, I embarked upon a two-and-a-half year research project entitled 'Becoming a Channel Swimmer'.[3] This marked the beginning of my research career as what *The Guardian* newspaper described as an 'aquatic sociologist' (Arnott, 2010), through which I immersed myself – literally and metaphorically – in the marathon swimming world. Using my own body 'as tool of inquiry and a vector of knowledge' (Wacquant, 2004, p. viii), I documented in autoethnographic detail both my own embodied process of transformation whilst training for swims of the English Channel (2010) and the Catalina Channel (2011), my increasingly passionate immersion in the social world of marathon swimming and my changing relationship with the sea (and other bodies of open water). In the course of the research, I also carried out 'observant participation' (Wacquant 2004, p. 6) at a number of key training sites and sea swimming communities in the UK, Malta, Ireland and southern California, conducting formal interviews with 45 swimmers, partners, coaches, pilots and other involved individuals, as well as keeping notes of uncountable informal conversations (see also, Throsby, 2013a, 2013b). This more conventionally ethnographic data performs a supplementary function for this chapter, which draws primarily on the autoethnographic elements of the research, taking advantage of the detailed critical self-reflection of the fieldnotes that would otherwise be inaccessible through interviews or observation alone (Sparkes, 2009). It is, therefore, a highly individualised account that aims not towards a generalisable account of *the* path to marathon swimming, but rather, a very specifically contextualised exploration, via Becker's three-stage thesis, of how an individual came to find pleasure in something that is not self-evidently pleasurable in the first encounter.

In what follows, I incorporate Becker's explanation of the three stages to explicate my own experiences of becoming a marathon swimmer via the lens of each, including some commentary on the possibilities and limitations of this stage-structure for understanding the process of becoming a marathon swimmer.

Stage One: Learning the Techniques

Becker argues that a novice marihuana smoker 'does not ordinarily get high the first time he smokes marihuana [...]' (1963, p. 46). This is, he suggests, because it is not smoked 'properly', with many novices mistakenly smoking it like a cigarette and failing to draw the smoke in deeply enough to be effective. The first step, then, in becoming a user 'is that he must learn to use the proper smoking technique so that his use of the drug will produce effects in terms of which his conception of it can change' (p. 47). In a similar vein, lacking many of the skills and techniques of

---

3   ESRC ref: RES-000–22–4055. See: http://www.warwick.ac.uk/go/channelswimmer.

marathon sea swimming, my first training swims gave me none of the pleasures that other swimmers had reported.

In April 2009, I joined a specialist training camp for long-distance swimmers on the island of Gozo in Malta. This was not my first sustained engagement with sea swimming. Prior to this I had been on organised, leisurely sea swimming holidays in warm, beautiful locations, with stunning swims punctuated by delicious food and relaxation. However, the Gozo trip was my first experience of sea swimming in marathon swimming mode. In my mind, this was not holiday; this was *training* and the sea was my proving ground. Already committed to an English Channel swim attempt in August 2010, I had come to see what I could do, how I would cope and to learn as much as I could in the colder waters of the springtime Mediterranean.[4] I recorded one of the first training swims of the trip in my fieldnotes:

The boat took us out of the harbour to a spot a couple of hundred metres offshore. We stripped down to our costumes and began the rituals of swim preparation: sun cream first, with its social dance of mutual back-slathering, and then standing, arms up and apart, while a latex-gloved guide smeared globs of Vaseline under our armpits, costume straps and around the backs of our necks to prevent chafing. Already, I had forgotten one of the first lessons we'd been taught on day one – get your cap and goggles on before you grease up so you don't get smudges on your lenses. Absent-mindedly, I straightened my costume straps, getting Vaseline smears on my fingers before reaching for the goggles perched on top of my kit bag. Beginner's error. I rummaged in my bag for a spare pair, cursing my stupidity and embarrassed at my obvious display of novice status. Safety boats were untethered from the boat and we were given our orders: a two-and-a-half hour swim up the coast towards a promontory in the distance and into a bay, setting off in pace groups marked by hat colour. Then, 'Jump!' Not wanting to appear tentative, I hurled myself off the dive platform and into the air, away from the boat, breaking the surface in an ungainly splash before resurfacing with a horrified gasp. COLD – so much colder than the sheltered, shallower waters of the bay we'd swum in on the first day of the trip. I gave a couple of hyperventilating gasps, straining to catch my breath; my skin burned and prickled and my forehead throbbed with an 'ice cream' headache. Unwilling to be left behind, I started to swim after my fellow yellow-hats, turning my arms furiously to catch up and to try and shake off the shock of cold.

A second problem: the sea was chaotic and choppy, and I was unbalanced and disorientated by the motion across every plane and axis. My months of pool training and careful stroke work seemed useless in the face of this impossibly mobile environment. I mistimed a breath and gulped down a mouthful of sea water,

---

4   The water was about 15° Celsius (58° Fahrenheit) and was, therefore, seen as good preparation for an English Channel swim, which would usually be between 15–18° C.

which made my stomach heave; I gagged and the tension of coughing creased my face, letting water seep under the seal of my goggles into the corner of my right eye. Cold, nauseous, sore-eyed misery crawled through me. I was falling behind my group and, each time I sank into a trough between waves, I lost sight of the safety boat and the reassuring cluster of yellow heads in front of me; my fingers felt fat and stiff with cold and I seemed unable to manage more than a handful of consecutive strokes before being upended by a wave or having to pause to orient myself. Everything I had read told me that I should learn to 'listen to my body' and know my own limits as a marathon swimmer, but I was at a loss as to how to interpret this barrage of unfamiliar bodily signals or where my limits might possibly lie amidst all this novel unpleasantness. All I could think about was how utterly miserable I was and how stupid I had been to think that I could swim the Channel. Self-pityingly, I distracted myself from my suffering and incompetence by drafting a letter in my head to my English Channel boat pilot, withdrawing from my 2010 swim.

The necessary techniques of marathon sea swimming fall into two separate but interconnecting domains: firstly, and at the risk of stating the obvious, you have to be (or become) a competent swimmer to be a marathon sea swimmer; and secondly, the swimmer needs command, honed by personal experience and idiosyncratic preference, of a wide range of preparatory, in-water and post-swim routines and practices that minimise the potential for harm or discomfort for the swimmer and facilitate sustained endurance, as well as signalling social belonging.

Even (or perhaps especially) the most confident and competent swimmers devote at least some training time to ongoing technique work – for example, using repetitive, mindful drilling in order to embody 'good' swimming habits that both enhance pace and efficiency and mitigate injury risk. Even for a relatively confident swimmer like myself back in 2009, I lacked the techniques specific to *sea* swimming. As my swimming apprenticeship progressed, I learned to breathe out slowly underwater to quell the drive to hyperventilate when I jumped into cold water. In choppy water, through instruction from experienced others, careful observation and trial and error, I learned to adapt my stroke to the conditions: for example, by training myself to breathe bilaterally (to either side) in order to be able to breathe away from incoming waves, and by increasing the body's roll along the long axis to help both the mouth and the recovering arm clear the water more easily in rough conditions. These are techniques, like the act of swimming itself, that can be described and imitated, but that can only be acquired effectively through time in the water, during which the body acquires the capacity to make the 'fleeting improvisations' (Lorimer and Lund, 2003, p. 142) of habitual movement.

This process of technique acquisition highlights the ways in which the work of becoming appropriately skilled is never simply a matter of perfect repetition of a careful honed movement but rather, demands the ability to constantly adjust and adapt bodily movement (see, for example: Downey, 2005, p. 49; Throsby 2013a, p. 13). As Lea, following Deleuze, argues in her analysis of Thai Yoga Massage

(TYM) training, appropriate technique involves being able to 'conjugate with the context' (Lea, 2009, p. 467) and this process is as much about embodied 'feel' as objective knowledge. As has been documented in other diverse domains of skill acquisition including becoming a barista (Laurier, 2003), piano playing (Sudnow, 2001), surfing (Ford and Brown, 2006; Humberstone, 2011), Capoeira (Downey, 2005) and dance (Potter, 2008), the acquisition of sea swimming technique is a long, slow passage through various degrees of competence, beginning with the self-conscious watchfulness of the novice and eventually reaching a point where the swimming body seems able to find its own way in the aquatic world. It becomes 'a strategy without a strategist' (Sudnow, 2001, p. x). This aspect of technique acquisition is missing from Becker's account, which speeds quickly over this first stage in just a handful of pages, focusing on direct teaching, discrete observation and imitation as vectors for the cognitive acquisition of the correct inhalation techniques, but without any account of the process through which those techniques pass from the domain of intentional theorising.

The techniques of sea swimming are not the only skills that the marathon sea swimmer requires. Other skills include, for example, the rituals of 'greasing up'; in-water feeding regimens and techniques; or post-swim changing routines that minimise heat loss (hat first, then the top half of the body, then the bottom half). The 'rules' constitute techniques of the body that neutralise, or minimise, aspects of marathon sea swimming that would otherwise make it more difficult or more uncomfortable and are, therefore, essential techniques in the process of successfully 'becoming'. Just as Lea found with the TYM textbook she was given to study (2009, p. 469), the 'rules' and their limitations only come to life through practice. For example, the preparatory ritual of 'greasing up' involves both a generalisable rule – always use Vaseline (or similar) before even a short sea swim to avoid painful chafing – and a series of idiosyncratic adaptations including not only favoured products but also an intimate knowledge of likely chafing spots. This skill acquisition can also be seen as part of what Stevenson (2002) describes as the 'conversion' process, during which novices acquire the specialist vocabularies, practices and values of the group or activity as part of their growing 'entanglement' with it.

These techniques of the body, then, constitute the foundations for the next stage in Becker's taxonomy – learning to perceive the effects.

Stage Two: Learning to Perceive the Effects

Becker argues that there are two elements to 'being high': 'the presence of symptoms caused by marihuana use and the recognition of these symptoms and their connection by the user with his use of the drug' (1963, p. 48). Even with the proper technique, novice users frequently reported failure to get high, even when those around them perceived them as self-evidently stoned. In response, the novice would begin to listen intently to other more experienced users as they described the sensations caused by the drug, thereby acquiring 'the necessary concepts with which to express to himself the fact that he was experiencing new sensations caused by the drug' (p. 51). In time, the novice develops a 'stable set of categories for experiencing the drug's effects' (p. 52), which in turn enable the user to 'get high with ease' (p. 52).

Given the reliance of the acquisition of swimming technique on 'feel', the distinction between the first and second stages here lacks the clean delineation of the model as set out by Becker, operating in iterative rather than cleanly linear relation to each other. Nevertheless, learning both to recognise and calibrate the effects of marathon swimming is a key element in the process. As described in the earlier fieldnotes extract, one of the primary challenges, especially for the novice, is the unintelligibility of the barrage of novel sensations. This is exemplified by the case of cold.[5] In everyday, non-swimming life, even a modest sensation of cold is usually a prompt to action – closing a window, putting on a sweater, turning up the heating. More overt physiological responses to a fall in body temperature such as goose bumps or shivering are generally experienced as a pressing call for rewarming action. However, in the case of marathon sea swimming, the effect of cold is calibrated very differently. This was brought home to me in 2011, when I worked as a guide on the same training camp in Gozo that I had participated in as a novice swimmer in 2009. During a chilly 6-hour training swim, one of the participants broke from the swim circuit in the bay and paddled her way over to the beach intent on getting out early. She sobbed miserably that she was too cold to continue and she held up her arm, covered in goose bumps, as evidence of her suffering. Another of the guides, a very experienced swimmer who was in the water with the group, headed her off, holding up his goose bumped arm alongside her own: 'We've all got those. You're fine. Keep swimming!' Thwarted, she slid her body back into the water and headed out into the bay to rejoin the training circuit, going on to safely complete her first 6-hour swim. What we usually understand as 'cold' does not apply in this context and swimmers have to learn to recalibrate if they are to go on to find marathon swimming pleasurable; they have to understand the effects on the body differently.

In the weeks following my own Gozo training camp in 2009, I swam several times a week in much colder water in local lakes, watchfully exploring the effects of cold on my body and trying to identify these new, unintelligible boundaries of cold. I described the effects in my fieldnotes: the 'sausage-fingers', clawed hands, ice cream headaches, the numbness at my peripheries as my body held the warm blood protectively at my core. The cold was recorded in my fieldnotes as tingling, biting, burning, searing. Minutes after leaving the water, I learned to recognise the

---

5   Not all marathon swims take place in cold water but water temperature is a primary concern for many of the iconic marathon swims (e.g. the English Channel), and acclimatisation is a crucial part of the training process.

dramatic post-swim shivering of the 'afterdrop',[6] and tense-jawed and fumbling, bundled under layers, I would try to pour hot chocolate from my flask into a cup, slopping liquid over the sides like a drunk. However disconcerting and frightening in the first instance, both to the novice and to the uninitiated around them, all this, I learned, is normal. This is how it is supposed to feel, especially in the early season while the water is still inching out of its winter lows. Occasionally, I pushed the envelope too far and became too cold-addled and thick-fingered to dress myself without help. I tried to remember the feeling of cold that preceded it – the slowing of my stroke and the numbness creeping up my limbs. Like all swimmers, I learned to read the cold based on my body's own reaction to it, recalling the connoisseurship described by Becker among his marihuana smokers, who claimed to be able to distinguish between different qualities and strengths of marihuana (1963, p. 52). In this way, I began to delineate boundaries of 'safe' cold as an effect of swimming, expanding the safe possibilities of time in the sea and the pleasures that it brings.

Experience also teaches novices to embrace what Potter describes as a 'shifted sensorium' (2008, p. 459; see also Throsby, 2013a). As Merchant notes in the context of scuba diving, immersion in water demands 'a reorganization of the land-based or travelling sensorium' (2011, p. 216). This is significant in the process of becoming a marathon sea swimmer because reliance upon a conventional land-based sensorium effectively renders marathon sea swimming an experience of sensory deprivation; indeed, this provides the basis of many of the outward-facing stories of suffering that are told (for example, on charitable fund-raising websites) to illustrate the 'toughness' of the challenge. Engaging the 'travelling sensorium' on the other hand reveals new dimensions of sensory experience. For example, hearing (in its land-based sense) is dulled during a long sea swim. However, an unexpected cacophony of new sounds gradually becomes audible to the swimmer: the musical rhythms of swimming as hands tap-tap-tap into the water; the sound-sensation of exhaled bubbles rolling up the cheeks; the watery crackles and ticks of submersion (Merchant, 2011, p. 227); the hiss of pebbles being dragged along the ocean floor. Marathon sea swimming, then, is far from quiet but not always in immediately perceptible ways. Over time, these sounds become integral to sea swimming itself. A brief experiment with ear plugs in 2011 after recurrent bouts of 'swimmer's ear' failed miserably, when I found myself unable to find the rhythms of long swimming without the sounds that it had taken me so long to become attuned to.

Learning to perceive, interpret and respond to the effects of being a swimming body in water is, therefore, a central element in the process of becoming a marathon sea swimmer, both in terms of recalibrating what counts as a problem

---

6   After exiting cold water, the body begins to recirculate the warm blood held at the body's core out to the peripheries, driving the cold peripheral blood back to the core, causing a drop in body temperature (the 'afterdrop'). Swimmers learn to use the short window before the afterdrop to change as quickly as possible to maximise heat retention.

and embodying a reconfigured swimming sensorium. This highlights an aspect of the process that is missing from Becker's framework – the transformation of the body itself. Writing of marathon running, Reischer argues that cycles of training cause the body itself to undergo profound changes, including a decreased resting heart rate, increased oxygen capacity, altered blood chemistry, increased metabolism, improved muscle tone and changed body composition; the body, 'from the micro-cellular to the gross anatomical level, is transformed' (2001, p. 27). These transformations affect how the body experiences the effects of swimming, which in turn contributes to the transformation of the body. For example, while the swimmer is learning to perceive and delineate the effects of cold on the body, the process of regular immersion simultaneously produces physiological adaptations to the cold, producing marginal but appreciable increases in tolerance (Hong, Rennie and Park, 1987; Makinen, 2010). This highlights both the dialectic, iterative relationship between the acquisition of technique and learning to feel the effects, and the embodied transformations that occur in the course of producing those effects. This iterative embodied process is missing from Becker's more linear model but, nevertheless, these preliminary stages are the necessary precursors of the final stage in the process.

Stage 3: Learning to Enjoy the Effects

> The taste for such experience is a socially acquired one, not different in kind from acquired tastes for oysters or dry martinis. The user feels dizzy, thirsty; his scalp tingles; he misjudges time and distances. Are these things pleasurable? He isn't sure. If he is to continue marihuana use, he must decide that they are. (Becker, 1963, p. 52)

Marathon swimming is undoubtedly an acquired taste and there are many aspects to it that are not easily categorised as pleasurable: cold, pain, nausea, sleep deprivation, fatigue and fear are all common occurrences for even the most experienced and accomplished of swimmers. Technique, practice and familiarity mitigate some of these negative experiences to a certain degree and swimmers become accomplished in making particular kinds of pain and suffering an 'active absence' (Aalten, 2007, p. 118), forcing them into the background. But they are also an integral part of the activity itself and to eliminate them is to change the practice to the point where it is unrecognisable as marathon swimming. Consequently, rather than pleasure being contingent on the elimination of those aspects of the sport, novice participants learn over time to re-evaluate them. Without this transition, following Becker, they are unlike to continue in the sport. There are two dimensions to this re-evaluation: (1) recoding conventionally negative experiences as enjoyable or as evidence of productive activity; and (2) the appreciation of novel, activity specific pleasures that have been made accessible via the earlier stages in the process.

Pain and discomfort are an inevitable part of marathon swimming as muscles fatigue and joints and sinews strain under the repetitive motion of tens of thousands of strokes. As part of the connoisseurship of becoming, marathon swimmers (as with many other endurance athletes) learn to distinguish between different kinds and degrees of pain, differentiating between the injurious pain that is a threat to continued participation and the 'burn' that is experienced positively and actively welcomed as evidence of a job well done (Reischer, 2001; Crossley, 2004; Hanold, 2010). The generic discomforts and pains of long swimming such as aching muscles and drained energy reserves become satisfying evidence of having pushed against limits and having engaged wholeheartedly in a swim. As my own training progressed, I started to actively anticipate the deep, post-swim fatigue of my 6-hour training swims. Hard training produces a bone-tiredness that makes every surface look like a tempting spot for a nap and facilitates a luxuriously thick, profound night's sleep. In a similar process of recoding through experience, rough water becomes a site for play or challenge; cold water becomes 'refreshing' or 'invigorating'; and the depleting effects of a long swim become the grounds for the collective consumption and sharing of food (Throsby, 2013b).

Humour is also an important part of the process of recoding the swimming experience as pleasurable. For example, swimmers commonly experience 'saltmouth' after long periods of immersion. The mouth and tongue thicken and ulcerate from sustained exposure to salt water, eventually culminating in the sloughing of a layer of dead cells from the tongue a couple of days later. These effects, unpleasant and alarming in other contexts, are not only symbolically rewarding (as evidence of long swimming) but also collectively pleasurable as sources of both sub-cultural belonging and in-group humour. It is not uncommon for swimmers to stick out their furred-up tongue on the beach to pantomime shouts of disgust from the swimmers around them or to post photographs on social media. Similarly, images of the 'swimmers' tan' (white goggle rings around the eyes and a pronounced hat-stripe across the forehead) or video clips of dramatic post-swim shivering circulate widely as humorously self-deprecating statements of sub-cultural belonging.

This points to the second way in which swimmers learn to enjoy the effects of marathon swimming: by focusing on novel, activity-specific pleasures that are perceived as outweighing any negatives even whilst being inextricably linked to them and the context in which they occur. This is demonstrated in fieldnotes written following a 6-hour sea swim[7] in Cork, Ireland at the end of a 9-day training camp in 2010 involving almost 100 km of swimming. The swim took the form of 1-mile laps around the island of Sandycove, supported by volunteers on one corner of the island, who passed us our pre-prepared bottles of drink and snacks as we beached ourselves hourly at their feet.

---

7   All prospective English Channel swimmers have to complete a 6-hour qualification swim in water below 16° Celsius. Consequently, many training camps conclude with a 6-hour qualification swim.

The first two hours was nothing but slog. Tired from the week of hard swimming, I felt disjointed and awkward in the water, like a wind-up bath toy, and had already resigned myself to a trudging swim, counting down each lap towards the finish. But into hour three, at last, my body seemed to 'find' the water and my limbs reconnected; I was swimming with my whole body now. I relaxed downwards, like someone finally settling into a chair they hadn't trusted to bear their weight; I let myself be held there, between the opposing forces of gravity and saline buoyancy, between air and sea water. Every movement felt smooth and powerful, as if I were sliding on a gentle downhill slope. Imagine a big tub of ice cream left out in the sun momentarily to soften, and then running a scoop gently down the surface to expose a long, smooth furrow. Swimming felt like travelling, frictionless, down that ice cream furrow. On the outside of the island, facing out into the Atlantic, large swells started rolling in, churning up the water as the island stalled their progress, so I moved further out, where the water had a steadier rhythm into which I could fold myself. It was a clear, sunny day, and the light travelled down through the water in shafts; shoals of tiny fish zipped across my field of vision. The time between feeds gradually collapsed, and I felt for a brief few hours like the best swimmer in the world, like I could swim forever.

Within the swimming community, these elusive intervals of euphoric pleasure are widely recognised and valued. They are referred to as experiences of 'flow' or being 'in the zone' but are notoriously difficult to capture and describe, not least because they occur precisely in those moments when swimming is not happening self-consciously. It is recounted through similes in the interviews, it is like flying, dreaming, dancing. There is not the time and space to do justice to the extensive literature on 'flow' here (see, for example, Csikszentmihalyi, 1988; Logan, 1988; Jackson and Csikszentmihalyi, 1999; Hunter and Csikszentmihalyi, 2000; Game, 2001; Humberstone, 2011) but the significant point is that those highly pleasurable and rewarding states are the product of the very specific interconnections of embodied skills, learned sensory perceptions, the mobile, living, breathing aquatic environment and a specific style of engagement with that environment. This is the taste that I have acquired and those sensations, however provisional, of perfect smoothness and infinite capacity are a key motivator for my continued participation in the sport.

This 'taste', for me, is inextricable from my personal context. I live a 4–5 hour drive away from a good, safe sea swimming location and my everyday training is carried out either in 25-metre chlorinated indoor pools or in local lakes, swimming from buoy to buoy in repetitive 700 m circles. Consequently, my engagements with the sea tend to be highly purposeful. I go to the sea to train (or to undertake a specific marathon swim), swimming for long periods in order both to make the long drive worthwhile and to get the most out of my time-limited access to the unique aquatic environment of the sea. The pleasures that I have learned from sea swimming then are inextricable from long swimming, and the idea of 'dipping' in the sea holds very little appeal for me. I have learned instead to relish the unexpectedly luxurious pleasures of having nothing to do that day but swim.

To finish here is to risk a romance narrative – 'I've never lived by the sea; sea swimming was awful at first; then I learned to love it – ta dah!' This fails to capture the precariousness of the process of 'becoming'. The joyous ice cream smoothness of being 'in the zone' is unpredictably elusive and, on some days, the more mundane pleasures of simply finishing a swim have to be enough. Then there are the bad days – the days when nothing feels right and I seem to be back to the floundering novice state of my first training swims in Gozo in 2009. Becker observes this too, noting that some long-term users had occasional bad experiences with the drug 'which go beyond any conception he has of what being high is and is in much the same situation as the novice, uncomfortable and frightened' (1963, p. 56). He suggests that this can prompt a re-evaluation of the way in which they are using the drug or even a complete cessation of use. In May 2013, for example, I attempted to swim the Cabrera Channel[8] but I was unprepared for the unseasonably low sea temperatures, which sent me into a spiral of hypothermic cognitive impairment and eventually forced the end of the swim after 6 miserable hours. I recalled afterwards feeling like I was being eaten from the inside by cold and I was shocked and frightened by my swift and inexorable decline. In the weeks that followed, I had to force myself to repeat my early experiments around the safe boundaries of cold to rebuild my confidence and capacities, without which the sea held few possibilities for pleasure. The process of 'becoming' a marathon swimmer, then, is never complete or predictably linear.

Conclusion

Taking Becker's work on 'becoming a marihuana user' as a framework, this chapter has explored the process of my becoming a marathon swimmer. Following Becker, I have argued through my embodied experiences that the process of 'becoming' required, firstly, the acquisition of a constellation of skills and techniques that enabled me to be in the water for long periods of time (and to recover effectively afterwards). Secondly, I had to learn to recognise the effects of marathon swimming and then to delineate between different kinds of effects and recalibrate their significance. Finally, in order to continue engagement in the sport, I learned to find pleasure and enjoyment in those effects. These pleasures are multifaceted, ranging from social belonging to satisfaction in the challenge of completion to the euphoric experiences of being 'in the zone'. These are never static and bad experiences (injury, hypothermia) can change the relationship

---

8   The Cabrera Channel is a 25-km swim from the island of Cabrera to Mallorca (Ballearic Islands, Spain).

with the activity – for example, by prompting a return to earlier stages in the process or revising the boundaries around what can or cannot be categorised as pleasurable.

Becker's model of 'becoming' is not without its limitations in this context. In particular, his model focuses on the learned interpretations of the effects of the drug but in doing so, positions the body as relatively static. 'Perception', then, for Becker, emerges as a system of signal decoding rather than an active reordering of the sensorium, and there is very little sense in his discussion of how drug use might change the body itself, or how bodily changes (for example, ageing) might affect the action of drug on the body. In the case of swimming, bodily transformation is much more self-evidently a part of the process and my own body has been marked and reconfigured by the many hours I have spent in the water. I have large shoulders and upper back muscles; I retain a layer of insulating body fat to protect against the cold (Throsby, 2013b); and the skin on my back displays a costume-shaped cross that fades but never disappears. I am literally shaped by the sea (and other bodies of water) in ways that Becker's account cannot easily incorporate.

Nevertheless, Becker's framework is a useful model for thinking about this process of 'becoming'. It is an effective counter against the mystification of ultra-endurance sport, which tends to rely on narratives of suffering and struggle, and on the mobilisation of innate capacities to endure and overcome (Throsby, 2013a). Becker's model disrupts this by demonstrating, firstly, that the process of 'becoming' is a profoundly social one; the marathon swimmer is made, not born. Secondly, this highlights the role of pleasure in the continued engagement with the sport, not only in the accomplishment of a long swim, but also in the act of long swimming itself. This pleasure is not innate to either swimming or to the sea but is a learned process. In a social and cultural moment when there is considerable anxiety about low participation in sport and physical activity and where non-participating individuals are increasingly pathologised for their lack of engagement, this analysis should give pause for thought. Perhaps the question should not be 'how can we get people to exercise?' but rather 'how can people be helped to find exercise pleasurable?' – a reformulation of a question that is both more pragmatic and humane than the prevailing rhetorics of coercion and blame (see also, Throsby, 2013b).

My own experience of the sea as a marathon swimmer is a very specific one, forged around the idiosyncratic pleasures and possibilities of long swimming. And some things never change – I still hate boats. My transformation, then, is highly contingent, marking a very particular process of becoming and a particular kind of relationship with the sea, far outside of the flags.

References

Aalten, A., 2007. Listening to the dancer's body. *Sociological Review*, 55(S1), pp. 109–25.

Arnot, C., 2010. Swimming the Channel in the name of research. *The Guardian*, 5 July 2013. Available at: http://www.theguardian.com/education/2010/jul/19/research-extreme-sports [accessed 3 November 2013].

Baldwin, C.K., 1999. Exploring the dimensions of serious leisure: 'Love me – love my dog!' *Journal of Leisure Research*, 31, pp. 1–17.

Becker, H.S., 1963. *Outsiders: Studies in the Sociology of Deviance*. [online] New York: The Free Press. Available at: Amazon.co.uk: http://www.amazon.co.uk [accessed 2 January 2012].

Crossley, N., 2004. The circuit trainer's habitus: Reflexive body techniques and the sociality of the workout. *Body & Society*, 10(1), pp. 37–69.

Csikszentmihalyi, M., 1988. The flow experience and its significance for human psychology. In: M. Csikszentmihalyi and I.S. Csikszentmihalyi, eds, *Optimal experience: Psychological Studies of Flow in Consciousness*. Cambridge: Cambridge University Press, pp. 15–35.

Dilley, R.E. and Scraton, S.J., 2010. Women, climbing and serious leisure. *Leisure Studies*, 29, pp. 125–41.

Downey, G., 2005. *Learning Capoeira: Lessons in Cunning from an Afro-Brazilian Art*. Oxford: Oxford University Press.

Ewald, K. and Jiobu, R.M., 1985. Explaining positive deviance: Becker's model and the case of runners and bodybuilders. *Sociology of Sport Journal*, 2, pp. 144–56.

Ford, N. and Brown, D., 2006. *Surfing and Social Theory*. London: Routledge.

Game, A., 2001. Riding: Embodying the centaur. *Body & Society*, 7(4), pp. 1–12.

Gillespie, D.L., Leffler, A. and Lerner, E., 2002. If it weren't for my hobby, I'd have a life: Dog sports, serious leisure and boundary negotiations. *Leisure Studies*, 21(3–4), pp. 285–304.

Hanold, M.T., 2010. Beyond the marathon: (De)construction of female ultrarunning bodies. *Sociology of Sport Journal*, 27, pp. 160–77.

Hockey, J., 2005. Injured distance runners: A case of identity work as self-help. *Sociology of Sport Journal*, 21, pp. 38–58.

Hong, S.K., Rennie, D. and Park, Y.S., 1987. Humans can acclimatize to cold: A lesson from Korean women divers. *Physiology*, 2(3), pp. 79–82.

Hughes, R. and Coakley, J., 1991. Positive deviance among athletes: The implications of overconformity to the sport ethic. *Sociology of Sport Journal*, 8, pp. 307–25.

Humberstone, B., 2011. Embodiment and social and environmental action in nature-based sport: Spiritual spaces. *Leisure Studies*, 30(4), pp. 495–512.

Hunter, J. and Csikszentmihalyi, M., 2000. The phenomennology of body-mind: The contrasting cases of flow in sports and contemplation. *Anthropology of Consciousness*, 11(3/4), pp. 5–24.

Jackson, S.A. and Csikszentmihalyi, M., 1999. *Flow in Sports: The Keys to Optimal Experiences and Performances*. Leeds: Human Kinetics.

Laurier, E., 2003. *Field Report 1: The Basics of Becoming a Barista*. Glasgow: University of Glasgow. Available at: http://www.academia.edu/2755223/Field_Report_1_the_basics_of_becoming_a_barista [accessed 3 November 2013].

Lea, J., 2009. Becoming skilled: The cultural and corporeal geographies of teaching and learning Thai Yoga massage. *Geoforum*, 40, pp. 465–74.

Logan, R., 1988. Flow in solitary ordeals. In: M. Csikszentmihalyi and I.S. Csikszentmihalyi, eds, *Optimal Experience: Psychological Studies of Flow in Consciousness*. Cambridge: Cambridge University Press, pp. 172–80.

Lorimer, H. and Lund, K., 2003. Performing facts: Finding a way over Scotland's mountains. *The Sociological Review*, 52(1), pp. 130–44.

Makinen, T.M., 2010. Different types of cold adaptation in humans. *Frontiers in Bioscience*, 1(2), pp. 1047–67.

Merchant, S., 2011. Negotiating underwater space: The sensorium, the body and the practice of scuba-diving. *Tourist Studies*, 11(3), pp. 215–34.

Mortimer, G., 2008. *The Great Swim*. London: Short Books.

Potter, C., 2008. Sense of motion, senses of self: Becoming a dancer. *Ethnos*, 73(4), pp. 444–65.

Raisborough, J., 2006. Getting onboard: Women, access and serious leisure. *Sociological Review*, 54, pp. 242–62.

Reischer, E.L., 2001. Running to the moon: The articulation and the construction of self in marathon runners. *Anthropology of Consciousness*, 12(2), pp. 19–35.

RNLI, 2011. *On the Beach. Your Guide to a Safe and Fun Time at the Seaside*. Dorset: RNLI. Available at: http://rnli.org/SiteCollectionDocuments/Beach-safety-On-the-Beach-2011.pdf [accessed 3 November 2013].

––––––– 2013. *Respect the Water*. Available at: http://rnli.org/safetyandeducation/stayingsafe/Pages/Respect-the-water.aspx [accessed 3 November 2013].

Sparkes, A., 2009. Ethnography and the senses: Challenges and possibilities. *Qualitative Research in Sport and Exercise*, 1(1), pp. 21–35.

Stalp, M.C., 2007. *Quilting: The Fabric of Everyday Life*. Oxford: Berg.

Stebbins, R.A., 2007. *Serious Leisure: A Perspective for Our Time*. New Brunswick: Transaction Publishers.

Stevenson, C.L., 2002. Seeking identities: Towards an understanding of the athletic careers of masters swimmers. *International Review for the Sociology of Sport*, 37(2), pp. 131–46.

Sudnow, D., 2001. *Ways of the Hand: A Rewritten Account*. Cambridge, MA: The MIT Press.

Throsby, K., 2013a. 'If I go in like a cranky sea-lion, I come out like a smiling dolphin': Marathon swimming and the unexpected pleasures of being a body in water. *Feminist Review*, 103, pp. 5–22.

––––––– 2013b. 'You can't be too vain to gain if you want to swim the Channel': Marathon swimming and the construction of heroic fatness. *International Review for the Sociology of Sport*, 5 July 2013. Available at: http://irs.sagepub.com/content/early/2013/07/05/1012690213494080 [accessed 3 November 2013].

Turner, B.S. and Wainwright, S.P., 2003. Corps de ballet: The case of the injured ballet dancer. *Sociology of Health and Ilness*, 25(4), pp. 269–88.

Unruh, D.R., 1980. The nature of social worlds. *The Pacific Sociology Review*, 23(3), pp. 271–96.

Wacquant, L., 2004. *Body & Soul: Notebooks of an Apprentice Boxer*. Oxford: Oxford University Press.

Willig, C., 2008. A phenomenological investigation of the experience of taking part in 'extreme sports'. *Journal of Health Psychology*, 13(5), pp. 690–702.

Chapter 12

'Do we keel haul the little %$#@ or chuck him in the chain locker?' How Life at Sea Becomes 'Stories to Live By' for a Woman on a Fishing Vessel

elke emerald and Fiona Ewing

Fe's energy fills a space. She is big – as in, personality big. Her life force is strong. I cannot imagine being in a room and not knowing she is there. I guess that is one of the reasons she was so successful at sea. I am thinking it is not a place for shrinking violets or wallflowers. And, she swears – not too much, but to effect. So do not read further if you are offended by salty parlance. We are on about our fifth cup of coffee as Fe tells me the story of 'this guy':

As an observer on board these fishing vessels we are in someone else's space you know. The boat is their workplace, as well as living, eating and sleeping quarters. You do everything you can to respect that. Pitching in with meals, doing your work quickly with as little disruption to the crew as possible. It's an unspoken rule. If I can't add value to the space, then I just keep out of the way ... The mere fact of my presence on the boat means that the crew are being held up in their work, they are being inconvenienced in pursuit of their livelihood, but more, they are best suited to make what you need to happen, happen. They know their working environment and they are the experts here. You have to work collaboratively, be a contributor. Not this guy. He was from a large research agency. I can't even remember his name. He just had no respect. Carlos and I were on this particular trip as scientific observers. This guy was there conducting some complementary research. The research equipment he had took up a big chunk of the working deck of the boat, which was an inconvenience to begin with. He didn't even bother to explain anything about his research to the boys. And he'd make them wait – like when it was time to come down on deck and take little jars off the buoys, he'd make them wait, you know. Do it in his own fucking time, you know. These guys are working 18 hours a day and through the night and crazy shit and they are accommodating him and cooking for him and then he leaves them just hanging, waiting in the cold, for him to do his thing before they could get on with their thing – which is their livelihood. Just no idea. He was on the boat for 10 days.

And after a few days Carlos and I forced him, absolutely forced him to make a meal, we had this conversation, you gotta do something – he just didn't get it. No fucking idea. We'd be measuring fish, Carlos and I, and eventually this guy would come down and help, that's what you do, you pitch in and make things happen, when your work is done you pitch in with others. So eventually he'd come down and help. Oh my God, and he'd just be a complaint about it. Carlos tried to show him by example. No matter what's going on, Carlos's way of being is upbeat and friendly and charming and he's got millions of fabulous sea stories from South America and he's a good storyteller. So we'd be measuring fish and Carlos'd be telling stories you know. And this guy still didn't get it, he still complained, I mean, we've gotta do the work, it's not fun work, but complaining won't make it more fun. He was just a black hole this guy.

Fe stopped for a breath, a mouthful of coffee, and then,

He had this whizz-bang digital measuring board and one night the skipper came down to help him with some stuff, this guy was such a blockage that the Skipper stepped in to move things along. And this guy makes some comment about the digital measuring board being too complex for the Skipper! Shit! Can you imagine! Have you got any idea the complex world that Skippers negotiate? The complex fucking machinery and shit in that wheelhouse, sounders and radars and satellite whatevers and crew issues and negotiating catches and quotas and sales and government departments. This thing was basically an electronic ruler! After days of this crap, this was like the last straw. The Skipper turns to me and he says all kinda wry and laconic; 'What do you reckon Fe, do we keel haul the little %$#@ or chuck him in the chain locker'.

Fe rocks back in her chair and laughs heartily – it is a cliché, but really she does. Tears stream down her face. She flicks them away. We are sitting at Fe's kitchen table. It is rough wood, beautiful, solid, impossible to lift. It seems to be made out of most of one tree. 'That was a blast of trip', she continues, 'I have never laughed so hard at someone else's expense, not vindictive you know, just, this guy was such a … I don't know …' she shakes her head searching for words, 'and he just didn't get it! Carlos summed him up in his singing Argentine accent "You can see Fe, he has come straight from the arms of his mother, into the arms of his wife"'.

I laugh with Fe and rest my eyes on the bay outside her door, reflecting on the embodied nature of Fe's professional knowledge. Her professional knowledge is, as Clandinin and Connelly (1998) remind us 'composed of relations among people, places and things'; it is 'both an intellectual and a moral landscape' (p. 151). I reflect on Clandinin and Connelly's (1998) discussion of their work as narrative inquirers researching teachers, classrooms and schools and translate that insight to Fe's seascape. Fe shows regard for the ongoing stories. She sees that the story of each vessel is a living narrative a 'changing organism composed of multiple nested stories' (Clandinin and Connelly, 1998, p. 161). Each member of the crew has an ongoing story, that story itself a complex and interwoven set of stories and relationships with complex relations of time, space and sociality. Their individual stories are shaped by and, at the same time, construct, the long- and short-term story of this vessel, this fishing trip and this time. As an observer in this context, Fe knows she disrupts the story of this vessel in its midst. She disrupts the routine of the fishing, takes someone's bed or cabin, is another mouth to feed and takes up space and time on the busy working deck. As much as possible she must 'join the parade' to paraphrase Clandinin and Connelly's metaphor, 'dance wisely in the parade' (p. 162) or, in her own words, 'do everything you can to make that smooth'. This is in contrast to her unwelcome colleague, 'that guy', who simply 'parachuted in' (Clandinin and Connelly, 1998) with no apparent understanding of the ongoing story, the interrelated lives and his impact on them. Fe knows she has dipped into the story and will dip out again; but must leave welcome to return. As much as her colleague does not, Fe knows that she must work relationally. In her story, I hear that she knows that she too will become a part of the ongoing story of those individuals and that vessel, just as her colleagues and 'that guy' are now characters in her own ongoing story.

Fe and I were at school together once, way back. We sat side-by-side in maths class, admiring Mr Cole's enthusiasm and earnestly trying to find the area under the parabolic curve, but nevertheless counting the minutes to the bell, the ritualised imbroglio of our trip home on the bus full of boys from the school next door and a late afternoon splash at the beach on our doorstep. But now, two oceans separate and connect us and I have travelled across those oceans to her home to ask if she will share her stories of life at sea. I am asking her to recreate her lived world through her stories, so I can dwell with her there a while (Barone, 2001). I understand narrative to be a powerful way of knowing, 'as powerful as scientific knowing but different from it' (Bruner, 1986, p. viii). It is one of the ways we come to understand our lives and understand others' lives. I elicit Fe's stories through narrative interview as a means to capture the layerings and richness, the 'situatedness, the contexts, and the complexities' (Lyons and Kubler LaBoskey, 2002, p. 3) of her life. The Narrative Inquiry approach to story respects and privileges the *telling* of the experience. I recognise that meaning is not necessarily inherent in an act or experience alone, but can be constructed and refined through the act of the telling. As Bamberg (2004) notes, 'lives are lived, but stories are told' (p. 354). In the telling of her experience, and placing it in the context of some whole, she and I set out to form and reform both the experience and its meaning. Further, the telling of a story is a context of knowledge production. In the telling of our stories we can often hear ourselves articulate what Riley and Hawe (2005) refer to as indigenous theory. That is, we hear our ordinary everyday theorising in making sense of our world (Gubrium and Wallace, 1990).

Anyway, this table and the telling of stories is a familiar ritual for us. I have sat around this table for many years, hearing Fe's stories and telling my own. As friends we have narrated our lives for each other, storying the months or years since we last sat around this table. Now I am hearing Fe's stories as a 'social researcher' and she is telling them as a 'co-author'. What impact will this have on the stories and on the senses we can make? When I step into a scene as an ethnographic researcher, I do not naively imagine that my presence is without impact, although I work to make that impact benign (Ellis, 2004; Richardson, 2001). There is no pretence of an objective observer in our social research. Once you have stepped into the river, it is not the same river and you are not the same person. As a narrative inquirer I understand that stories are fluid and contextual; both *contexted* in space, time and social relationships (Clandinin and Rosiek, 2007) and implicit in *creating* space, time and relationships. Storying is not an isolated activity. It is a social activity that 'embodies the relationship between a particular life experience and the social and cultural world the narrator shares with others' (Kelly, 2005, p. 185). I have no expectation that stories reflect some inviolate 'truth': few would be so bold in postmodern times. I take it as given that people may exclude details of events or exaggerate aspects of stories (Ezzy, 2000; Riley and Hawe, 2005) and am alive to Clandinin and Rosiek's (2007) claim that narrative 'describes human experience as it unfolds though time' (p. 40). Thus, just as Fe is conscious that she steps on to a boat in the midst of its story, I am conscious that I hear Fe's stories in their midst, that is, Fe's meaning making through storying these events does not begin the day I arrive nor end as I leave (Clandinin and Connelly, 2000). Meanings are not fixed. Murray Orr and Olsen remind us that it is in the telling and retelling that stories take on meaning and enable growth and change (Murray Orr and Olsen, 2007, p. 822–3).

Fe knows this too. She is not a sociologist or ethnographer, she is a marine scientist. Fe is by training and character a 'meaning maker' – she searches for meaning and she is fearlessly self-reflective. She does not shy away from self-critique. As her laughter eased over that 'blast' of a trip she says: 'well I didn't behave too well on that occasion – I am not too proud of some of my behaviours then'. More than reflective, Fe is reflexive. She actively seeks to understand and expose the filters through which she makes meaning. She engages in the reflexive practice of 'objectivation of the knowing subject' (Deer, 2008, p. 201). Perhaps she embodies the 'flexible or reflexive habitus' that Adkins (2003) and Sweetman (2003) propose. They propose, in different ways, that many contemporary practices train us in reflective and reflexive thought: workplace reviews, portfolio careers, therapy, critical literacy; as such, the contemporary individual may be one for whom reflexive practices are habituated.

So, as we sit around the table this time, Fe is not just telling me her stories as we usually do. This time, we deliberately step into our storying, knowing that narrative inquiry is a 'method that can provide a theoretical and practical framework for (re)interpreting our lived experience' (Shields, 2005, p. 179). This time, she and I have a distinct and particular purpose in her telling. I have asked her to tell me her stories so that I can understand the 'knowing' in her practice (Clandinin and Connelly, 1998, p. 150). As Clandinin and Connelly and colleagues have sought to mine the 'professional knowledge landscape' (p. 150) of teachers, seeking to gain some insight into its history, its moral, emotional and aesthetic dimensions, I seek to fathom Fe's 'seascape'. And, we have a chapter to write, we have a deadline.

'When is the chapter due to the editor?' she asks me.

'September.'

It is now only February and Fe thinks we have ample time. I know, however, that September is tomorrow in the life of an academic and ethnographer and I foresee my scramble come mid-September.

I cannot pretend that Fe's stories are my data, scooped up, fresh and untainted, in a net and stored on ice for processing at my leisure. Fe's stories are by no means Silverman's (2007) naturally occurring data. They would not exist in this telling, in this form, had I not come and asked for them, for this purpose. We might conceive of her stories as field texts (Clandinin and Connelly, 2000), co-constructed around this table. Sitting around this table with us are our interwoven histories, our families, our knowledge of each other. Fe's 'natural' reflexivity gives her stories a certain hue, as does our explicit search for 'stories to live by'.

'I want to understand', I say to Fe, 'How life at sea steps on to land with you. What steps off the boat with you? How do your experiences at sea become stories to live by?'

As a method then, an ethnographer and a scientist, friends for nigh on 30 years, swim amongst Fe's stories in search of a particular form of sense, in search of 'stories to live by'.

We have been sitting at the table all morning and right now, we need to walk, so we grab the dog lead and head out towards the bay. Fe and her partner are what I would call working scientists. They are average Australian workers with modest wages and four weeks' leave a year. But they live in a priceless paradise. Many years ago, through research, determination and hard work, thrashing a struggling kombi down every side road and dirt track, they found a tiny corner of paradise and bought an ordinary little house. Through years of frugal living, self-sustained permaculture gardening and DIY house renovations, they have created a work-in-progress utopia. Development crept out from the city to swamp them, but they and some neighbours fought it off by forming a collaborative and mortgaging themselves to the gunwales. So, because of their foresight, we now have the luxury of stepping out of their kitchen and across the deck to walk along a pristine bay. A sea eagle hovers over the water and I watch a stingray glide past me as I wade knee-deep. I collect a magenta-pink scallop shell as big as my hand as a souvenir of this visit. I will place it alongside the other nine on my bedside table! I suspect, again, that I am breaking some law collecting shells; I really must check that out some time.

We release Patsy from her lead as we reach a secluded spot where she can run and, as we watch the waves lap at the bay, Fe takes up her reflections. 'Here's a story to live by', she says, 'I am too old to piss in a bucket'. Her laugh rings across the bay.

I. Am. Unwilling. To. Piss. In. A. Bucket. I will not go on a boat without a flush loo now. I'm too old to piss in a bucket, waaay too old. Take Charlie's boat, that was small, there were only three of us on that boat. We could all fit in the wheelhouse if we were standing up. It was the size of a kitchen table.

Fe's laugh punctuates her story,

I used to just hide behind the wheel house with a bucket. I never did the hanging over the side thing – how can you relax dangling over the side, 20 miles off shore! So to have a pee, I would time it, they were gentlemen about it anyway. I would time having a pee so they were both busy over there.

As a younger woman, I was about 25 when I first started going to sea, I was stretching my boundaries because I did not know what they were. You find the boundaries in that process. Yes, it was about proving myself and doing a good job and all that, and now with the wisdom of looking back, and watching my son stretch to find his boundaries, I see that it was also about finding where my boundaries are, that's what I was doing.

She finishes her story succinctly, the scientist providing the findings. 'That learning comes right onshore with me: "I'm too old to piss in a bucket" means for me "I need to be clear about what my boundaries are in any situation"'. 'I think I need that on a bumper sticker', I say and we laugh again, both at Fe's metaphor and her succinct, scientific rendering of some great life advice. I file that away for future reference, for next time my socialisation prompts me to say 'yes' when really I should say 'I am too old to piss in a bucket!'

As Fe tells it, she adopts the metaphor of stories-to-live-by in a very personal way. I tell Fe about Clandinin and colleagues' work with teachers (Clandinin et al., 2006). How they talked about teacher knowledge that can be accumulated as a personal attribute, acquired skills or gathered experiences, but still not change the way teachers 'know' their classrooms, their schools, their students, their colleagues and their professional lives (Clandinin and Connelly, 1998). Whereas it seems to me, as Fe voices it here, in her visceral and very embodied story of one of the basic human realities of life on a small boat, far out to sea, that her knowledge, her professional practice, is a shift in point of view, an epistemological shift, a shift in the way she knows herself.

As the water laps my toes, I contemplate the relationship between our storying of experience and the knowings that experience/story come to represent in our lives. I contemplate the ebb and flow of storying and meaning making. Fe charges up the beach to retrieve Patsy from a joyfully escalating dog-pack. 'I'll just get her back before this ends in a vet bill', she shouts back at me. When she and Patsy return, both puffing, but only Patsy looking pleased, Fe says to me 'I'll tell you about knowing yourself but let's crack the champagne first'.

When we're settled back in the golden evening light with the bottle open and cheeses and fruit at hand, Fe continues: 'When I am at sea I feel most me – without the pretences and cover stories.' I raise my eyebrows over the rim of the glass and she continues:

It's hard to explain, but I'll give it a go. It's about the 'feel' of the ocean. Ocean currents are fascinating. They are almost alive. Their energy is a living energy. A current is a body of water being driven through the ocean, like a river flowing through the water. Each current has distinct features, a distinct temperature, salinity and nutrient profile. These things are both created by where the current has been and reflect where it has been. You can kind of read a current – you can read its history and its journey and its impact on the environment, and it is the environment.

So currents have their own physical, biological and chemical characteristics and they also react to the topography of the bottom of the ocean. They are in conversation with the ocean, and yet they are the ocean. Life in the ocean reacts to the currents. Fish are guided in their migration, whales head south for food in summer, north for babes, tuna follow nutrient rich currents.

Then there's the swell. The swell is very different to the waves. The waves are slop on top caused by wind. Surfers catch waves and little boats bob about on top of the water on the waves in the bay. The swell is a deeper movement of water. It's very powerful. You can feel it on the boat when you are in the deep ocean. You feel the power of the swell. It's very different to being in the surf catching a wave. When I am out in the deep water in a boat, I am closer to the ocean, to the whole earth, than when I am in the surf. Even scuba gear comes between me and the ocean. It's a deeply felt, moving connection. I feel deeply connected to everything, to the ocean, to the earth. When I am on that boat in the deep ocean, gently rising and falling, I feel like I am connected to the movement of the planet.

The ocean breathes, there is a deep pulsing, you can feel this deep strong rolling pulse, you lift and fall with it. You have this awareness, this deep sense, in your body. And the strange thing is, I feel this through a manmade object – the boat. The boat does not come between me and the experience. It's like I am connected to the breath of the ocean, I am connected to the engine that drives the whole planet, and I can feel it in my body, I sense it in my body.

Sometimes, very rarely, very rarely, the skipper will shut everything down, all the boat's engines, the gear, everything, you are just floating in the middle of the ocean, no anchor. It's not like you can hit anything, there's nothing out there. And you're lying there and the boat becomes an amplifier, you can hear the slap of the waves on the metal hull, I've even heard dolphins, and this deep, deep slow pulse, rising and falling with the swell.

I am my environment.

My environment is me.

The current and the swell are the big stories – they are the life forces that run through us, run through our lives. The waves are the slop on top. Waves are caused by the wind. Water doesn't move in a wave, the energy moves, the water itself cycles or rolls as the wave of energy passes through. Water does not travel with the waves, it travels in the current. In the waves the water moves in circles ... they are the little stories, they are the ones we fight, we label, we rant against – but they're just the waves, just the slop on top – the daily worries, the frustrations, the things we think matter – our ego, our job, all the ephemeral stuff. Like arguing with your kid over violin practice, as if that matters in the big scheme of things – what matters is, is he healthy, happy, strong, centred; a good person, whatever that is. Who cares whether he's played violin for 15 minutes today. How about this? If the wind is in the same direction as the current, the surface is smooth – no waves. If the wind is in a different direction to the current, it's choppy and messy on the surface. That's all it is, mess on the surface. But we get caught up in it, tossed around, we name it, we call it good or bad, or right or wrong, we think it's so damn important.

The swell and the currents are my big story – I am in deeply connected relation with this planet, you know. The deepest oceans touch us, they mean something. The swell connects us to the universe – the moon pulls the water this way and that, huge bodies of water shift around the planet, moving nutrients, fish, changing temperatures, interacting with the ocean floor. There is world down there, volcanoes, mountains, deep, deep fissures. Humans have no idea what's down those fissures. And the sky, it's vast out there in the middle of the ocean. Earth is a grain of sand in this huge story and humans are just specks. This huge life force moves the whole universe. We barely understand it, but we are very, very connected to it. And we are so arrogant. We screw it over, you know. We think we can do what we like, fish to extinction, warm the whole globe. I can feel that in the silence when I am out in the deep ocean, feeling the boat gently lift and fall in response to the swell. I am sure I can feel the current moving underneath me. I lie there, no light from humans, only the stars and moon, so if there's cloud, it can be pitch, pitch dark. I can feel the earth spinning, the ocean moving and I feel completely at one, totally true. Just in place, content, connected, right. I feel huge and vast and connected and I feel small, a tiny cog in a huge machine, but a cog just the same, in my place, doing my thing, doing my bit. The big story is vast and each of us has a perfect place in that big scheme. I couldn't give a toss about the small stories, the violin lessons, homework, ego shit when I am there.

I am surprised to hear Fe's use of big stories and small stories and I wonder how her metaphor relates to Bamberg's big and small stories (Bamberg, 2006). I make a note to follow this up but cannot dwell on it now, the champagne is flowing and so are the stories.

So I am at 'one' [she makes the 'quotation marks' sign with her fingers]

when I am out there, either in that utterly quiet peaceful state or busy in the flow of my work. You see, on land, my underlying story to myself is that life is hard work. But what's really, really interesting is, I don't experience that at sea. And that work is hard, it's fucking hard. Seriously, anybody would say, that work is physically exhausting, it's demanding, there are safety issues, it's dangerous, but I love it, I don't experience it as hard work. The rest of the time, on land, that underlying conversation of 'life is hard work' is with me all. the. time. It is constant. I have to work to give up, give up, give up that story. It's even 'hard work' to give up the story of 'hard work'. But not at sea.

At sea, I found out that I can be more than my own expectations of me.

'Do tell', I prompt.

In the early days I had these two bosses, Jeremy and Geoff, they ran some of the research surveys that I used to work on. I did several trips for them and my role and responsibilities expanded on every trip. They had a bigger expectation of me than I had for myself. I found that I could be more than I knew myself to be, in a work context in a resilient context, long hours, hard work, physical labour, rough conditions.

At sea, it's a given that things go wrong. So, my first reaction, straight from the 'life is hard' story is 'I can't deal with this'. But then, when at sea, straight away, I'd have this other voice: 'you have to Fe, you have no choice'. I know I am committed to something here; the outcome of the research, just keeping people happy or looking competent, so I have no choice, there is no way out, there is no alternative. I am on a boat in the middle of the fucking ocean you know. I have no alternative.

And in the early days with Geoff and Jeremy, one day I was all 'I can't do this, what if I can't use that equipment' whatever, Geoff just turned to me and said 'of course you can Fe, you're a dead set legend!' His story of me was so much bigger than my story of me. It stopped me in my tracks you know. And I just had to live it – live the dead set legend – so when I am at sea, my conversation with me is 'you'll be right Fe, you're a dead set legend'. I can bring it forward as a way of being. So I took this on to land. I consciously, explicitly, draw on that experience at sea to empower me on land when I have some overwhelming task. Not as effectively as I do at sea. But I know I can do it at sea, so I take that little key of knowing on to land. I can authentically say that that's a story that Fe lives by.

The stories in the 'it's too hard' soap opera still appear, of course they do, but not with the same grabness and intensity. And it's waaaay easier to give them up. It gets easier every time I do it. When I am really connected, when I am not in that soap opera, I see it for what it is, nonsense, just stories we make up to keep ourselves busy and in drama, and prove things about ourselves, stories we tell to create the situations that gather more evidence for the stories we tell about ourselves. The small stories. The wind slop.

You know, sometimes, one of the things I am committed to is just looking like a dead set legend! Once you have experienced yourself in one way you can do it again. Once you know yourself one way you can't unknow yourself, even if you like to pretend sometimes, or forget a little.

Fe shows how a story can be a transformative space. In offering a story we not only make a claim about who we are, an identity claim, but a story is often a presentation of characters as becoming, that is, 'undergoing processes of transformation' (Bamberg, 2004, p. 357). Her understanding of who she is as a worker and a person shifted in the moment of the 'dead set legend' story. That story has now become an anchor, helping her moor that new knowledge of herself. But as Fe says in her story of her story – epiphanies are rarely permanent. She can forget herself as a dead set legend and return to the drama of the small 'it's all too hard' soap opera. But this knowing of herself as greater than she knew is a space she returns to, to renew her transformation. Fe can tell herself the story of herself as a dead set legend in order to re-member herself as such.

I chose the sea and the sea provides me with choices. It provides me with the opportunity to be a better person than I ever thought I could be. Growing up, my mother had a very clear and well-articulated intention that I should have more choice than she, a woman, born in the 1920s. Without this opening of 'choice', I never would have even entertained the notion of a life at sea. There was an allowment, an enabling of Fe not being constrained or limited by her gender.

It has been three full days of stories and food and the bay. It has been a rich time, visiting Fe's world through her stories, and now we're heading to the airport. Fe's husband is driving. He is a marine scientist too. He asks me that question familiar to many qualitative researchers, 'Well, did you get what you need?' I never know how to answer that one.

'I got what I got.'

'What did you learn?' He is the scientist in search of findings.

'I thought I might get a bunch of juicy stories about "a woman in a man's world." I am not sure yet what I learnt about that, about sex and gender and negotiating bathrooms on boats, but I did learn a lot about how stories can make meaning in our lives.'

'Well', says Graeme, 'I'll tell you about Fe and gender ...'

Graeme is a thoughtful guy; you never get an unconsidered response from him. Today his words flow smoothly, fast and deliberate and, of course, I did not have my recorder on. So later, I asked him again and he emailed me:

Whenever Fe steps onto the deck of a fishing boat she is an ambassador – an ambassador for women, for science, and for government regulation on behalf of all of us who collectively own the coastal seafood resource being exploited, and for whom it must be managed sustainably (both ecologically and economically). While there are exceptions, the skippers and crew with whom she sails generally have strong negative opinions around all of these: women, science and government. Further, borne on the inherent risks of plying our local treacherous seas for a living, many are still deeply superstitious, despite modern engineering and electronics mitigating risk. Consequently, opposition to a female researcher on board generally surpasses the inconvenience of one less bunk, another mouth to feed, an inexperienced worker in the way on the heaving deck, the presence of the regulatory enemy in their midst; for some, opposition to a woman on board is held far deeper than opinion – for some, it is 'just not right' and touches a primal fear.

I too spend time on commercial fishing boats as a fisheries researcher and know well how strong the antagonism from crew can be. That Fe has such a reputation and acceptance in the fishing community is a testament to her strong interpersonal skills and to her integrity as a stand for women's ability to excel in traditionally male arenas. Fe has not achieved this by being more butch than the blokes, by swearing harder than their best, nor by pandering for their sympathy or fluttering her eyelashes. She has met them eye to eye, on their own turf, has worked hard through unimaginably adverse sea conditions, has endured the lack of any toilet facilities, the communal bunkroom with the snoring blokes while occupying the bed under the leaking hatch. She has met these challenges with grace, dignity, without complaint, and with respect for the integrity of the unwritten fishermen's code of behaviour both on board and ashore.

Having earned the respect of the fishing community, Fe's subsequent contribution to the fishing sector's understanding of the necessity and role of research and regulation cannot be underestimated. More impressive still, her contribution to an acceptance of women in the fishing industry has paved the way for women into this and other male-dominated industries. It is little wonder that in the local fishing circles I am known as 'Fe's husband'.

As the plane lifts on the first of two flights, crossing the first of two oceans, I allow my mind to drift over the stories I have heard: the generosity of spirit of the late-night coffee-maker on the Russian boat, who after an 18-hour shift of his own, helped Fe through the long working nights by taking the time to brew and share a real coffee from his personal stash, not the chicory usually on offer, and sit a while and talk with the little English he had; a month at sea on a Japanese vessel, the only woman and the only English speaker on board, the cause of great and inexplicable merriment, never mind the too-fucking-hot onsen; the deep satisfaction of belonging played out in the unscheduled bear hug reunions on lonely southern fishing wharves 'You remember that Fe, you were there'; hearing the stories of redemption, love, family and connection from men who she would normally be frightened of, 'you know the ones, they have "love" and "hate" prison tattoos on their knuckles'. So many lush stories.

I play with bumper sticker versions of stories-to-live-by: 'If you can't add value to the space, just keep out of the way'; 'I am too old to piss in a bucket'; 'Move with currents, ride the waves'; 'I am my environment, my environment is me'.

I am tired now, there has been too much coffee, too much champagne, too many rich creamy cheeses and too many stories; too many for one chapter. As the force of uplift pushes me back in my seat, I wonder which stories will make it into Barbara and Mike's book.

References

Adkins, L., 2003. Reflexivity: Freedom or habit of gender? *Theory, Culture & Society*, 20(6), pp. 21–42.

Bamberg, M., 2004. Considering counter-narratives. In: M. Bamberg and M. Andrews, eds, *Considering Counter-Narratives: Narrating, Resisting, Making Sense*. Amsterdam and Philidelphia: John Benjamins Publishing, pp. 351–71.

———— 2006. Biographic-narrative research, quo vadis? A critical review of 'big stories' from the perspective of 'small stories'. In: K. Milnes, C. Horrocks, B. Roberts and D. Robinson, eds, *Narrative, Memory and Knowledge: Representations, Aesthetics, Contexts*. University of Huddersfield, pp. 63–79.

Barone, T., 2001. Science, art and the predispositions of educational researchers. *Educational Researcher*, Oct, pp. 24–8.

Bruner, J., 1986. *Actual Minds, Possible Worlds*. Cambridge, MA: Harvard University Press.

Clandinin, D.J. and Connelly, M., 1998. Narratives of experience and narrative inquiry. *Educational Researcher*, 19(3), pp. 2–14.

———— 2000. *Narrative Inquiry: Experience and Story in Qualitative Research*. San Francisco: Jossey-Bass Publishers.

Clandinin, D.J., Huber, J., Huber, M., Murphy, M.S., Murray Orr, A., Pearce, M. and Stevves, P., 2006. *Composing Diverse Identities: Narrative Inquiries into the Interwoven Lives of Children and Teachers*. London and New York: Routledge.

Clandinin, J. and Rosiek, J., 2007. Mapping a landscape of narrative inquiry: Borderland spaces and tensions. In: J. Clandinin, ed., *Handbook of Narrative Inquiry: Mapping a Methodology*. Thousand Oaks, CA: SAGE, pp. 35–76.

Deer, C., 2008. Reflexivity. In: M. Grenfell, ed., *Pierre Bourdieu: Key Concepts*. Stocksfield: Acumen Publishing, pp. 199–212.

Ellis, C., 2004. *The Ethnographic I: A Methodological Novel about Autoethnography.* Walnut Creek: Alta Mira Press.

Ezzy, D., 2000. Illness narratives: Time, hope and HIV. *Social Science & Medicine*, 50(5), pp. 605–17.

Gubrium, J. and Wallace, J.B., 1990. Who theorises age? *Aging and Society*, 10, pp. 131–49.

Kelly, S.E., 2005. 'A different light': Examining impairment through parent narratives of childhood disability. *Journal of Contemporary Ethnography*, 34(2), pp. 180–205.

Lyons, N. and Kubler LaBoskey, V., 2002. *Narrative Inquiry in Practice: Advancing the Knowledge of Teaching.* New York and London: Teachers College Press.

Murray Orr, A. and Olsen, M., 2007. Transforming narrative encounters. *Canadian Journal of Education*, 30(3), pp. 819–38.

Richardson, L., 2001. Getting personal: Writing stories. *International Journal of Qualitative Studies in Education*, 14(1), pp. 33–8.

Riley, T. and Hawe, P., 2005. Researching practice: The methodological case for narrative inquiry. *Health and Education Research Theory and Practice*, 20(2), pp. 226–36.

Shields, C., 2005. Using narrative inquiry to inform and guide our (re)interpretations of lived experience. *McGill Journal of Education*, 40, pp. 178–88.

Silverman, D., 2007. *A Very Short, Fairly Interesting, and Reasonably Cheap Book about Qualitative Research.* Los Angeles: SAGE.

Sweetman, P., 2003. Twenty-first century dis-ease? Habitual reflexivity or the reflexive habitus. *The Sociological Review*, 51(4), pp. 528–48.

Chapter 13

Embodied Narratives and Fluid Geographies

Barbara Humberstone and Mike Brown

It is our hope that this collection of narratives provides new ways to contemplate *with* the sea rather than on or at it. In the preceding chapters, the authors have conveyed a variety of perspectives regarding how their lives have been influenced through their relationship with the sea. As editors we have been deeply impacted by the depth and diversity of narratives of the authors' lived-experiences. We have come away with new perspectives and ways of thinking about our own personal connections with the sea and how they were affected by, and effected our collective representations.

During the process of compiling this volume on seascapes we have been concerned to offer narratives and ideas that may provoke different ways of thinking about and researching human–sea relationships, rather than providing any final words on narratives and seascapes. Consequently, in these closing remarks we are unwilling to offer any definitive conclusion on human relations with (on, in, through) the sea. Rather our intention is to open up the possibilities to wider and broader understandings of the sea (and our relations with it) through methodological approaches that celebrate the sentient and affective and that engage critically with human/non-human relations and acknowledge the sea as 'more-than-human' space (Peters, 2014).

The vision underpinning *Seascapes: Shaped by the Sea* is based upon our own life-long engagements in various ways with the sea and our consciousness that the sea is much more than a watery space. It is energy that provides for fluidity, transformation and the potential for social and environmental awareness and change.

The authors in this book come from a variety of fields of study and background experiences yet most have spent much of their lives engaging with the sea. Their commitments have been for pleasure, for voluntary or paid work, whilst for some the sea has been the vehicle through which personal and even family histories have been made and are in the making. These embodied narratives, informed, in many cases, not only by experience but also by social theory, highlight a potent form of research that is much 'more-than-representational' (Carolan, 2008, p. 409). Contributors are transcending their particular disciplinary boundaries through interrogating their water-based lived experiences from diverse conceptual frameworks, whilst using eclectic forms of narrative to create alternative knowledge of what constitutes seascapes (see Sparkes and Smith, 2014).

In a number of ways, the purposes/principles underpinning *Seascapes* have much in common with the thinking behind 'Mobile Methodologies' (Fincham, McGuinness and Murray, 2010). The authors in Fincham et al.'s text are occupied with 'mobile' contexts where they are concerned to 'access a subject experience that is, by definition, momentary and passing-by, issues of authenticity, of recounting corporeal, sensorial and emotional responses of participants rather than passive observations …' (McGuinness, Fincham and Murray, 2010, p. 170). Whilst the authors in *Seascapes* are engaged herein with corporeal and sensuous relations with the sea, additionally they have been immersed in relations with the sea for much of their lives. Each *Seascapes* author's active, reciprocal engagements with the fluid contexts of the sea are not only momentary. They are also continuous, embodied and embedded.

A major inspiration in producing this compilation is to unsettle conceptualisations of the sea as alien 'other', as featureless wilderness. The varied, embodied and situated accounts co-construct the centrality of (and even permeability with) the sea, affording our contributors the means to render the sea as mobile living energy, a phenomenological part of their being and becoming. Whilst the sea is intimately implicated in each author's personal stories, the social phenomena co-constructed through these autoethnographic accounts speak to issues of race, gender and migration as well as ecological consciousness.

Little-researched and under-theorised dimensions of the sea are made accessible through each author's personal narratives that aim to do more than represent an individual's intimate corporeal knowledge of their seascapes. Some of the reflective accounts provide stories that trouble popular discourse on gender, whilst all highlight the multiple interconnections of social issues and seascapes. Being with the sea in these accounts is being in the social and material world. Far from exposing seascapes as a featureless wilderness, these narratives exhibit and co-construct pulsating social and embodied life-worlds that are intrinsically intertwined with other 'scapes'. Demonstrated repeatedly by each contributor to this collection, seascapes permeate the very fabric of our being. Making these stories available and accessible presents challenges. Nevertheless, they open up opportunities to learn to think in alternative ways about our individual and collective relationships with the watery world.

Thus our desire is for the autoethnographic accounts herein to evoke nuanced perspectives of seascapes as more-than-human space and to be inspired to also engage in methodological approaches drawn upon by each author to likewise reflect upon and co-create human and non-human relations in nature. We hope readers can take forward these processes of being and becoming in more-than-representational manner, interrogating the world for potentials for social and environmental awareness and action.

References

Carolan, M.S., 2008. More-than-representational. Knowledge/s of the countryside: How we think as bodies. *European Society for Rural Sociology*, 48(4), pp. 409–22.

Fincham, B., McGuinness, M. and Murray, L., eds, 2010. *Mobile Methodologies*. Basingstoke, UK: Palgrave Macmillan.

———— 2010. Conclusions: Mobilising methodologies. In: B. Fincham, M. McGuinness and L. Murray, eds, *Mobile Methodologies*. Basingstoke, UK: Palgrave Macmillan, pp. 169–73.

Peters, K., 2014. Taking more-than-human geographies to sea: Ocean natures and offshore radio piracy. In: J. Anderson and K. Peters, eds, *Water Worlds: Human Geographies of the Ocean*. Farnham, UK and Burlington, VT: Ashgate, pp. 177–91.

Sparkes, A.C. and Smith, B., 2014. *Qualitative Research Methods in Sport, Exercise and Health. From Process to Product*. London: Routledge, Taylor & Francis Group.

Index

For Product Safety Concerns and Information please contact our EU
representative GPSR@taylorandfrancis.com Taylor & Francis Verlag GmbH,
Kaufingerstraße 24, 80331 München, Germany

Printed and bound by CPI Group (UK) Ltd, Croydon, CR0 4YY
08/05/2025
01864522-0001